D1253915

DISCARDED

UNIVERSITY OF WINNIPEG
PORTAGE & BALMORAL
WINNIPEG 2, MAN.   CANADA

DISCARDED

MINERVA SERIES OF STUDENTS' HANDBOOKS

No. 19

General Editor

PROFESSOR
BRIAN CHAPMAN
MA, D.PHIL (*Oxon*)

THE SCIENCE OF SOCIETY

by the same author

TECHNICAL EDUCATION AND SOCIAL CHANGE

Minerva Series

HM
51
·C65
c. 1

THE SCIENCE OF SOCIETY
AN INTRODUCTION TO SOCIOLOGY

By
STEPHEN COTGROVE
Professor of Sociology
Bath University of Technology

London
GEORGE ALLEN & UNWIN LTD
RUSKIN HOUSE   MUSEUM STREET

FIRST PUBLISHED 1967
SECOND IMPRESSION 1967
THIRD IMPRESSION 1968
FOURTH IMPRESSION 1968
FIFTH IMPRESSION 1968
SIXTH IMPRESSION 1969
SEVENTH IMPRESSION 1969
EIGHTH IMPRESSION 1970

This book is copyright under the Berne Convention. All rights reserved. Apart from any fair dealing for the purpose of private study, research, criticism or review, as permitted under the Copyright Act, 1956, no part of this publication may be reproduced, stored in retrieval system, or transmitted, in any form or by any means, electronic, electrical, chemical, mechanical, optical, photocopying, recording or otherwise, without the prior permission of the copyright owner. Enquiries should be addressed to the Publishers.

© *George Allen & Unwin Ltd, 1967*

ISBN 0 04 300005 3

PRINTED IN GREAT BRITAIN
in 10 point Times Roman type
BY CLARKE, DOBLE AND BRENDON LTD
PLYMOUTH

PREFACE

If sociology is a relatively new star in the academic firmament, it is one which is rising rapidly. It lacks therefore the settled and established perspectives of the older disciplines. It is also a subject with a voluminous literature, and the task of selecting what is most appropriate in an introductory text is especially difficult.

Two main criteria therefore, have guided the selection and presentation of the material. Firstly, there is the claim that sociology is a science; that it is, in fact, possible to apply the perspectives of science to the study of social systems. Throughout, the emphasis had been on getting across the sociological perspective rather than conveying a mass of factual information. Science is essentially analytical. It involves the isolation of variables, tracing their relations with other variables, and in this way mapping out systems and sub-systems of interrelated elements. The 'rag-bag' notion of sociology as being the study of the odds and ends left over by economists, historians, and political scientists has been decisively rejected. Nor is sociology simply 'political arithmetic', counting heads and providing demographic data for governments. But if it is developing a distinct perspective, it must of necessity develop a special language. It is no more possible to undertake sociological analysis without special language symbols than it is possible to study physics or chemistry.

There has been no hesitation then in using the vocabulary of sociology. But technical terms have been introduced in a context which indicates their meaning and have been italicized when first used. Where the word italicized is a familiar word, such as *culture*, this serves also to draw attention to the fact that it is being given a precise and special meaning.

There is one further guiding principle. Science, like other intellectual activities, can be exciting. The excitement of discovery, of pitting one's intellectual resources against a tough problem, is one of the most rewarding aspects of science for the scientist. It is not easy to preserve this excitement in an introductory text. But it is perhaps easier in sociology than in some subjects because its study inevitably involves new ways of looking at familiar things. Attention has been directed therefore wherever possible to recent researches and to the problems that are now attracting the interest of sociologists, in the hope that students may catch some of the excitement of scientific research by some exploration at the frontiers of knowledge.

Finally, the emphasis throughout is on the sociological study of industrial society, with particular reference to modern England. It is hoped that this text may be one of an increasing number which attempts a more systematic and analytical approach, and tries to tread a middle way between highly theoretical and abstract studies and the all too voluminous largely descriptive literature whose relations to sociological perspectives are hard to find.

It will be necessary for the advanced student to undertake some further reading, selected from the recommendations for each chapter. The aim has been to provide a systematic framework to which wider reading can be related. (Suggestions for basic reading are marked with an asterisk.) There is little point in incorporating detailed summaries of readily available texts. Moreover, the exercise involved in relating the perspectives of this book to the sometimes differing approaches of the supplementary reading is an essential experience in developing a critical approach. No attempt has been made to keep footnotes to a minimum. On the contrary, these are important indications to the student of where to look for a more detailed development of the points briefly made in the text.

The indebtedness of the textbook writer to others is always extensive. The footnotes and references are some indication of this. But this book owes more than most to the help and encouragement of others. In particular, I must acknowledge my debt to a group of former students, who became the founder members of a graduate seminar at the Polytechnic in which many of the perspectives to be found in this text were hammered out. Distinctions are always invidious, but I must mention in particular Steven Box, Penri Griffiths, Stanley Parker, Noel Parry, and Douglas Young, some of whom have still further increased my gratitude by reading and criticizing draft chapters. I am also grateful to Anthony Taylor for his valuable assistance with Chapter 5, and to Mary Couper, Theo Nichols and Dr Ram Srivastava for reading draft chapters. Any inadequacies and errors are, of course, my own. I would also like to express my appreciation to Mrs Avril Fordham who patiently typed a none too legible manuscript, and, by no means least, to my wife and family for their forbearance during the many months of intensive preoccupation with its production.

Finally, I wish to thank *New Society* and Mr S. Parker for permission to reproduce in Chapters 2 and 4 parts of an article written jointly with Mr Parker, 'Work and Non-Work'.

Bath University of Technology
July 1966

CONTENTS

ABBREVIATIONS

A.J.S.—American Journal of Sociology
A.S.R.—American Sociological Review
B.J.S.—British Journal of Sociology
Soc. Rev.—Sociological Review

Chapter 1

THE SCIENCE OF SOCIETY[1]

What is sociology? It's not surprising that we are so often asked this question. Sociology is not a subject which is generally taught in schools. And until recently, it has not been widely studied in British universities, although there has been a very rapid expansion in the 1960s. Moreover, its complexities, plus its relative newness, mean that there are still considerable differences of opinion among people calling themselves sociologists as to precisely how the subject is to be approached.

This chapter is one of a number of possible answers to the question. Whether it is the correct answer or not, only the future development of the subject will show. It outlines briefly the variety of answers to specific questions, while at the same time stressing some major perspectives among contemporary sociologists. It will attempt answers to three main questions. Firstly, what is the subject matter of sociology? Secondly, how is this subject matter approached? And thirdly, why do we study it—what is its justification?

The answer to the first question can be deceptively simple. It is really no answer to say that sociology studies human society, because so do history, and anthropology. Nor is it enough to say that it studies human social behaviour, because so does social psychology. We really want to know what is its distinct perspective. What is the distinctive way in which sociology looks at man and society and their interactions? What is the distinctively sociological perspective on, for example, marriage and the family?

SOCIOLOGICAL PERSPECTIVES

A marriage seems at first sight to be an intensely personal affair. Boy meets girl, they fall in love, marry, set up house together. After a few years she stops working and has a baby, followed by a second

[1] I am indebted to Penri Griffiths for valuable suggestions for the organization and content of this chapter.

and possibly a third at intervals of about two years, while the husband continues to work.

But although each feels that he is freely choosing, each is, in fact, fitting into a pattern which would be quite different in other societies. In India, for example, boy does not meet girl and fall in love. Parents arrange marriages, and will choose a husband or wife for their daughter or son after consulting horoscopes and entering into negotiations with the other family.

Every step in this complex process is in fact, regulated by powerful social pressures. Courtship, marriage, and subsequent relations between wives and husbands, all are the subjects of laws, convention, and expectations, which if broken will bring a variety of sanctions ranging from imprisonment to ridicule. It is this coercive nature of society which Durkheim saw as its chief characteristic. For Durkheim,[1] sociology is the study of such *social facts*, which he defined as ways of acting, thinking and feeling, general in a society, which exert coercion on the individual to conform. Birth-rates are a good example of such social facts. In the nineteenth century, for example, wives usually had three or four children, sometimes ten or more. Today, the majority have one, two or three. Such facts cannot be explained simply by reference to individuals. Wives today are just as capable of having large families. But society today is different in many ways from Britain in the nineteenth century. And it is to these differences in their social context that individuals are responding when they take steps to limit their family size.

'Boy meets girl' then is a social fact. The biological changes which are involved in this event are common to healthy men and women in all societies, but there will be considerable differences in the permitted ways of sexual behaviour. Some societies permit plural mating (polygamy) and allow husbands to have more than one wife (polygyny) or wives to have more than one husband (polyandry).

'Boy meets girl' then within the context of a set of rules and usages or *institutions* which define what is considered 'normal' by any particular society. The social grouping which results from this regulation of sexual behaviour is the family. At each stage in its formation, and throughout its life, the behaviour of boy and girl, husband and wife, parent and child, will conform more or less closely to a pattern of norms and expectations which will define the way in which each will act out his *roles*. 'Boy' will have learnt what is expected of him as a 'lover' (and even ways of making love vary in different segments of society). He will expect to experience the

[1] E. Durkheim, *Rules of Sociological Method* (1950).

emotions of romantic love with one particular girl, whom he will then ask to enter into a life-long (monogamous) relationship with him in which he will expect her to look after his home, cook his meals, possibly defer to his judgment on major issues, and probably give up her career. She in turn will expect him to keep alive his romantic attachment by remembering wedding anniversaries, and any deviation from a strictly monogamous relationship may be interpreted as a fatal blow to the marriage, and recognized by the law as a 'matrimonial offence' giving grounds for divorce.

We learn to play adult roles during childhood. During play, for example, we engage in *anticipatory socialization* by acting as mothers and fathers, or teachers. Indeed, it is instructive to watch children at play to see just how they define adult roles. To say that we play the role of husband or wife implies that this is simply an act. At first it is, and we may not feel the emotions which we have come to expect. But with time, the 'act' becomes a part of us, an element in our *identity*, just as the newly qualified doctor at first self-consciously plays a part very different from that of his student days, but comes in time to *be* a doctor, thinking and behaving like one. Social systems are, in fact, remarkably successful in moulding people who will fill a wide variety of social roles—assembly-line workers, research scientists, witch-doctors, warriors, hunters. Such differences can certainly not be explained as inborn.

It is perhaps a somewhat exaggerated analogy to liken individuals to puppets, pulled by social strings, and acting out parts written for them by society. But they have come to know their parts so well, that they are no longer aware of the pulls and pushes, and unlike puppets, an internal machinery has taken over and moves them from inside. They have *internalized* their roles. All of this is an oversimplification, but it serves to illustrate an important element in the sociological perspective—the coercive nature of social systems which structure the behaviour of individuals in their pursuit of biological and other satisfactions.

Social systems

Perhaps the key concept in the sociological perspective is the notion of a *social system*. A system is a whole whose parts are interrelated. A simple example is Boyle's law in physics, which states that under certain conditions there is a mathematical relationship between the temperature, pressure and volume of a gas. An increase in temperature is a *function* of an increase in pressure, as for example, when you blow up a bicycle tyre and the valve gets hot.

This brings us back to the question, what precisely are the elements of social systems? And what are its boundaries? All science involves an abstraction of certain aspects of complex phenomena. In the example just quoted, the physicist has abstracted certain measurable aspects—temperature, pressure and volume and has ignored odour and colour. To some extent the question of what constitutes a system is a question for empirical study. For example, researches have discovered an association between social class and early school leaving. To investigate this more fully, we would have to translate the notion of social class into variables which could be observed and measured. The earliest inquiries simply related early leaving to fathers' occupation. But not all boys whose fathers are unskilled workers leave early. If we compare the early-leavers with those who stay on, we discover other variables. For example, boys whose mothers had a secondary grammar school education are less likely to leave early, or those who were allocated to an 'A' stream. In this way, we will uncover the elements in the system, and when we have accounted for all the variance in early-leaving we will have isolated the 'system'.

It would be more precise to say that we have isolated a sub-system, because many elements in the system will be functions of larger systems. Whether a school practises streaming or not, for example, will depend on a number of variables, including the current state of educational theory and whether the school is in a predominantly middle or working class area. In sociology, it is usually more difficult to isolate a system to discover its boundaries, and to deal with it as though it were a closed system. For this reason, the concepts 'internal' and 'external' system are preferred by some sociologists.

The class can be studied as a sub-system of the school, and the school as a sub-system of the educational system. But the major structural elements in the social system are those organizations clustering round the major functions which must be performed if any society is to survive. Thus, in addition to the educational system, and the kinship system, there are the economic and political systems, each of which will be the subject of more detailed study in later chapters of this book.

Not only are sub-systems such as schools and factories related to the major systems of which they are parts, but the major systems themselves are interrelated. We shall see later, for example, that the family greatly influences a child's scholastic attainments, the school socializes the child to perform work roles in the economic system, while the job a man does influences his family life and relations with his wife. This, in fact, is the major task of sociology—to bring to light the interrelations between the elements in systems and sub-systems. As a framework for such analysis, the vocabulary of sociology provides a number of other useful concepts which enable us to identify the major components of social systems.

Structure

If we focus attention on a major sub-system of society, such as the economic system, we can identify a number of separate *organizations*, such as firms, and trade unions. Each of these will have a definable *structure*. That is to say, there will be a hierarchy of *positions* or *statuses* such as managing director, secretary, or bench worker. Moreover, there will be recognized norms defining what is expected of each position. When an individual acts according to such ex-pectations, he is carrying out his role as managing director or secretary. *Role* is the acting out of *status*.[1] Not only may each organization be viewed as a structure, with a regular relation be-tween its elements, but we may also conceive of the total pattern of the sub-systems—the kinship, economic, political, and educational sub-systems as constituting the *social structure*, or the broad frame-work within which individuals occupy statuses and act out roles.

Culture

The behaviour of actors in a social system will be oriented to their perception of what others expect of them. Actions will also be oriented towards the pursuit of valued ends or goals. Members of a trade union, for example, join to achieve better wages and condi-tions. The shared norms and values of members of a social system are a most important aspect of a society. Shared norms, values, and beliefs are referred to as the *culture* of society—and here the word is being used in a technical sense.

The culture of a society plays a major part in structuring the social actions of its members. In the small group such as the family, as well as in the wider society, activities will be directed towards the achievement of valued goals. In a society in which material posses-sions such as cars, TV sets and refrigerators are highly valued, indi-viduals will be motivated to want them. Such shared goals help to integrate the activities of individuals in a social system. Members of a family who all want the same kind of holiday will all bend their energies in the same direction. But there must also be agreement on means as well as ends. Norms of conduct prescribe some means and

[1] See L. A. Coser and B. Rosenburg (eds), *Sociological Theory: a Book of Readings* (1957), Chapter 8.

prohibit others. Only some means of achieving valued goals such as TV sets are legitimate. Morals, fashions, conventions, laws, all regulate conduct according to prevailing norms. Consensus on means (shared norms) together with consensus on ends, channel social actions and help to promote integrated systems of action. Where there exists such shared norms, regulating the behaviour of actors in a specific context, we refer to the existence of a *social institution*.

Types of persons

Both *culture* and *structure* are highly abstract concepts. In the last analysis, a school is an organized system of relations between individuals. Values and beliefs do not exist in vacuo: they are socially significant only to the extent that they exist in the brains of men and women. A third and extremely important way of looking at a social system is from the perspective of the individual social actors. But for the sociologist, this means looking at *typical* individuals not isolated individuals. It is the family life of car-workers, or the educational achievements of working-class students that interest us. If class influences educability, then this effect will be detectable among numbers of working-class students. We will be able to talk about what is typical—although we will normally do this in the more sophisticated language of statistics.

When we look at the social system from the perspective of the individual, we can start either by locating his *position or status* in the social system (manual worker in the economic sub-system, for example), or we can examine the way in which he acts out his status—his *role*, or we can look at the characteristic personal qualities that he brings to his role (such as his beliefs about the value of trade unions). We must, in fact, take both his role and characteristics into account. The way in which an individual acts in a social situation will depend on the way *he* defines it. If a child believes that his mother does not love him, this is the *real* situation for him.

Many theories of society have, in fact, stemmed from certain assumptions, about the characteristics of the individuals who compose it. Theories of economic behaviour, for example, influenced by the utilitarians and classical economics, have assumed that man is motivated primarily by the desire to maximize his material satisfactions. 'Economic man' rationally pursues economic goals. For Thomas Hobbes,[1] man was primarily a 'security seeker', for some sociologists, he has been defined primarily as a 'status seeker', while for Freud, sex instincts were seen as the primary explanation of a

[1] *The Leviathan.*

variety of social phenomena, including religion and civilization.[1]

Such explanations are clearly an over-simplification of human motivation. Moreover, they fail to take account of other characteristics of the individual actor in a social system, such as his definition of the situation. Manual workers, for example, may restrict output and thus fail to earn production bonuses and to maximize income. But this does not mean that they are uninterested in economic rewards. It may be that they prefer to sacrifice income for security. They define the situation as one which calls for restrictions on output.[2]

But in any case, we cannot adequately explain the behaviour of a social system simply in terms of the characteristics of the individuals who compose it.[3] The actor is himself the product of a social system. His motives and perspectives, and the ways in which he legitimizes and justifies his actions can only be understood as a result (in part) of the lengthy processes of socialization which has moulded his characteristics, of the social expectations to which he responds which derive from his position in the social structure, and of the prevailing culture which influences the ways in which he defines situations, the goals he values, and the means which he accepts as legitimate. The total *social system* that is to say, embraces structures, culture, and persons. (Figure 1.1.)

Social and non-social
When we discuss courtship patterns in sociology, we take as given the biological basis of courtship—puberty and sexual maturation. What interests us is the fact that different societies impose different patterns of courtship, and channel and control the biological sexual drive in different ways. We can never overlook the biological basis of human behaviour. But biology cannot explain the social expectations which result in distinctive courtship patterns, differing between societies. Biology cannot explain *social* facts. Sex is a biological drive; monogamy or celibacy are social facts.

Quite elaborate theories have been developed which attempted to explain social movements in biological terms. Racial theories of history, for example, have tried to explain the rise and fall of civilizations as due to changes in the racial (inborn biological) composition of peoples. One weakness of such theories apart from the lack of evidence is the fact that social changes frequently take place far too

---

[1] *Civilisation and its Discontents* (1963) and *Future of an Illusion* (1962).
[2] See Chapter 4 for a discussion of 'occupational strategies'.
[3] This approach is known as psychological reductionism.

FIGURE 1.1

A MODEL OF A SOCIAL SYSTEM

Social structure
Political system
(Machinery of government, parties, pressure groups)

Culture
Values (ends)
Norms (means)

Economic system
(Firms, the market, trade unions)

Knowledge, beliefs,
ideologies

Kinship system
(Families, kinship networks)

Cultural system
(Schools, colleges, churches, broadcasting corporations)

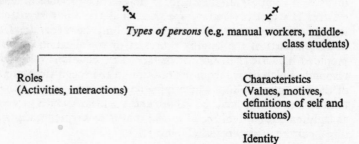

Types of persons (e.g. manual workers, middle-
class students)

Roles
(Activities, interactions)

Characteristics
(Values, motives,
definitions of self and
situations)

Identity

quickly for them to be due to biological changes which take scores of generations. We cannot, for example, explain the fall in the size of the family from 1870 in biological terms. This has been far too large to be explicable as the result of any decline in reproductive capacity.[1]

Geographical factors, too, have entered in sociological explanations. And in some ways, the sociologist must take them into account. We may observe, for example, that suicide rates are higher in hot than in temperate climates. If we could demonstrate that climate was indeed the significant variable, then we would need to turn to biology and possibly psychology to determine how the human organism responds to temperature in ways which affect the tendency to suicide. The explanation would not then be sociological. In fact, we find a number of other variables which are not themselves causally related to climate but which are associated with suicide—such as social norms on the morality of suicide, and the degree of integration between the individual and society. These are all sociological variables.

[1] For a review of such theories, see M. Ginsberg, *Sociology* (1934); P. Sorokin, *Contemporary Sociological Theories* (1928).

This does not mean that sociologists can ignore geographical or biological factors. They constitute factors which individuals in societies have to take into account. But it is the differential response of societies to, for example, arid conditions, or skin colour, which interests the sociologist. A lack of rainfall is a geographical fact; an irrigation system is a social product. A hand is a biological non-social phenomenon; and hand-shake is a social fact, a symbol, communicating meaning and intention from one individual to another.

Sociology and the social sciences

The relation between psychology and sociology is obviously close. The basic unit of society is the individual. And it is the behaviour of the individual that preoccupies the psychologist. He studies the ways in which individuals learn, perceive, and react to frustrations. The sociologist too is interested in these phenomena, but only in so far as he needs to take account of them in studying the interaction between individuals in social situations. Sociologists and psychologists are concerned with different levels of analysis. The sociologist is interested in the individual as an element in a social system. He needs to take account of the way in which an individual perceives a situation, since this will influence his reaction to it. But he leaves the study of the mechanisms of perception to the psychologist. Sociologists in other words, are trying to build a body of theory to explain the behaviour of social systems—while psychologists want to explain the behaviour of individuals. Individuals, in fact, are always parts of social systems. Both psychology and sociology involve different ways of looking at individuals. This is what science is—a way of looking at and talking about phenomena. It involves abstracting certain elements from complex reality (e.g. whether a man dominates his wife) and trying to relate these to other elements. For example, wives who are economically dependent are more likely to be subordinate. This is a sociological explanation—relating typical unemployed wives with a typically subordinate role. We are not, in this case, concerned with whether any particular wife has psychological characteristics which can be described as a submissive personality.

It is less easy to differentiate between sociology and anthropology. The simplest basis of distinction is to say that anthropology has concentrated on the study of pre-literate societies. Because of the small size of such societies, the absence of a shared culture with the investigator, and the absence of written records, this has involved the development of specific techniques of inquiry, in which observation and interviewing have played a dominant role.

Economics, unlike sociology, studies only one segment of a social system. But it also differs in its perspectives.[1] Classical economics was largely deductive, starting with basic assumptions about economic rationality, and deducing from these an elaborate theory of economic behaviour. The theory of price, for example, assumes that individual buyers will buy less if the price rises and that producers will produce more. Price under perfect competition is determined by the inter- action of the curves derived from plotting changes in supply and demand in relation to price movements. The theory of the firm shows how profits can be maximized given various relations between fixed costs, average costs and marginal costs. Whether entrepreneurs actually behave in this way, is another matter.

Economics, then, provides us with models of behaviour in limited circumstances and under stated assumptions. It has developed more sophisticated theory than sociology, and has also gone further in the use of mathematics. But sociology and economics are coming closer together. In trying to bring its models more closely into line with what actually happens in the real world, economists have increasingly tried to measure economic behaviour (econometrics) and to modify their theories in the light of empirical data. On the other hand, there has been a growing interest among sociologists in the study of the economic system. Sociologists are particularly interested in the interaction between the economic system and other aspects of the social system, and stress the non-economic assumptions and bases of economic behaviour. (Contractual relations in a market economy, for example, take place within the framework of a set of social rules.) There are many areas which are studied by both economists and sociologists—especially in such fields as labour relations and the organization of the firm. But each discipline has developed distinctive perspectives, concepts, and theories. Economics talks about allocating scarce resources to given ends and the relation between units of input and units of output. Sociology applies a different perspective. It is interested not so much in efficiency measured by input and out- put, but rather in the firm (for example) as a social system—the goals of the organization, the ways in which roles are distributed among the personnel, the factors which ensure the compliance of individuals with their roles, and the factors influencing innovation and stability.

The convergence between sociology and economics can be seen in a number of ways. Problems of economic growth in under-

[1] For a fuller discussion, see N. J. Smelser, *The Sociology of Economic Life* (1963), Chapter 2.

developed countries have forced economists to widen their perspectives and to pay attention to the non-economic context of production—the way in which the extended family, for example, may
hinder mobility of labour. On the other hand, the possibility that
models of economic behaviour may be capable of computer analysis,
and the more sophisticated theories of economics are tempting
sociologists to work more closely with economists and to try to
apply some economic perspectives, such as input-output analysis
to the study of social systems.

History and sociology have a long and close association. The
difference is mainly in the kind of question asked. The historian asks
'what happened?' and strives to achieve a chronological recon-
struction of events. One extreme view of history would be that its
task is simply to describe the minutiae of events. Sociology places
more emphasis on 'how' questions, and on building general theories
of social systems. Many historians would adopt a more analytical,
rather than purely descriptive, approach, and seek to establish
relations between events and to investigate the causes of events.
Many works by historians and by sociologists, in fact, are indistinguish-
able in their approach. Indeed, it may be that historians will increasingly adopt a sociological perspective in their study of the
past.[1] Similarities, however, are largely confined to the works of
those sociologists who have studied historical societies. But to the
extent that sociologists are mainly concerned with the study of
contemporary societies, their perspective is becoming increasingly
distinctive as they concentrate more and more on distinguishing the
elements in social systems and formulating and testing theories about
the relations between them.

THEORIES AND METHODS

How then does the sociologist study social systems? What kinds of
explanation does he attempt? It has been generally claimed that
sociology is a science. But there is by no means consensus on the
implications of this for sociology. Moreover, problems about the
nature of proof and scientific explanation are questions of current
philosophical debate. Such problems cannot be discussed in detail
here, but it is important to stress right at the outset that an introductory text must of necessity over-simplify in the interests of clarity.

[1] See, for example, the recent studies at Cambridge: P. Laslett, 'The history
of population and social structure', *Int. Soc. Sci. J.*, Vol. XVII, No. 4, 1965,
and *The World We Have Lost* (1965).

A rather more pressing and practical question is how far can the ways of studying phenomena which have proved so successful in the natural sciences be applied to the study of man and society?

Science claims superiority over other kinds of knowledge on the grounds that it is derived from the observation and recording of phenomena. The ultimate test of a scientific proposition is its verifiability. This means that scientific propositions are limited to statements that are capable of verification. The proposition 'Five million angels can dance on the head of a pin' is not verifiable. Nor is the statement 'You ought not to gamble'.

Theory versus empiricism

Much social research has been mainly of a fact-gathering kind into the 'condition of Britain' question, to discover, for example, exactly how many people were living in poverty, and the factors such as low wages and irregular employment which led them to this condition. Such inquiries into the health of towns, labour conditions in factories, and the conditions of the poor have been undertaken largely outside the universities, by government departments, by amateur investigators like Booth and Rowntree, or by statisticians like Bowley. They have provided a mass of factual data which has had a substantial influence on social legislation. Booth's inquiries into the nature and causes of poverty for example, were reflected in the social legislation of 1911.[1]

Current researches closely related to this tradition include studies of family life in industrial cities, and the researches into the problems of old people, widows, and poverty. But it would be misleading to describe such recent studies simply as political arithmetic—counting heads—although they are certainly concerned with providing data for legislators. Such studies have also been influenced by the perspectives of anthropology and have placed great stress on the use of interviews as the method of making intensive inquiries into various aspects of the life of the community. Their approach has, however, been mainly descriptive.

Now it can be argued that science is more than observation and recording. And however important political arithmetic may be, it does not as such contribute greatly to the development of a science of society. It undoubtedly provides us with much raw material. The difficulty in sociology is that in the past there has often been an inverse relation between the significance of an inquiry and its methodological and theoretical rigour. Inquiries into important

[1] M. Abrams, *Social Surveys and Social Action* (1951).

questions of family life have been theoretically naive, while many theoretically rigorous researches have investigated trivial questions. A strong case can be made for bringing these two traditions closer together.

Recent studies of family life can be taken to illustrate the relations between theory and empirical research. Young and Willmott, for example, have shown that kinship is still a powerful force in East London. Married daughters still visit their mothers a good deal; in fact, much of the leisure time of the women is spent with mothers and close relatives. When the young families are moved to new housing estates in outer London, these ties with 'Mum' are weakened. But this is not the only change. The role of the husband and his relations with his wife also change. Husbands participate more actively in the household tasks, and are to be seen pushing the pram at weekends.

These studies raise some interesting questions. Why do husband-wife relations and roles change when families move to new housing estates? We could formulate a number of hypotheses. It may be that new estates have fewer pubs, and so husbands are forced back into the home. Or the new houses encourage them to spend more on furniture and decorations or to work in the garden, so they become home-centred. At about the same time as the Young and Willmott study, Elizabeth Bott was asking questions of this kind. The conclusion from her inquiry was that the kinship network determined husband-wife (conjugal) roles. In East London, kinship ties are strong and persist after the couple are married. This pulls the wife away from her husband. Husband and wife pursue separate activities, that is to say, there is a pattern of segregated conjugal roles. In the new housing estates, the pull of kinship is weakened and husbands and wives develop changed patterns of integrated activities.

If we are to discover the relations between elements in a social system, we need to approach our inquiries with this aim in mind. A predominantly descriptive approach is not enough, although descriptive studies may provide clues for more analytic inquiries, and even raw material for secondary theoretical analysis. One way in which theoretically oriented studies may be superior to descriptive studies is in their economy of effort. If we have a definite hypothesis in mind, we can collect data specifically to test it. The social survey approach frequently collects a large amount of descriptive information which cannot be related to any theoretical perspective.

The sociological imagination
What has been said is not meant to imply that only theoretically

rigorous analyses are of use to the sociologist. The break-throughs in scientific theory are the result of hunches and guesses that may be triggered off by the most unlikely events. If we are to be intellectually creative, we have to cultivate our ability to see relations which are often far from common-sense. To stimulate our 'sociological imagination',[1] we may talk to experts in other disciplines. We may get clues on the working of social systems by discussions with experts in cybernetics. Or we may read novels. Sillitoe's *Saturday Night and Sunday Morning* for example, suggests that the way in which Arthur Seaton spends his week-ends is very directly the result of the boredom and tedium of his work at the lathe from Monday to Friday. A rigorous inquiry to test this hypothesis is likely to yield more useful results than a large-scale survey which can do little more than relate the statistics of leisure activity to previous education, occupational categories, and income. But what differentiates the imaginative insights of the novelist and the activities of the sociologist, is that the latter must eventually put his theories to the test of the most rigorous empirical inquiries that he can devise. This, in turn, does not decry the value of the more speculative and interpretative studies such as Hoggart's *The Uses of Literacy* or Whyte's *Organization Man*, or Riesmann's *Lonely Crowd*. It does mean that we have to be aware of the fact that studies have varying degrees of reliability.

Verification and refutation

This brings us back to some of the current controversies in the philosophy of science. This chapter has inevitably taken a position on some of these questions. It implies, for example, that the perspectives of the natural sciences can be applied to the study of society. At this point it may be useful to direct attention to some recent ideas on the nature of science which are particularly relevant to the social sciences. It has just been argued that science involves testing hypotheses, and evolving theories. Such activities involve imagination, and conjecture. Now, in order to test such conjectures, we may construct an experiment or collect data, to *prove* our theory. The danger is immediately obvious. In order to guard against this, Karl Popper has argued that our task should be to seek to disprove our theory, to look for data which, if found, would show we were wrong.

In practice, of course, it is very difficult for the scientist to do this, whether he is a natural or social scientist. But science is a social activity in which the work of one scientist is read by others. A scientific report will indicate the nature of the research, its main

[1] C. W. Mills, *The Sociological Imagination* (1959).

findings and the conclusions which the researcher draws from these data. Other scientists may check on the validity of the conclusions or may replicate the inquiry. Sometimes research findings are put to a practical test. If this produces unexpected consequences then the researches will be called in question. In this sense, science is a self-correcting activity. Its findings are being constantly checked against experience.

Sciences and values

Science is concerned with questions of fact. Propositions about values—prescriptive propositions—are logically distinct from descriptive propositions. Of course, in making a judgment about what is good, or what ought to be done, we need to take account of all the relevant facts. But the distinction remains. Most philosophers would agree that we cannot derive an 'ought' proposition from an 'is' proposition. This is to commit what Moore called the *naturalistic* fallacy. Crime is a fact which exists in all societies and is in this sense 'natural'. Pain is 'natural'. In neither case can we logically jump to propositions about the goodness or badness of such phenomena.

Sociology then is concerned with studying the nature of social systems, not with passing moral judgments about what it finds. Of course, sociologists are themselves members of a society, and will have moral attitudes towards the questions they study. What is clearly important is that they carefully distinguish between facts and values. When engaged in scientific research into social questions, they will need to take every precaution to avoid bias both in collecting and interpreting data. Indeed, scientific method devises techniques to minimize distortions. In writing up a report, for example, on the effects of divorce on children, it would be essential to avoid mixing up statements about the observed consequences which can be verified, with moral judgments, which cannot.

Of course, this is not meant to imply that the only worthwhile propositions are those which are capable of verification. It may be prudent to base our behaviour so far as possible on knowledge of this kind. All we are saying is that science involves a distinct kind of discourse. And since sociology claims to be the application of the scientific perspective to the study of society, this involves efforts to maximize detachment and objectivity.

Some sociologists will argue that impartiality is impossible. O. R. McGreggor, for example, in his book *Divorce in England* states that it 'does not claim to be impartial (whatever that may mean); it does claim to be candid because throughout it attempts to

distinguish between cant and opinion. . . . But there can be no excuse
for unscientific explanations of such data as exist or for the substitu-
tion of dogma for empirical knowledge in this crucial area of human
behaviour.'

One way in which values do enter into the work of the sociologist
is in his selection of topics which he thinks worth study. McGregor
thinks that divorce is a 'crucial' area of behaviour. He has studied it
because he thinks it is important. Moreover, he clearly has definite
views on the subject. But this has not prevented him from taking a
cool analytical look at the facts.

Some sociologists would go further than this and argue that
sociology ought to concern itself with problems which are significant
for the human condition, and not simply of academic interest. But
however much values influence the choice of areas for study, the
researchers themselves must comply with the canons of science.

One way in which values are likely to intrude unnoticed is in the
use of value-loaded terms. Many words used in sociology are taken
over from public language. A word like 'civilization', for example, is
very difficult to define in a purely descriptive way. It includes not only
reference to certain characteristics of society, but to those which are
highly valued. What is a civilized society? The answers would be a
list of those characteristics which the individual values, and although
this may tell us something about the individual's values, such a term
is of little use for classifying types of society. 'Democracy', 'psycho-
path', are further examples of such words.

Prediction and probability

The claim by sociology to be a science does not go unchallenged. It
implies that it is possible to construct models and establish theories
that will enable us to predict the behaviour of social systems—and
this means ultimately, of individuals. This conflicts with our deep
conviction that we are each free and self-determining.[1] In its more
extreme form, such a view is clearly untenable. Some measure of
predictability is in any case essential in normal human relations. We
come home from school or work, knowing that the bus or train can
be relied upon (within limits) and that a meal will be served at the
usual time. We know that the chances of a boy achieving good
'A' levels whose father is a professional are about thirty times better

[1] For a thought-provoking discussion of the implications of sociology for
the problem of free-will, see P. Berger, *An Invitation to Sociology—a Humanist
Perspective* (1963).

than those of an unskilled worker's son with the same IQ.[1]

The argument may shift. In each of these cases, we are dealing with probabilities. We can't say for certain that John Smith will leave school without good 'A' levels, only that the chances are say 30:1 that he will. But the natural sciences, too, deal in probabilities. When, however, you are dealing with millions of molecules which are relatively simple, statements can be made with a very much higher order of probability than when you are analysing a system made up of a few hundred very complex men and women.[2]

Interpretation and understanding

A more fundamental attack on the position that sociology is a natural science comes from those who argue that human beings differ in a crucially significant way from molecules—they are conscious beings whose actions have meaning for them. When the natural scientist studies molecules, he can only do so from the outside. When the social scientist studies individuals in social systems, he wants to know, among other things, why the individual behaves as he does— what meaning his action has for him. Some social scientists[3] have argued that a sociological explanation must therefore go beyond the kind of explanation sought by the positivists, who considered the task of sociology was to establish statistical regularities. We also need to *understand* the meaning which the action has. Now this does not necessarily amount to an attack on sociology as a natural science. In the form in which this view was originally stated, it does

[1] Statistics provides us with methods of establishing whether such differences are greater than could be expected by chance. Chi-squared tests, for example, may be used under some circumstances to enable us to say that 'the probability is only 1 in 100 (or 1,000, etc.) that the difference could occur by chance'.

[2] A simple experiment will demonstrate what have been referred to in a recent series of broadcasts on thermo-dynamics as the 'Laws of Disorder'. Take two jars, one containing four black balls and one, four white balls. Pour one into the other, shake thoroughly, and then pour half back into the empty jar. There is a finite number of possibilities. You may have 3B+1W, 2B+2W, or 4B or 4W, or 3W+1B.

There is one chance in 35 that the balls will separate out so that you again get all the white in one jar and all the black in another. Increase the numbers to eight in each jar, and the chance is one in 6,435. Now take half a jar of water and half a jar of ink and pour one into the other. When the molecules are thoroughly shaken up, pour half a jar of liquid into the empty jar. The chance that all the black molecules will end up in one jar is simply not a finite chance.

[3] Notably Weber, influenced by Dilthey and Rickert. For a more recent re-statement of this position, see P. Winch, *The Idea of Social Science* (1958). For a discussion of the positivist position, see the work of A. Comte, the inventor of the word 'sociology', and J. S. Mill, *Logic* (book 6).

put sociology in a different category. It was argued that meaning could only be grasped by intuition and empathy. Because the sociologist is like the individuals he is studying, he can put himself in their shoes and intuit the meaning of their actions—can understand them in terms of the motives and feelings which he shares with those he is studying. This is something the natural scientist can't do, but the social scientist must do.

There are some obvious objections to this procedure. In the first place, the 'intuition' of meanings or motives is frankly guess-work. There's no harm in guessing, and indeed we may turn to the insights of novelists, politicians, magistrates, or anyone else for ideas about possible motives. But science is concerned with verification, and it would be essential to discover some way of verifying our 'intuition' empirically. There is, however, a more fundamental objection. When we say we 'understand', we are referring to a subjective state in which we feel that things make sense. This, it can be argued, is a long way from scientific proof, which depends on the demonstration of interrelations. Indeed, in some fields, such as cosmology, the explanations of science are very far from 'understandable'. (Those who take this position then would reject the Weberian view that sociology is concerned with understanding human action.) But it does not follow that we are not interested in the meaning and significance which a social action has for the individual. Thus, if we observe that boys in 'C' streams in schools leave at age 15, we want to go beyond the statistical correlation between streaming and early leaving. We will want to know how such boys define themselves, see the school, and their image of the world outside, that is to say, the meaning which their action has for them. But intuition is not enough. We must establish their 'definition of the situation' (to borrow W. I. Thomas's term) by empirical investigation, by interviews, questionnaires, and the various other tools of social research. In this way, we can fill in the intervening variables between 'C' stream and 'early leaving', and this in turn will enable us to see in more detail whether this is likely to be an invariant relationship.

None of this is meant to imply that sociology does not face special difficulties in its attempt to apply the methods of science to the study of social phenomena. A more detailed study of some of these difficulties is to be found in text-books on methods of research.[1] A few may be mentioned briefly. The fact that the objects of sociological

[1] C. A. Moser, *Survey Methods in Social Investigation* (1958); J. Madge, *The Tools of Social Science*; W. J. Goode and P. K. Hatt, *Methods in Social Research* (1952); M. Duverger, *Introduction to the Social Sciences* (1964).

study are aware that they are being investigated may well change their conduct. A person being interviewed may well give replies which he thinks will please the interviewer. But such problems, though more frequent in social science, have their parallels in the natural sciences. Electrons, for example, are affected by the light which is used to observe them (Heisenberg's principle of indeterminancy). Sometimes a result may be brought about simply because it is expected. Children put into 'C' streams in schools sometimes do less well because little is expected of them. Their poor achievement confirms the original impression that they are less able. This is what Merton calls a *self-fulfilling prophecy*.[1] Despite such difficulties, which are, in any case, not peculiar to the natural sciences, the achievements of the social sciences in recent years on very modest budgets may be felt to be the most convincing evidence for their claims to recognition.

Types of explanation
Sociology seeks to analyse the relations between variables in social systems. We can, for example, demonstrate that there is a relation between a boy's social class and his educational achievement. We could say that class is a *cause* of under-achievement, meaning that working-class boys fail to achieve the same degree of success attained by middle-class boys of comparable ability. To take another example, if we observe that there is a relation between whether a wife works and the extent to which she is dominated by her husband, we could say that the employment of wives is a *cause* of their emancipation from male dominance. But we could equally well say, that it is their emancipation from being tied to the kitchen ('a woman's place is in the home') which has *caused* more of them to go out to work. One way round this difficulty is to refer to a functional relation between female employment and male dominance. This leaves open the question of the direction of causation, and indeed, whether there is, in fact, a direct causal relation between the two variables at all. This is to use the word *function* in a mathematical sense—a way which has not, in fact, been favoured by social scientists. If a mathematician says that A is a function of X, he simply means that there is a regular relationship between A and X.

In the social sciences, the concept of function has more generally been used in a way borrowed from biology. We may speak of the function of the digestive system, meaning the contribution which it makes to the maintenance of the body as a functioning system. In the

[1] R. K. Merton, *Essays in Social Theory and Social Structure* (1957).

same way, sociologists talk about the function of, for example, religion in society. This particular usage has given rise to a number of difficulties, which will be examined later in the discussion on *functionalism*.

Two other kinds of explanation are widely used in sociology. Suppose, for example, that we are interested in exploring the factors which lead wives to go out to work, or which lead some young people to become delinquent. As we have seen, the explanation of a social action requires an analysis of two main variables. We need to discover the characteristics of the actors, and we also need to know something about the situation to which they are responding. We may, therefore, compare numbers of delinquents with numbers of non-delinquents to see whether the delinquents possess any specific characteristics, either innate (genetic) or acquired. We would also need to compare all those who have similar characteristics, who become delinquent with those who don't, to discover whether there are situational (environmental) factors which can account for the adoption of delinquent behaviour. This approach attempts to account for the *aetiology*[1] of delinquent acts, that is to say, the antecedent factors which lead to the emergence of delinquent behaviour. This is the approach used in medicine when an explanation is sought for the causal factors leading to a specific disease. This type of explanation can be expressed by the formula:

Action = function of (actor + situation)

We may, on the other hand, be interested rather in the distribution of some particular kind of behaviour. We may observe that delinquency is concentrated in the lower working-class areas of cities. Or we may wish to explain why fertility rates were high in the nineteenth century, and very low in the 1930s, or why middle-class boys have high rates of educational achievement. This corresponds to the interest of medicine in epidemics, and leads to an *epidemiological* explanation.[2] Here, we try to discover what characteristics of the social system in the nineteenth century were associated with high fertility rates and the corresponding conditions of the social system in the 1930s associated with low fertility rates. A sociological explanation, that is to say, explains rates as functions of a social system.[3] A pioneer and classical study of this kind is Durkheim's

[1] In American texts, this is spelt 'etiology'.

[2] See Chapter 9 for a discussion of the aetiology and epidemiology of crime and delinquency.

[3] For an example of this approach see the analysis of reproduction in Chapter 2.

analysis of suicide, discussed more fully in Chapter 9. If we use the concept of function in the mathematical sense, such explanations are of course, functional explanations.

Concepts, paradigms, models
Science involves the abstraction of some characteristics (variables) from complex reality and the attempt to establish laws about the probability of there being regular relationships between such variables. Boyle's law, for example, provides a mathematical formula for the relations between the temperature, pressure, and volume of a gas. 'Temperature', 'pressure' and 'volume' are each *concepts*. They are verbal symbols which stand for characteristics. If such characteristics are to be observed, and if possible measured, we have to translate them into criteria which can be perceived by the senses— whether it be the movement of a dial on a pressure gauge, or the thread of mercury in a thermometer. Similarly, if we are to investigate social systems, we must formulate concepts which symbolize the variables we wish to examine, and state the criteria by means of which such characteristics can be observed.

Suppose we are interested in the relations between husbands and wives (conjugal roles) and the influence of the husband's occupation. We would need to decide what aspects of husband-wife relations might possibly be related. We can identify a number of possible variables, such as the power relations between spouses (equality/ dominance), the evaluation of wives by husbands (intrinsic/instrumental), and the kinds of functions wives perform for their husbands (companions, hostesses, servants). The next step would be to decide on criteria which would provide us with indices of such variables for research purposes (to 'operationalize' the concepts). Out of such concepts, it might be possible to construct a ·model or *paradigm* which described in a systematic way all the variables we would need to investigate in exploring our problem. We could go further than this and hypothesize some possible relations between the variables. For example, 'where the husband is dominant, the wife is more likely to be a "servant" than a "companion".' Or 'where the husband's occupation involves influencing others, his wife is likely to function as a "hostess".' The formulation of concepts and models, and the further step in hypothesing relations between variables, are all steps in the process of theory building—the hallmark of the scientific perspective.

Models are a half-way house in theory building. They are very tentative descriptions of what a system looks like, and suggest possible relations between variables for empirical research.[1] Figure 1.1 for example, is a tentative model of a social system which will be used for the subsequent analysis in this text. Concepts and models are *heuristic* devices—essential aids in the process of analysis. The fact that subsequent researches prove them to be faulty doesn't matter. What is important is that they provide us with first approximations which we can test and out of which we can build theories which have more powerful explanatory value. The fact that the Niels Bohr model of the atom (neutron with electrons in orbits) is no longer acceptable to modern physics in no way detracts from the fact that it was a major step with enormous power to generate further theory and research.

Types of sociological theory

'Sociology comes into being with the extension of the scientific method . . . to the social world of man himself.'[2] It was during the early part of the nineteenth century that systematic attempts to evolve a science of society led to the emergence of sociology as a distinct perspective, and its claim to differentiation from philosophy, history, political economy and other social sciences. From this date on, sociology's search for a distinct identity has been accompanied by the formulation of a variety of theories about the nature of social systems and the methodology appropriate for their study.

There is no space in an introductory test to do more than to mention some of the earlier theories, and to sketch a little more fully models and theories of more contemporary interest. Many of the perspectives of contemporary theory have their roots in the work of the 'founding fathers' of the nineteenth century. The germ of the idea of society as a system whose parts are interrelated is to be found in the work of Comte (*Cours de philosophie positive*, 1830–42). Herbert Spencer elaborated the concept of society as an organism with structures which become differentiated as society evolves and performs increasingly specialized functions.[3] Durkheim's emphasis on the way in which society exercises constraints on the individual is, as we have seen, one of the most forceful statements of the existence of social factors as distinct from biological, geographical or psychological facts.

---

[1] Much of Parson's work falls into this category. His contribution has been to provide sociologists with concepts and models and in this way to help lay the foundations for theoretical developments.

[2] Don Martindale, *The Nature and Types of Sociological Theory* (1960).

[3] L. A. Coser and B. Rosenburg, *op. cit.* (1957), Chapter 15.

Two broad theoretical schools demand particular attention for an understanding of contemporary sociological perspectives—*functionalism* and *social behaviourism*. As we have seen, if we conceive of society as a system or structure, this leads rather naturally to the study of the functional relations between the parts and the whole. It is the body of theory which has grown up around this way of looking at society which has come to be known as *functionalism*.[1] It would be wrong to imply that what has emerged constitutes a tightly knit cohesive theory. Many, in fact, would argue that functionalism is not a theory at all. It is rather a perspective which is helpful for some kinds of sociological analysis, and has served to clarify a number of useful concepts.

One of the leading exponents of functionalism in contemporary sociology has been Talcott Parsons.[2] In every social system, he argues, there are four basic problems (*functional imperatives*) which must be met if the system is to continue in existence. These are:

G. Goal attainment

A. Adaptation

I. Integration

L. Latency (Pattern maintenance and tension management)

Goal attainment is the end of any cycle of social action. The problems here include the adaptation of means appropriate to ends and the allocation of resources to various goals.

Adaptation involves coming to terms with the external situation and environment, and includes devising appropriate techniques for the achievement of ends.

Integration is concerned with maintaining internal relations between the units in a system, for example, between managers and workers in a factory.

Latency or *Pattern maintenance and tension management*, refers to the problem of maintaining adequate motivation among the elements in the system and resolving the tensions which are generated by interaction between the units and the system.

G and A functions can be described as *instrumental* functions, allocating means for the achievement of ends.

I and L functions are *expressive* functions, concerned with main-

---

[1] *Ibid.*

[2] The following account is based on M. Black (ed.), *The Social Theories of Talcott Parsons* (1961)

taining appropriate emotional states of the units for the performance of instrumental tasks.

If we look at the total social system, we can see that these functions are distributed among the major structural elements. Thus the economy provides the material means for the achievement of societal goals in the shape of a variety of goods and services, the polity mobilizes the resources and allocates them to a hierarchy of goals according to some judgment about priorities, while the kinship system and cultural organizations contribute to the *latency* problems of maintaining morale and integration.

The earlier cruder formulations of functionalist theory were open to a number of criticisms. By discussing some of these, we can indicate the way in which functionalism has evolved. One simple error is to confuse a structural element with its function. It is argued, for example, that religious organizations perform important integrating and tension management functions. And since these are essential functions in any society, therefore religion is a functional necessity. What this argument overlooks is the possibility of functional alternatives. For example, a pen functions as a writing instrument, so does a typewriter. Indeed, one of the tasks attempted in Chapter 6 is to see how far secular ideologies such as science and political ideologies may function as alternatives to religion.[1]

Not all elements in a society are necessarily functional. Some writers have tried to find a function for every social phenomena. We have to recognize that some practices may be survivals which no longer have any significant function, such as the buttons on the sleeves of a man's jacket, although even these may perform a minor function as status symbols by enabling us to differentiate tailor-made from mass-produced suits. Or practices may be functional for some groups and dysfunctional for others. Trade unions and employers' associations function, for example, to protect the interest of their members. But in so doing their actions may have consequences which are contrary to the interests of other groups.

A very important distinction between *manifest* and *latent* functions has been made by Robert K. Merton. He points out that in addition to the intended and recognized consequences of social action, there may be unintended and unrecognized *latent* functions. We may go further than this, and incorporate a term used by Malinowski. The *charter* of social institution can be thought of as the objectives which are generally recognized by society, the official objectives. Thus the

[1] R. K. Merton, *Essays in Social Theory and Social Structure* (1957).

memoranda and articles of association lay down the charter or objectives of public companies.

The second important type of theory is *social behaviourism*.[1] The distinctive mark of social behaviourism is its emphasis on the study of the social individual—the social actor in the social system. In this, it was reacting against the rather vague formulations of the nineteenth century with their discussions of the relations of parts and whole and ill-defined social entities. Of its various branches, *symbolic interactionism* has had an especially powerful influence, and indeed, continues to flourish. Particularly important has been its contribution to our understanding of the way in which social individuals are formed through interaction with social structures.[2] Cooley and Mead, for example, have provided us with powerful tools for the analysis of the ways in which society moulds the individual with their analysis of the socialization process, the influence of primary groups, and the influence of 'significant others' as models for the 'self'.[3] Other contributions of symbolic interactionism include the concept of roles, and an understanding of the importance of symbols such as language in social interaction. In the hands of Erving Goffman, symbolic interactionism has proved a powerful tool for an understanding of the way in which social structures such as mental hospitals bring about changes in the personality of inmates.[4]

The second main branch of social behaviourism, *social action* theory includes many of the big names in sociology—Max Weber, Veblen, and Mannheim, and more recently, Riesman and C. Wright Mills, as well as part of the work of Parsons and Merton. The distinctive perspective of this branch was its emphasis on the study of *social actions*—or more explicitly—*meaningful social actions* (whereas symbolic interactionism has concentrated more on the characteristics of the actors). We have already looked briefly at Weber's view that the meaning of a social action to the actor is an essential feature for its understanding. From this, Weber went on to study social actions according to their relations to ends and values, and to relate these to the analysis of social structure. Thus he saw bureaucracies as examples of rational systems of action in which

---

[1] For a summary and analysis, see D. Martindale, *op. cit.*, part 5, especially Chapters 14 and 15.

[2] L. A. Coser and B. Rosenburg, *op. cit.* (1957), Chapters 7 and 8.

[3] This is discussed in Chapter 2. For a more recent statement, see A. M. Rose (ed.), *Human Behaviour and Social Processes* (1962).

[4] *Asylums* (1961). See also Chapter 8 for examples of the use of symbolic interactionist perspectives. See also, L. A. Coser and M. Rosenburg, *op. cit.* (1957), Chapter 8.

tasks were rationally distributed and co-ordination for the efficient pursuit of the goals of the bureaucracy.

JUSTIFICATIONS FOR SOCIOLOGY

Finally, we come to the question: Why study sociology? There are three main answers to this question—conservative, revolutionary, and pragmatic. Sociology came into existence as an essentially conservative answer to the problems of revolution and change at the beginning of the nineteenth century.[1] For both Comte and Spencer, society was a natural system with its own laws of evolution and change. In the hands of Spencer, sociology lent strong ideological support to nineteenth century laissez-faire economics. Any attempt at social amelioration, for example, would be an interference with the laws of natural selection and the survival of the fittest, and would threaten the health of the social organism. Much contemporary American sociology is basically conservative and anti-revolutionary, or at least stems from implicit value commitments to the American conception of democracy.[2]

Not surprisingly, this has stimulated a concern with a more radical sociology, seeking inspiration from Marx, and 'committed' to radical comment. Such commitment has little patience with the scientific claim to a 'value-free' sociology, and is impatient of empiricism with its preoccupation with the smaller issues. Its preference is for involvement with the fundamental problems of war and peace, and concern with the broad drift of capitalist society.[3]

The prevailing tradition in Britain has been pragmatic—to find an answer to social problems. This is best exemplified by the Fabians, and the investigations of philanthropists such as Booth and Rowntree into the 'condition of Britain' question. Studies of poverty, factory conditions, and urban living have, to a large extent been pioneered outside academic sociology, which has until recently shown little interest in such questions, having its roots rather in the nineteenth century philosophy of history and a concern with the broad pattern of social change and development. Largely under the influence of Professor Titmuss, the investigation of social problems has now become academically respectable and is exemplified by the work of the Institute of Community Studies.

[1] D. Martindale, *op. cit.*, p. 122.
[2] See, for example, D. Bell, *The End of Ideology* (1960).
[3] One of the most powerful and challenging exponents of this position is C. Wright Mills. See his *Power Elite* (1956) and *The Causes of World War III* (1958).

The perspective outlined in this book attempts a possible fourth answer. The methods of science have proved their power in the field of the natural sciences. Their rigorous application to the study of society has barely begun. Science is born of the marriage of theory and research. In many areas of social investigation, the two have barely met. The ends to which the knowledge of science is applied may be good or ill. A science of society *may* provide man with the knowledge which he needs to guide his own future. Whether he is yet ready for such knowledge and how he will use it, are matters which the individual must judge for himself.

SUMMARY AND CONCLUSIONS

At the present stage of development of sociology, there is a variety of views on the nature of the sociological perspective, on its subject matter and on how this is to be approached. Any attempt to crystalize an emerging consensus must necessarily be tentative. Above all, sociologists differ on the implications of such claims to scientific status, and on the kind of theoretical models which can most fruitfully be used as a first step to theory building. Some have been primarily preoccupied with attempts to arrive at a systematic theory which will enable the integration of available empirical data, while at the other extreme, much energy has been devoted to the empirical investigation of problems of social policy, with little attempt to relate such findings to any broader theoretical perspectives.

Attempts to arrive at a holistic view of society have borrowed a number of models, including the analogy between society and organisms. The concept of society as a system whose parts are functionally related appears to provide the most promising starting point. Among the major sub-systems of society, we can focus attention on the relation between the various structural elements, which provide the organized framework for social action, and include the family, economic, political and cultural organizations. The cultural sub-system constitutes the shared values and norms which play an important part in the integration of individual action into co-ordinated systems, while the personality sub-system directs our attention to the fact that in the last analysis, social systems are made up of social actors, individuals who occupy roles and who possess characteristics moulded by the socialization process.

Cognate disciplines such as economics, anthropology, history, and psychology differ in the perspectives which they bring to bear on the study of human society. Intellectual study involves specific ways of interpreting phenomena, according to distinct frames of reference. These have grown up by a consensual process as a result of the interaction between professional members who identify with a particular discipline, and who in this way help to hammer out its distinctive approach. The historian, for example, may take the view that human behaviour cannot be reduced to generalized laws. All we can do is to immerse ourselves in the complex web of events and attempt some intuitive grasp of their interrelations, especially the connexion between contiguous periods. There are signs, however, of a convergence of perspectives and a breaking down of barriers between traditional disciplines.

The attempts to apply the perspectives of science to the study of society have resulted in a variety of approaches. At the one extreme, accurate observation and recording with a minimum of theoretical analysis can be contrasted at the other extreme with theory building which presents major difficulties of empirical verification. There appears to be a growing recognition of the need to bring these approaches closer together, and to integrate theory and research. The effort to develop a more rigorous science of society is not without its special difficulties, including the problem of objectivity and detachment, but such difficulties do not by themselves constitute fatal objections to the claim of sociology to be a science. Such a claim can only be refuted in the last analysis by sociology's failure to develop a body of theory. And all the evidence suggests that the time is now ripe to pursue such an objective with increased effort and resources.

QUESTIONS AND EXERCISES

1. What do you understand by the concept 'social system'? How does it differ from the idea of social structure?
2. 'The concept of "role" enables us to avoid the false dichotomy between the individual and society.' Discuss.
3. What part does 'culture' play in the social system?
4. How useful do you think functionalist theory has been in sociological analysis?
5. Write notes on: (a) functional imperatives
    (b) manifest and latent functions
    (c) functional alternatives.
6. 'Whether sociology is a science depends on how the term "science" is defined.' Discuss.
7. 'Sociology can never be a natural science, because it is never enough simply to observe, describe and formulate generalizations about the

behaviour of members of societies. To "understand" human behaviour, we need to know its meaning and significance for the individual.' Discuss.

8. What are the relations between sociology and (a) history, (b) economics, (c) psychology?

9. Write notes on: (a) the sociological imagination
                            (b) objectivity in the social sciences
                            (c) social behaviourism
                            (d) symbolic interactionism.

READING

*P. Berger.—An Invitation to Sociology: A Humanist Perspective (Doubleday, 1963). A thought-provoking, readable and stimulating discussion of the sociological perspective and its implications for the idea of free-will.
*E. Chinoy.—Sociological Perspectives (Random House, 1964). An easy introductory discussion.
L. A. Coser and B. Rosenburg (ed.).—Sociological Theory (Collier Macmillan, 1964).
M. Duverger.—Introduction to the Social Sciences (Allen & Unwin, 1964).
A. Inkeles.—What is Sociology? (Prentice Hall, 1964). A short, concise, but closely written discussion of the scope, perspectives and nature of sociological analysis, and guide to literature.
D. G. MacRae.—Ideology and Society (Heinemann, 1961) Part I: includes an account of the development of sociology in Britain.
D. Martindale.—The Nature and Types of Sociological Theory (Routledge, 1964). An advanced text, to be used very selectively by the beginner as a book of reference.
C. W. Mills.—The Sociological Imagination (OUP, 1959).
C. A. Moser.—Survey Methods in Social Investigation (Heinemann, 1958). The standard text on methods of social research.

THE SOCIAL SYSTEM

Chapter 2

THE FAMILY

THE FAMILY AND THE SOCIAL SYSTEM

In every society, culture defines the rules which pattern the relations between husbands and wives, parents and children. The role of husband or wife is prescribed by society, and the relations between them are structured by their mutual expectations as to what constitutes 'wifely' or 'husbandly' conduct. Each acts out his role within the prescribed limits, or suffers the sanctions applied to deviants.[1] Moreover, each thinks that his or her behaviour is perfectly 'natural', yet the wide differences in family roles between societies, or even between different segments of the same society underline the *social* structuring of family life.

In Western societies, for example, it would be strongly condemned if a husband took a second wife without divorcing the first. Yet in some Middle Eastern societies up to four wives are allowed. Or again, in the West, we think of the family as a unit comprising husband, wife and children, yet in many societies, the family extends to embrace a much larger group, comprising several generations and collateral kin.

The family and culture

Part of the explanation, as we have already seen, is to be found in the *culture* of society. Culture includes a set of shared norms and beliefs about marriage and the family, defining the behaviour which is generally expected in a variety of situations. Thus, there are norms

[1] This point has already been illustrated in Chapter 1.

about the selection of partners (including courtship and incest taboos), about husband/wife and parent/child roles (including numbers of partners to the marriage, division of labour, and the distribution of authority, and extra-marital sex relations), and lastly there are norms about relations with kin. Culture defines both what we can expect, and what is considered to be legitimate. And although these institutionalized norms vary widely between societies, the majority of members of a society accept the norms and beliefs as perfectly natural and largely unquestionable.

Culture then, goes some way to explain the persistence of family patterns. It is a very important variable for explaining the very substantial consensus and uniformity in societies. But it cannot explain how the specific patterns of behaviour emerged in the first place. In the West, we accept monogamous marriage as the only conceivable form of marriage. The existence of entrenched cultural norms, underpinned in this case by law and religion, may explain the persistence of monogamy. But how can we account for the decline in the patriarchial family, and a world trend towards conjugal family patterns? To do this, we must look for those factors which reinforce or challenge existing practices. We shall find, for example, that a number of changes in the nineteenth century led to a challenging of the prevailing norms condemning the practice of contraception and eventually to a change in the norm. We also find a shift to a more equalitarian relationship between husbands and wives. For a clue to such changes, we shall later examine the interaction between the family and other parts of the social system, particularly its interactions with the economic system.

The foregoing paragraph may be taken to imply that culture is a passive, dependent variable, adjusting to pressures to change. Although this may be true in the long run, in the short run, we have to treat culture as an independent variable, exerting an extremely powerful influence. Moreover, cultural beliefs and norms do not exist in isolation. Beliefs about the family, for example, are frequently associated with religious beliefs. In fact, in some societies, the latter may determine the former, resisting pressures for change.

A major determinant of monogamy in the West derives from the influence of religion. Long before the Christian era, both Greek and Roman religion exerted a powerful pressure towards life-long monogamy. It was believed that the spirits of the dead depended for their well-being on the care of the living. The veneration and care of ancestors constituted the religion of the family, but such tasks could only be carried out by the sons of a 'religious' marriage.

Consequently, irregular sex relations by wives were punished.[1]

The traditional Christian doctrine has stressed the inherent sinfulness of sexual behaviour and has sought to confine it within the marriage relation and to direct it towards the procreation of children.[2] Such doctrines have had a substantial influence on marriage laws, and on marriage relationships. The contemporary family then is in part a function of such normative and legal elements in society.

Of course, we could go farther back and ask why Christianity came to teach particular views on marriage and the family. But we have to draw a line somewhere, and this particular question is not of major relevance for the study of contemporary social systems. A more significant question would arise from the observation that contemporary religious views on the family are undergoing change. In 1908, for example, the report of the Lambeth Conference of the Church of England condemned the practice of birth control. In 1956, the same conference concluded that family limitation was compatible with Christian doctrine. The sociological issue here is how far religion can be treated as a dependent variable, and how far social changes will bring about a modification of religious teaching on the family. It will clearly be difficult for society to accommodate a substantial discrepancy between precept and practice. Meanwhile, we can observe that pressure from religious organizations and viewpoints has considerably shaped legislation, especially on the question of divorce.[3]

This stress on the institutional pressures which structure the family has led some to argue that the stability of the family derives very largely from such a legal framework and system of moral rules. The 'institutionalists' argue that any weakening of such rules, by liberalizing divorce laws for example, would lead to a fatal weakening of family ties and would contribute substantially to the disintegration of family life. This is precisely the kind of question which requires empirical sociological investigation, and to which we will return later.

Within this framework of legal and social rules, there are considerable variations in the patterns of marriage and family life. In some localities for example, husbands and wives share a variety of activities, and arrive at important decisions such as budgeting the family income after joint decision. In other areas, husbands share few

[1] F. de Coulanges, *The Ancient City* (1956).

[2] O. R. McGregor, *Divorce in England* (1957), Chapter 1 reviews the history of divorce and marriage in England.

[3] *Ibid.*

activities with wives, treating the home mainly as a place for bed and board, and a base from which they go to work or for leisure activities which they share with their work-mates. Their wives do not know what their husbands earn and receive a fixed 'wage' for housekeeping.[1]

One explanation of such differences would be that the traditions of family life vary. Men and women will have learnt particular ways of playing roles as husbands and wives through their upbringing and will perpetuate these in their own marriages. Moreover, they will respond to the 'sub-culture' of their locality where there will be generally accepted *norms* or rules of family behaviour (the husband should be the boss), *values* attached to various aspects of married life (companionship is one of the most rewarding aspects of family life), and various *beliefs* about marriage (that men are by nature polygamous). Different segments of society certainly vary, and such sub-cultures will exert pressures on those who live within them. They will reinforce some patterns of conduct and inhibit others. Where the men spend their evenings in the pubs, leaving their wives at home, it will be difficult for one to be odd-man out. But this does not explain why the patterns differ, only the fact that, once established, they will be resistant to change.

Family and Kinship
Some have tried to explain different patterns of marriage by relating them to social class.[2] A number of studies of working-class areas, such as Bethnal Green[3] have described the three-generation 'mum-centred' family, in which married daughters remain closely related to their mothers, while husbands spend much of their leisure-time outside the home. Such facts have been used as evidence that kinship is still a powerful force in the older industrial areas. Young and Willmott noticed however, that when Bethnal Green families moved to new housing estates on the outskirts of London, the close ties with 'mum' weakened. Mogey[4] observed a similar change in his study of Oxford families. But more significant, the relations between husbands and wives changed. Husbands began to spend more time in the home, and to share in the household tasks, including care of the children. In more technical terms, *conjugal roles* became *joint*

[1] For a detailed account of such differences, see J. Klein, *Samples from English Culture* (1965).
[2] The concept of class will be examined in Chapter 7. The terms 'working-class' and 'middle-class' will be used to refer to manual and non-manual occupations.
[3] M. Young and P. Willmott, *Family and Kinship in East London* (1957).
[4] J. M. Mogey, *Family and Community* (Oxford, 1956).

or *integrated* instead of *segregated*, and marriages became *home-centred* instead of *mum-centred*.

Why was this? In posing such questions, we can begin to move from description to analysis. We can begin to identify a number of variables and to ask questions about the relations between them. Elizabeth Bott,[1] for example, considers that the relation between the nuclear family and the wider community of which it is a part is the main determinant of the way in which the husband and wife parcel out the household tasks, and the relationships which are established between them. The close network of social ties with kin and neighbours which exists in an area such as Bethnal Green means that spouses continue to be drawn into external activities after marriage. Marriage is super-imposed, as it were, on a previous pattern of social ties, interactions, and interrelations, and these are so strong that they persist after marriage. Each spouse continues to be pulled outside the home so that the development of joint activities is inhibited. Conjugal roles follow the segregated pattern. Removal to a new housing estate then will weaken the links binding husband and wife to the social network, and the emotional support which this provides, making it more likely that each will turn to the other for help and support. In this context joint or integrated conjugal roles are more likely to develop.

More recent studies have questioned Bott's interpretation of the nature of the relationship between the social networks and conjugal roles. According to Bott, it is the connectedness of the social network which prevents the development of joint conjugal roles. We can certainly agree that where spouses, especially the wife, interact frequently with her kin, that this would be incompatible with joint conjugal roles.[2] But it could also be argued that in traditional working-class areas, role segregation within the elementary family is accompanied by role segregation in the social network, and that it is the latter which maintains the high degree of connectedness in the social network.[3]

A rather different interpretation is given by Rosser and Harris. They argue that a major factor is the domestic involvement of the wife. Segregated roles have been particularly characteristic of working-class families in the past, with 'the wife tied down at home with frequent pregnancies and a prolonged involvement in child-rearing

---

[1] *Family and Social Network* (London, 1957).

[2] C. Rosser and C. Harris, *The Family and Social Change* (1965), p. 207.

[3] H. Fallding, 'The Family and the Idea of a Cardinal Role', *Human Relations*, Vol. 14, No. 4, 1961.

whilst the husband went off to long, arduous hours at work and thence with his work-mates to club or pub'.[1] The more women are involved in domestic affairs, the more likely they are to lead separate lives from their husbands, and the more probable that they will interact with their mothers in an exchange of domestic tasks made possible by proximity of residence. The extended family is for such wives, a 'mothers' union', in which husbands are only marginally involved.

Family and the economic system

The discussion so far suggests that one important variable associated with the family structure, and the existence of extended kinship ties beyond the elementary family, is social class. This leads to the more specific question, in what ways does the husband's (and possibly wife's) role in the economic system affect family structure? The husband's occupation is a major determinant of the family's market situation. And in the past, especially in those areas where opportunities for female employment have been limited, the family has been economically extremely vulnerable, and even among the better paid workers, separated from poverty by little more than one wage packet. The extended kinship network has, in these circumstances, performed an important function as a mutual aid society, providing some small measure of insurance against unemployment or illness of the wage-earner.

The relationship between the *work-situation* and the family can be seen most dramatically in studies of what can be called 'extreme' occupations: those that make extreme demands on the individual. Data exists on two of these—coal-mining[2] and distant-water fishing.[3] In both cases we have a picture of work, at the coal face, and on trawlers, which is dangerous and damaging, and demands close co-operation on the job, where one man's mistake can cause the death of others. The men are strongly attracted to a job which pays well and which they define as virile manly work. But they also hate many aspects of it and seek the forgetfulness of alcohol in the long round of pub visits on Saturday and Sunday, wives left at home. To repair the damages exacted by his work, the miner expects a wife who will feed and comfort him, making few demands in return. Indeed, the relationship can be conceptualized as that of 'servant'. About the trawlermen, Tunstall says 'Some men quickly come to

[1] *Op. cit.*, p. 207.
[2] N. Dennis *et al*, *Coal is Our Life* (1956).
[3] J. Tunstall, *The Fishermen* (1962).

regard their wives mainly as providers of sexual and cooking services in return for a weekly wage'.

There is only scanty evidence on the influence of other occupations on family life. But what there is suggests that the extent to which a man finds his work an absorbing interest will be related to the significance of family life for him. The less a man is work-centred, the more likely is he to be home-centred and to treat his wife as a 'companion'.[1] It is possible, (though this is little more than a guess), that the small significance which work has for a large number of men may be causally related to the growth of the home-centred family. The growth of home-centredness is further facilitated by the rising standards of living and by the break-up of social networks resulting from increased geographical mobility. A man's occupation will also determine his *market situation* (income, security, chances of promotion), and this in turn has been shown to be a significant variable influencing the relations between husbands and wives.[2] Husbands higher up the occupational ladder have more resources available to bring to the family situation. Goode refers to this process as *role-bargaining*.[3] The control which a family can exercise over its members depends in part on their relative bargaining power—the reciprocal rewards which each can offer others. The working class family has few resources by which it can control its members. Unlike an agricultural community, in which sons are economically dependent on fathers, industrial society offers economic independence to sons, and the chance of bettering their father's position. Moreover, the creation of thousands of new jobs makes it less likely that the kin group can obtain appropriate jobs for its members.

By contrast, upper class fathers can offer both economic advantages and social position to their sons, who cannot strike a better bargain outside the family, which retains therefore a greater hold over them. 'Thus we have the apparent paradox resolved, that the families that are most successful in the industrialized and urbanized system are precisely those families which are farthest removed in pattern from the conjugal family which is thought to be so harmoniously adjusted to industrialization.'[4]

[1] S. Cotgrove, 'The relations between work and non-work among technicians', *Sociological Review*, Vol. 13, No. 2, July 1965.

[2] R. O. Blood and D. M. Wolfe, *Husbands and Wives* (1960).

[3] W. J. Goode, 'The process of role bargaining in the impact of urbanization and industrialization on family systems', *Current Sociology*, Vol. XII, No. 1, 1963–64.

[4] *Ibid.* There is a considerable literature which explores the similarity or contrast of forms ('isomorphism' and 'heteromorphism') between work and family

The economic position of both wives and adolescents has been greatly improved in recent years by economic expansion and full-employment. More wives are now working than at any time this century and young people are receiving relatively higher wages than ever before. Both now have more bargaining power in the family and this may well have contributed to the decline in the power of the husbands over wives and parents over children. Working wives are likely to try to change the division of labour within the family and to gain more co-operation from their husbands in household tasks. We can expect then in such families, a further shift towards joint conjugal roles, and away from the 'servant' towards 'companionship' relations. American researches suggest that the wife going to work is the most important single factor determining the decline in the power of the husband and a change in the division of labour between husbands and wives.[1]

The entry of women into the labour market is then a further way in which the family interacts with the economic system with important consequences for family life. It is to the factors underlying this trend and its consequences to which we must now turn.

Working wives

Two main trends can be noted. Firstly, there is an increase in the proportion of married women employed from 10 per cent in the 1930s to over one-third in the 1960s. Secondly, and closely related, married women now constitute a much larger proportion of the labour force than hitherto, and a much larger proportion of all working women are married.

Demographic changes are part of the explanation. The percentage of women never married is steadily falling, from 15 per cent in 1900 to (an estimated) 5 per cent in the 1970s. Moreover, younger marriages means that the number of single women is also declining. In 1951, one-sixth were married by the age of 20. By 1973, this proportion will have increased to around one-quarter. These changes mean that the numbers of single women available for recruitment to traditional female occupations such as teaching and nursing are declining, and such jobs will increasingly have to rely on married women.[2]

life. See R. and R. Rapoport, 'Work and Family in Contemporary Society', *A.S.R.*, June 1965, pp. 381–94. This question will be examined in more detail in Chapter 4.

[1] R. O. Blood and D. M. Wolfe, *op. cit.* (1960).

[2] C. M. Stewart, 'Trends in the employment of married women', *B.J.S.*, March 1961.

The growth of family planning, smaller families, and the concentration of child-bearing during the early years of marriage mean that more women are free to enter gainful employment after the age of 40, and are, moreover, faced with many years of active life after the completion of their traditional child-bearing function, which is no longer a full-time job.

Changes in the economic system have also contributed to the increased employment of women, both single and married. Full-employment in the post-war period has led many employers (often reluctantly) to employ married women, sometimes on a part-time basis. Changes in the economy have also increased the numbers employed as clerks, shop assistants, social workers, medical auxiliaries and similar occupations which lend themselves particularly to female employment. Women now outnumber men in employment in shops and offices, while nearly half of all employed women are in non-manual jobs, compared with less than 30 per cent of males.

But such changes do not necessarily imply a shift of interest on the part of women away from their traditional role as wives and mothers to a growing interest in and preoccupation with work. Although this may be a trend for women who have a professional training and career,[1] the great majority of working wives use work instrumentally as a source of income to be spent on the home—on refurnishings and decorations, durable consumer goods, holidays and clothing for the family, and only secondarily because they are lonely or bored. They work to raise the standards of their families, and some regard those who stay at home as muddlers and lazy.[2] The increase in working wives is in fact, perfectly consistent with the growth in home-centredness. Such women put their families first, and are not interested in promotion. This purely instrumental involvement is confirmed by the fact that the peak year for working wives is around age 42, with a steady decline after 45. By age 55–59, only 16 per cent remain employed.[3]

The consequences of the increase in working wives for conjugal roles have already been noted. As one husband expressed it, 'it makes (marriage) more of a partnership somehow.'[4] There is no evidence to suggest that for most women, the performance of two roles as wives and workers damages their family functions, though of course, many

[1] For a discussion of this predominantly middle-class group, see A. Myrdal and V. Klein, *Women's Two Roles* (1956).
[2] V. Klein, *Britain's Married Women Workers* (1965).
[3] *Census of Population*, 1951. One per cent sample tables.
[4] V. Klein, *op. cit.* (1965), p. 79.

find the situation one of strain. Social workers have failed to discover any adverse effects on the families of the majority of working wives, though there are exceptions, especially where mothers of pre-school children are forced to work from economic necessity. Nor is there evidence that delinquency rates are higher for the children of working mothers.[1] On the contrary, some research indicates that children may be harmed by excessive maternal care or over-protection.[2]

FUNCTIONS OF THE FAMILY

So far we have been looking at the ways in which the social system influences the family and kinship systems. But the relationship is not one-way: the family and kinship systems also perform important functions in the social system.

Reproduction
Every society must ensure that an adequate number of children are born. Furthermore, they must acquire the personal characteristics which are necessary for them to carry out their roles in adult society. These functions—reproduction and socialization—are the major functions which the family performs. In a few societies, such as the Israeli Kibbutzim,[3] the nuclear family may play only a small part in the subsequent upbringing and socialization of the child. But most societies ensure that children are born to parents who are in a stable relationship, reinforced by the norms of society—that is, are married.

The reproductive function of the family is in many ways the most fully documented aspect of its behaviour in industrial societies. Governments need statistics and forecasts of population growth to enable them to plan school building, houses, to make provision for the elderly, and for a variety of other decisions on economic and social issues. Census data is available in Britain from 1801, and demographers have amassed volumes of statistical data.

The main trends are clear enough. Since the 1870s the birth rate (numbers of children born per thousand population) has been declining. Behind this decline, the salient fact is a reduction in the average number of live births per married woman. Compared with an average of six children for those married in the 1870s, the typical family size for those married in the 1920s was a little over two, and

---

[1] For a detailed discussion of this group, see B. Thompson and A. Finlayson, 'Married women who work in early motherhood', *B.J.S.*, June 1963.
[2] B. Wootton, *Social Science and Social Pathology* (1959).
[3] See N. W. Bell and E. F. Vogel, *The Family* (1960).

has more recently gone up to rather less than three. At the earlier date, 24 per cent of mothers had 0–3 children, compared with 81 per cent for those married in 1925.[1] And while 33 per cent of Victorian mothers had eight or more children, only 2.3 per cent of those married after the First World War had similarly large families. In other words, today the typical family is two or three children (50 per cent come in this category). In Victorian times, families varied all the way from no children at all (9 per cent) to ten or more children (10 per cent) with about an equal percentage in all the intervening categories. However, because of the extension of education, the total number of years of dependency has declined less dramatically.

Now one conclusion emerges fairly clearly. Such a decline in *fertility* cannot be due to a decline in reproductive capacity. The contemporary mother, who has one, two, or three children (usually in the first ten years of marriage) could obviously, in the majority of cases, go on to have the six, eight or ten of her great grandmother. The fact that child-bearing is concentrated in the early years of marriage, and then ceases fairly abruptly, leaves little doubt that the smaller contemporary family is the result of deliberate decisions on the part of parents to limit conception. This conclusion is confirmed by an inquiry into family limitation which shows that the use of various methods of contraception has gone up. Only 15 per cent of wives married before 1910 practised some form of birth control, compared with 55 per cent of those married during 1940–7.[2]

Such facts do not explain why parents decide to limit their families. They suggest simply that the increasing availability and use of effective contraceptive means has enabled the typical family to be dramatically reduced in size. To discover why parents now limit their families, we have to ask in what ways the interaction between the family and society before the 1870s differs from the situation in the 1900s.

There was one main reason why the motive to use contraception was greatly strengthened in the nineteenth century. Advances in hygiene, and medicine had resulted in a marked decline in mortality, particularly among infants. A much higher proportion of children survived birth and were reared to maturity. In other words, in the past, mortality had effectively limited family size. The lesson of the nineteenth century is that centuries of established patterns of family

[1] Royal Commission on Population (1946). For demographic data, see also A. M. Carr-Saunders, D. Caradog Jones and C. A. Moser, *Social Conditions in England and Wales* (1958).

[2] *Papers of the Royal Commission on Population*, Vol. 1, Table 37.

behaviour could not be changed in a hurry—a lesson which is reinforced by the great difficulties in establishing population control
in the developing countries, where the decline in infant mortality,
unaccompanied by any compensating changes in the behaviour of
married couples, is causing an explosive growth in population.

To understand what seems to us to be the not very sensible practice
of having ten children, we must examine the interaction between the
family and the social system. Part of the explanation is to be found
in the interaction between the family and culture. Pre-industrial
societies are characterized by high levels of mortality. Moreover, the
population is threatened and periodically reduced by famines,
epidemics and wars. It is not surprising, that such societies should
urge child-bearing as a duty and condemn practices which aim at the
limitation of fertility. And England was no exception. Even today,
although families of the magnitude of Victorian times would be
condemned, the idea of marriage includes the idea of children, and
few voluntarily abstain.

Moreover, such cultural values have been incorporated into religious beliefs and in this way, have come to be part of religious dogma
and underpinned by religious sanctions. The marriage service of the
Church of England puts the procreation of children as the first of its
aims. The Church, too, has in the past strongly condemned contraceptive practices. As recently as 1908, the Lambeth Conference resolved: 'The Conference regards with alarm the growing practice of
the artificial restriction of the family, and earnestly calls upon all
Christian people to discountenance the use of artificial means of
restriction as demoralizing to character and hostile to national welfare.' Those who advocated the use of birth control were prosecuted,
and even today local authority clinics are permitted by a 1931 ruling
to give advice only to women for whom a further pregnancy would
be detrimental to health.[1]

Despite such prohibitions and condemnations, the practice of birth
control has spread. And concomitantly, the culture has been
modified and now adopts a more permissive attitude, as exemplified
by the encouragement to family planning in the report of the Lambeth
Conference of 1958. We still have to explain therefore, why the
practice has increased. One important fact provides a starting point.
Family limitation in the latter part of the nineteenth century was
predominantly a middle-class practice. It was not until the 1920s

---

[1] Quoted by O. R. McGregor and G. Rowntree in Welford, et al., op. cit.,
p. 404. See D. V. Glass, Population Policies and Movements in Europe (1940),
Chapter 1, for an account of the birth control movement.

that the wives of skilled manual workers report contraceptive practices as frequently as non-manual workers.[1] For those married in the early 1930s, there are no class differences (although these re-emerge subsequently). What then, led the middle classes to limit their families in the 1870s? And why did the manual workers not follow suit until a lapse of nearly fifty years?

The interaction between the family and the economic system provides the main clue. In an industrial society, the family ceases to be the main unit of organized production. Its economic function shifts from production to consumption. It is the family unit which consumes food, clothing and shelter, and such goods are bought mainly with the income of the male wage-earner. The larger the household, the more thinly a single income has to be spread,[2] unlike the agricultural family, where each child soon grows into a hand to work on the farm. In industrial England, child labour was gradually prohibited, first by the factory acts and then by the extension of compulsory education. As an increasingly high proportion of children survived birth, the total burden of pregnancies increased.

But it was not those who could least afford children who took the first steps to have fewer. Nevertheless, J. A. Banks[3] has argued that it was economic pressures which contributed to the decline in middle-class fertility after 1870. The middle-class had experienced rapidly growing prosperity in the 1850s and 60s. But the 70s saw the beginnings of a relative decline in the rate of growth of profits and increasing foreign competition. Moreover, many items in middle-class budgets, such as domestic servants and housing were becoming increasingly expensive. Faced with the desire to maintain and continue to improve their standards of living in a context of economic stringency and of families far larger than many parents desired, one practical solution was to limit family size. Moreover, the Bradlaugh-Besant trial and public controversy over birth control drew attention to this as a possible solution. Once begun, such practices gradually spread. Lower paid white-collar workers were under particular pressure to limit family size. As education became increasingly important for entry to middle-class occupations, middle-class parents became more anxious to bequeath the only inheritance within their

---

[1] *Papers of the Royal Commission on Population*, Vol. 1, Table 37.

[2] Even in middle-class homes, 'a large family still involves relative, if not absolute deprivation'. In larger working-class families, disadvantages are reflected in the lesser average height children and a greater incidence of respiratory infection. O. R. McGregor and G. Rowntree, in Welford, *op. cit.*, pp. 411–12.

[3] J. A. Banks, *Prosperity and Parenthood* (1954).

means to ensure that their children would be able to continue in middle-class occupations—a good secondary education. And this meant a very small family.

It is less easy to explain the tardiness of the manual workers in adopting family limitation on a similar scale. Skilled workers were enjoying rising wages in the last decade of the century. But about one-third of the manual workers in industrial cities were living under conditions of poverty. Over crowding, and poverty are not conducive to the foresight and planning which contraception involves. Short-term hedonism and passive acceptance of fate were the typical reactions to poverty.[1] These are not the conditions which favour a break from tradition and the introduction of innovating practices. And the subordinate 'servant' role of the manual-workers' wife tended to make her feel helpless at the prospect of successive unwanted pregnancies, and unable to take steps in the face of opposition and possible hostility from her husband. The segregated conjugal role structure of manual-workers' families defined the children as the wife's responsibility. Husbands paid over a fixed wage to their wives and it was for them to do the best they could.

The more recent increase in the birth rate must also be explained. In part, it is due to the fact that a higher proportion of women are married,[2] to the younger age at marriage, (from 23 in 1931 to 20 in 1962, for women) and the fact that women are having children at a younger age. Children who would have been born later are arriving earlier and the gap between generations is decreasing. These changes are themselves the result of rising incomes and the improvements in the supply of housing.[3] But the increase in fertility is not simply 'borrowing' children from the future. There is also evidence of an increase in family size. Younger marriages, of course, increase the risk of pregnancy, and married women are now faced with a longer potential childbearing period. There is some evidence that parents now want larger families. Incomes have risen, and welfare services have reduced, though not eliminated, the relative disadvantage of parenthood. Now that more can enjoy the material pleasure of affluence, some may begin to invest more in family life—becoming

[1] See Chapter 7 for a more detailed discussion of working-class subculture.

[2] Higher male infant mortality, plus the effects of the First World War, skewed the sex ratio so that in 1921 there were 894 males per 1,000 females. In 1951 the ratio was 1,089.

[3] Overcrowding has been greatly reduced since 1930, except in a few large cities. The current shortage of housing reflects the increase in effective demand due to rising incomes. Improved contraception and earlier physical maturation may also have contributed.

home-centred as a refuge from the anonymity of urban living and the meaninglessness of work. Such explanations must remain largely speculative until they have been tested by research.

The interaction between the family and the economic system is therefore very complex. There is no simple relation between poverty and fertility. There tends to be an inverse relation between wealth and family size. The high level of unemployment in the 1930s was accompanied by the rapid spread of contraception among manual workers. But the practice declined among those married from 1935 to 1947, and manual workers continue to have larger families than non-manual, although they can less well afford the cost. But other variables also operate, notably culture. And the relative value of children must be weighed against the sacrificed alternatives. The final equation will depend on both values and costs.

Illegitimacy

One corollary of the reproductive function of the family is the social condemnation of conceiving children out of wedlock. And a substantial increase in illegitimacy would indicate a change in the family's child-rearing function. Moreover, it would indicate a rejection of the prevailing norm which condemns extra-marital sexual intercourse. Crude illegitimacy rates indicate a substantial increase in illegitimacy during the Second World War, and larger numbers in the 1950s and 1960s compared with pre-1939. But all statistics require care in interpretation. Some maternities are conceived out of wedlock, but subsequently legitimized by the marriage of the pregnant bride. There has been a decline in the percentage of extra-marital conceptions thus legitimized. If the increase in the numbers of legitimate conceptions is also taken into account, we find that the percentage of all

TABLE 2.1

ILLEGITIMATE MATERNITIES AND PRE-MARITALLY CONCEIVED LEGITIMATE MATERNITIES, 1938 TO 1956, ENGLAND AND WALES*

	Illegitimate maternities	Pre-maritally conceived legitimate maternities	Total conceived extra-maritally %	Extra-maritally conceived legitimized %
1938	27,440	64,530	14·4	70·2
1946	55,138	98,626	11·8	44·1
1956	34,113	54,895	12·6	61·7

* Based on Table XI, Registrar General's *Statistical Review of England and Wales*, 1956, Part III.

extra-marital conceptions was less in 1946 than in 1938 and remained lower in 1956 (Table 2.1). Such facts do not, of course, enable us to draw conclusions one way or the other about 'morality', since there may have been an increase in sexual-intercourse among unmarried persons who may also have taken more effective steps to avoid pregnancy. The undoubted social problem of illegitimacy could be tackled either by achieving a reduction in extra-marital sex behaviour or by the more widespread use of effective contraception. The solution favoured will depend on the values and norms of society.[1]

Socialization
The family is not simply concerned with child-bearing. Child-rearing involves socializing the child to adopt the modes of behaviour appropriate for its age and sex in any particular society. We now know from anthropological studies that human personality is immensely pliable. Out of the biological raw material, a variety of different types of persons can be produced. We learn to play a variety of roles. Boys, for example, learn through identification with their fathers, how the behaviour of men differs from that of women in their society. Of course, societies have quite different norms of male and female behaviour. In one, the sex roles are the exact opposite of those in Victorian middle-class England. It is the men who sit idly gossiping and intriguing, putting flowers in their hair, and wondering what woman will glance in their direction, while the women work and hold the purse strings.[2] Whatever the norm may be, men and women will grow up believing that the sex roles they have learnt are 'human nature'. This process whereby society builds itself into our personalities teaches us specific ways of acting, thinking, and feeling, is the *socialization* process.

The socialization process is in fact, very complex, and can only be briefly sketched here in order to indicate the role which the family plays in socializing the child. From the day the child is born, he will begin to be socialized. For example, until recently, mothers were urged to feed their babies only at strictly regulated intervals. The majority of middle-class mothers followed such rigid feeding schedules, while working-class mothers did not. Anthropological studies indicated however, that demand-feeding may produce more secure personalities and fashions have swung in the opposite direction. Although rigid feeding schedules may not by themselves have a

---

[1] For a comprehensive analysis of illegitimacy, see V. Wimperis, *The Unmarried Mother and Her Child* (1960).
[2] M. Mead, *Male and Female* (1964).

decisive effect on personality, they are a part of a pattern of *'deferred-gratification'*, which middle-class children are likely to experience. At a later age, for example, they will be urged to sacrifice immediate pleasures to get on with their homework in order to pass exams which will ensure them a better job in the future.

The American philosopher G. H. Mead, and the founder of psychoanalysis, Sigmund Freud, have both contributed a good deal to our understanding of the socialization process. Mead stressed the great importance of language. If a mother wishes to stop a baby from some dangerous action, she will have to use physical restraint. An older child will respond to the verbal symbols 'Come back Johnny, you'll hurt yourself.' In fact, most social interaction is reaction to symbols, either verbal or expressive. It is, that is to say, *symbolic interaction*.

Very early in the socialization process, the child learns to differentiate between himself and others: what Freud call the *ego* emerges. He begins to build up an image of himself, an *identity*. A most important element in this image will be how he sees himself reflected in the eyes of others. If others respond to him by saying 'he's a clever boy', he may well come to think of himself as clever. This is what Cooley called the *looking-glass* self. Of course, we are more influenced by some individuals than others; especially those such as parents with whom we have a close emotional tie. These are our *significant others*. Later, as we extend our social circle, we come to be influenced by groups, such as school-friends. These are now our *generalized others*. Those groups whose membership we value and which can therefore, play a very important part in moulding our identity, Merton calls *reference groups*. We will consciously adopt those ways of behaviour which we hope will earn our acceptance by the group, such as styles of speech, and in this way engage in *anticipatory socialization*.

The role of the family in the socialization process is clearly crucial, particularly in what can be called *primary socialization*, that is to say, the development of those relatively stable elements in personality such as a sense of basic security. It has been observed, for example, that the middle-class are not only more likely to practise *deferred gratification*, but are more strongly motivated towards achievement. Researches show that this results when parents set high goals for their children, expect high standards of excellence, stress independence, and instil confidence.[1] By contrast, achievement motivation

[1] B. C. Rosen and R. D'Andrade, 'The Psychosocial Origins of Achievement Motivation', *Sociometry*, Sept. 1959, pp. 185–218.

is not developed in authoritarian 'father-centred' families, in which children receive little training in independence and achievement. Authoritarian fathers thwart their sons' efforts to be autonomous and self-reliant.[1] In other words, the family plays an important part in producing types of persons who have the characteristics appropriate for certain social roles.

Differences in the child-rearing practices between social classes have long been observed.[2] Recent studies[3] have brought to light some of the mechanisms involved in such differential socialization, and help to explain the more aggressive and severe socialization of working-class fathers. Fathers whose work gives them little autonomy, and who are controlled by others, exercising no control themselves, are found to be more aggressive and severe. Their sons less frequently admire such fathers or gain emotional support from them. These factors are in turn related to occupational aspirations. Mobility is maximum where socialization is moderate, parents share authority, sons identify with fathers and fathers are involved in their boy's emotional life.[4]

In all societies, other agencies besides the family contribute to socialization. In advanced industrial societies, formal educational institutions become very important indeed. The child is also exposed to other socializing media, such as TV. But the family remains extremely important, particularly at the level of primary socialization. Children whose home-life has been seriously disturbed are much more likely to become delinquent and to fail to achieve a satisfactory adjustment to society.[5]

Role-allocation

In many societies, for example in Mediaeval England, a man's position in society was largely determined by his family of origin. His status was *ascribed*, and birth was the major determinant.

In advanced industrial society, specialization and division of labour means that more and more jobs are filled by those with special talent and training. Status is generally *achieved*. But this does not mean that the family ceases to be important. As we shall see in more detail later, the family plays an important part in determining the

[1] Bernard C. Rosen, 'Socialization and Achievement Motivation in Brazil', *A.S.R.*, Oct. 1962, Vol. 27, No. 5. Also in W. J. Goode (ed.), *Readings on the Family and Society* (1964), Chapter 22.

[2] See J. Klein, *Samples from English Culture* (1965), Vol. II for a summary.

[3] D. G. McKinley, *Social Class and Family Life* (1964).

[4] See also Chapter 7 for a fuller discussion of the mobility process.

[5] B. Wootton, *op. cit.* (1959).

level of education achieved, and this in turn is closely related to occupational achievement. Although there is a good deal of mobility in the middle ranges of society, birth still confers great advantages in the achievement of positions at the top.[1]

Economic and sustaining functions

In pre-industrial society, production is usually organized on a family basis. The domestic system in Britain is a good example. Industrialization takes production out of the household into factories and offices. As a result, as we have seen, wives and adolescents are no longer completely dependent on the head of the family, with the resulting loss in his power. But the family remains the unit for consumption, consuming housing, food, and to some extent leisure on a household basis.

However, as we have seen, the supportive function of the family has been more important for manual workers in recent history. The mutual aid provided by the extended family in times of misfortune underlies some of the significance attached to kinship ties in traditional working-class areas.

Not only the does the family provide physical sustenance and shelter, it also cares for its members when ill and old. It is true that the resources of the family have been reinforced by the growth of specialized medical services, hospitals, and clinics, but it is still the husband, wife or parent who calls in the doctor, and receives the convalescent from hospital. Nor is there any evidence that children have ceased to care for their ageing parents.[2]

Affective functions

According to the marriage service of the Church of England, among the causes for which marriage was ordained, third place is given to 'the mutual society, help, and comfort, that the one ought to have of the other. . . .' Most married couples would probably place this somewhat higher on the list.

In some societies, especially primitive agricultural societies, the procreation of children to ensure the continuance of the male line is of over-riding importance, and a wife may well be selected for her husband by his parents with this aim paramount. Without a male heir, there will be no-one to inherit the family estate and to care for the ancestor's shrine.

Today, the emphasis is increasingly on companionship and com-

[1] Chapter 7.
[2] M. Young and P. Willmott, *Family and Kinship in East London* (1960).

patibility therefore becomes more important. We have already noted the shift towards a more equal relationship and the sharing of tasks in the home-centred family. In this context, husbands and wives become more and more dependent on each other for support and primary relationships. With increasing leisure, and the weakening of social networks, a wife becomes not only her husband's best friend, but also the one with whom he will spend an increasing amount of time. In one American research, 48 per cent of wives rated companionship as the most valuable aspect of marriage.[1]

Of course, as we have seen, some wives are *servants* rather than *companions*, where their role is to make good the damage done by his occupation. But a husband's occupation can make demands on his wife which are compatible with companionship. She may, for example, help her husband get ahead by entertaining business associates, acting as *hostess* companion or may actively collaborate with her husband in his work. Hostess wives appear to be most satisfied with their husband's companionship and working-wives least.[2]

Recent researches suggest that the family may provide an important outlet for the pent-up frustrations generated by the work situation. Semi- and unskilled workers enjoy few positive rewards from work, and little or no autonomy. One possible outlet for such frustrations is the family, and this may account for the more aggressive relations with wives and the more severe socializing techniques adopted by working-class fathers.[3] Thus in an industrial society, the family may become increasingly important for its tension-management function.

THE FAMILY AND SOCIAL CHANGE

It has already been indicated that industrialization has had a considerable impact on the family. But its precise consequences are still a matter of some controversy. Many argue that the family has been stripped of its functions. Some (usually moralists rather than sociologists) have gone so far as to say that the contemporary family is disintegrating. There is much more agreement on the fact that the process of industrialization is accompanied by the break-up of the traditional extended or joint family systems. But much depends

[1] R. O. Blood and D. M. Wolfe, *op. cit.* (1960).
[2] *Ibid.*
[3] D. G. McKinley, *op. cit.* (1964); R. Titmuss, *Essays on the Welfare State* (1961).

on the definition of the extended family. If by this is meant joint households, then recent studies show that the nuclear family is traditional in pre-industrial Europe, and that the 'multi-generational family of kin living under the same roof or in close geographical proximity may even be somewhat commoner in the contemporary industrial city than it was among the peasantry.'[1]

There is some evidence however, to suggest that kinship plays a more important part than some have supposed in the older stable working class areas of industrial cities. Young and Willmott, for example, show that family connections still count in getting jobs and accommodation in Bethnal Green. And in some trades, notably printing, family connections are almost essential for entry to apprenticeship. But there is already a wide range of jobs, including for example, the civil service, where entry is no longer by patronage and family connections but by passing competitive examinations. Moreover, house agents would be out of business if the kinship network could get us accommodation.

How many of these changes can be attributed to the industrialization process it is difficult to say. But it can be demonstrated that the nuclear or conjugal family is a relatively good 'fit' with the needs of an industrial society. Industrialization certainly requires a mobile labour force, and the resulting geographical and social mobility will strain extended kinship ties.

In discussing the effect of industrialization on the extended kinship ties, it is important to distinguish the control which the kin may exercise over its members from the affective bonds which may unite them. It may be perfectly true, as Litwak argues,[2] that occupational and geographical mobility does not necessarily weaken the affective ties which unite members of a family. But the changes discussed by Goode would appear to weaken the power which the kin can exercise over individuals in many segments of industrial societies. Rosser and Harris have shown that in South Wales, the extended family is still strong, in the sense that children still feel strong ties of affection to their parents and close kin. The three-generation family in which the elementary family still has strong affective links with the families of origin of the spouses persists. True, the structure is less close-knit, but it still performs an important function as a source of

[1] P. Laslett, 'The history of population and social structure', *Int. Soc. Sci. J.*, Vol. XVII, No. 4, 1965, and *The World We Have Lost* (1966).
[2] E Litwak, 'Occupational Mobility and Extended Family Cohesion', *A.S.R.*, Feb. 1960; 'Geographic Mobility and Extended Family Cohesion', *A.S.R.*, June 1960.

identity. And although the importance of the supportive function
has declined, the kinship network continues to give a sense of
stability and belonging.[1] Moreover, as Litwak has argued, this tie
can survive physical separation.

The thesis that industrialization has brought about the decline of
the extended family depends to some extent on definitions and criteria. Geographical mobility certainly reduces the frequency of
interaction—the criterion employed by Young and Willmott. Moreover, there is increasing social and cultural heterogeneity among its
members, as sons less often follow in their father's footsteps. But
this has not destroyed the very real sense of identity, which results in
frequent visits, telephone calls, or letters.[2] It is not, perhaps surprising, that the strong emotional ties with parents and siblings generated
by long years of childhood dependency, are not suddenly severed on
marriage. Moreover, the importance of kinship ties as a source of
identity is not confined to manual workers, but as Rosser and
Harris show, characterizes middle-class families too.

One result is that the individual is forced to make his way with less
family support—kinship places no hindrance on industry employing
the individual where he is needed. Moreover, the more close-knit
conjugal family knits in with the needs of industry by its emphasis
on affective support, which helps to restore the emotional balance of
individuals facing the strains and frustrations of industrial work.
Furthermore, the conjugal family specifies the status obligations of
its members in less detail than the extended family which assigns
specific tasks according to family position. Thus, the conjugal family
makes possible the wider variations in role performance which are
demanded by an industrial society with its emphasis on achievement.[3]

Industrialization may also go some way to explain the decline in
arranged marriages, and .the increase in divorce and re-marriage.
Families are not only less able to control their young, but as land
becomes less important, the advantages of family alliances have
declined. In the past, family lineages have had strong reasons for
fearing divorce and re-marriage because of its possible consequences
for alienating property or confusing inheritance.[4]

But this does not mean that the family will remain in its present

[1] *Op. cit.* (1965), pp. 226–33.
[2] *Ibid.*
[3] W. J. Goode, *World Revolution and Family Patterns* (1963), ch. 1.3, 'The
"Fit" between the Conjugal Family and the Modern Industrial System'. For a
more extended discussion, see B. F. Hoselitz and W. E. Moore, *Industrialisation
and Society* (1960).
[4] W. J. Goode, *op. cit.* (1963), p. 376.

form. Divorce statistics indicate that for some the pattern may be shifting from lifelong to serial monogamy; from one partner for life to a series of partners.

Divorce and Family stability

It is important however, to get the statistics in perspective. In the first place, they are not the only index of family stability. A marriage may be terminated by death. There was, in fact, a smaller percentage of divorced and widowed women in 1951 than in 1931, despite the enormous increase in divorce. Moreover, a wife who is no longer living with her husband may seek a maintenance order from the courts. Table 2.2 shows that whereas divorce petitions increased by more than thirty times, if these are aggregated with maintenance orders, the increase becomes about six times. It must also be remembered that the number of married persons has nearly doubled. The corrected ratio should therefore show a three-fold increase.

TABLE 2.2

PETITIONS FOR DIVORCE AND MAINTENANCE ORDERS, E. AND W.*

	Petitions for divorce	Maintenance orders	Total
1911–15	1,000	7,600	8,600
1951–54	33,100	14,500	47,600

* From O. R. McGregor, op. cit. (1957), p. 51.

Divorce statistics and court orders do not enable us to say anything about either the happiness of marriage or its de facto stability. They represent only those who for one reason or another have decided to seek legal recognition of the termination of their marriage. Changes in the law have, in fact, removed many barriers to the resort to divorce. The most important of these changes are the extension of grounds resulting from the Herbert Act in 1937, and the Legal Aid Act of 1949, which reduced the financial barriers. There has also been a change in public attitude and divorce no longer carries the stigma that it once did nor can it any longer threaten a career in public life. As a result of these changes, divorce is no longer the prerogative of the well-to-do, but is distributed proportionately through all sections of society. (Table 2.3.) In fact, the increase in divorce and maintenance orders since 1911 can be explained almost entirely as due to the growth of population and the removal of economic and social barriers.

The question remains which was raised earlier. Are the institutionalists right when they argue that any further liberalization of marriage laws would fatally weaken family ties? Historical evidence suggests that there could well be a further increase in divorce. But whether this would contribute to an increase in broken marriages is problematic. It might simply that more existing broken marriages become legally terminated.

The evidence also suggests that marriage may be becoming increasingly important and rewarding for the individual with the growth of the home-centred family in which companionship is increasingly valued. Satisfaction with the love, understanding, and standard of living provided by husbands is high even in America with its high divorce rates.[1]

TABLE 2.3

OCCUPATION AND DIVORCE (1951), E. AND W.*

	Prof. %	Farmers, shopkeepers %	Black- coated %	Manual % = 100
Divorcing	13·5	8·0	9·0	69·5
Continuing married	13·9	8·4	8·1	69·6

*O. R. McGregor and G. Rowntree in A. T. Welford, *op. cit.* (1962), p. 406.

On the other hand, it is arguable that the changing structure and functions of the family make stable marriage more difficult. As we have seen, in industrial societies, with the weakening of extended kinship networks, the conjugal family becomes increasingly important as a source of affective support for its members. With the shift from segrated to integrated conjugal roles, and the growing importance of companionship, husbands and wives interact more frequently and become more dependent on each other's company. These changes make greater demands on compatibility, compared with the more restricted interaction of husbands and wives characterized by a 'servant' or 'colleague' relation. Moreover, the tension management function can only be adequately discharged within the context of strong emotional bonds.

Such considerations may go some way to explain the fact that an increasing proportion of divorces takes place between those who have been married for over twenty years,[2] and that an increasing propor-

[1] R. O. Blood and D. M. Wolfe, *op. cit.* (1960).

[2] This is in part due to an increase in the expectation of life. As McGregor says, 'the divorce court is now taking over functions which, in the past, were the undertaker's prerogative', *op. cit.*, p. 50.

tion of divorcees re-marry. Marriage is more popular than ever, but the more exacting demands made upon it can only be discharged by spouses more adequately matched than the chances of cupid's bow necessarily ensure.[1] Moreover, there are always likely to be some who simply cannot match up to the heavy demands that marriage makes upon them.

SUMMARY AND CONCLUSIONS

The family can be viewed as a system of interrelated variables some of which are in turn related to the wider social systems. Sex roles are structured to a very high degree by the culture of the society, that is to say, by its norms, values and beliefs. The recognized patterns which result constitute the institutional complex of marriage and the family and reflect the normative expectations of members of society, some of which are reinforced by legal sanctions.

Within this broad framework, there are variations on the major themes. Husbands may be dominant, as in the patriarchial family, or the relationship may be more equalitarian. There may be a rigid sex division of labour or a sharing of household tasks. These variables are found to be related to the existence of social networks, and to the interaction between the family and the economic system. The nature of the husband's occupation and the demands which this makes on his married life, for example, may influence husband/wife relations, wives performing roles as 'servants' or 'companions'.

The family performs important functions not only for its members but also for society. Among the most important of these are not only procreation, but also the socialization of the child to fit him for adult roles. Furthermore, changes in the reproductive behaviour of the family and differences in the socialization process can be shown to be influenced by the interactions between the family and the economic and cultural systems. The evidence suggests that the socialization process in each stratum of society produces the personal qualities necessary to function in that stratum. It suggests that the upwardly-mobile working-class boy is hampered by much more than the relatively low income of his parents—as subsequent chapters will demonstrate.

The main trends in family life may be tentatively summarized as a decline in the close-knit extended kinship network, and in the sup-

---

[1] Researches into the factors associated with marital failure enable predictions to be made on the basis of data supplied by engaged couples. F. W. Burgess and L. S. Cottrell, Jr, *Predicting Success or Failure in Marriage* (1939).

portive function of the kin resulting in the privatization of family life, but the persistence of loose-knit affective kinship ties as a source of identity. The changing sex division of labour and an increasing integration of conjugal roles and the emergence of more equal relations between spouses reflects the decreasing demands of child-bearing and domesticity, expanded opportunities for wives to work and the break-up of stable communities. The growing importance of the affective functions of the elementary family, and the emergence of companionship as a major functional relationship between husbands and wives reflect a growing investment in family life with the declining saliency of work. The increasing frequency of the legal termination of unsatisfactory marriages results from the removal of barriers to divorce, and is consistent with the increasing saliency of satisfying marital relations in an urban industrial society.

QUESTIONS AND EXERCISES

1. Examine the relations between the nuclear family and extended kinship networks.
2. 'Husbands occupy roles in both the kinship and the economic systems.' Examine the implications of this for the family.
3. How would you account for the trend towards (a) integrated conjugal roles; (b) a more equalitarian relation between husbands and wives?
4. Explore the interrelations between the family and the economic system.
5. Examine the causes and consequences of the increased employment of married women.
6. Attempt a sociological explanation of trends in fertility since 1870.
7. Examine the role of the family in socialization in contemporary society.
8. Examine the contention that industrialization strips the family of its functions.
9. 'In all industrial societies, the nuclear family is emerging as the typical form.' Discuss.
10. 'Divorce statistics prove that the modern family is becoming increasingly unstable.' Discuss.

READING

*N. W. Bell and E. F. Vogel.—*The Family* (Free Press, Ill., 1960). A collection of essays and extracts. The introduction by the editors outlines a systematic and analytical approach to the study of the family. See especially Chapters 1, 5, 10, 11, 13, 19, 35, 41.

R. O. Blood and D. M. Wolfe.—*Husbands and Wives* (Glencoe, 1960). Empirical data on the variables, especially economic, influencing conjugal roles.

A. H. Carr-Saunders, D. Caradog-Jones and C. A. Moser.—*A Survey of Social Conditions in England and Wales* (OUP, 1958). A summary of demographic data up to 1951.

N. Dennis, F. Henriques and C. Slaughter.—*Coal in Our Life* (London, 1956). Chapter on the family life of miners.

*R. Fletcher.—*The Family and Marriage* (Penguin Books, 1962). A largely descriptive and historical study, setting out to challenge the thesis that the family is facing disintegration and moral decline. Useful source material on the conditions of the pre-industrial family in Britain.

H. Gavron.—*The Captive Wife* (Routledge, 1966).

*W. J. Goode.—*The Family* (Prentice-Hall, 1964), especially Chapters 5, and 7 to 10. Closely written but analytical in approach. Examines the relations between the family systems and social systems, drawing on a wide range of material from pre-industrial and industrial societies.

W. J. Goode (ed.).—*Readings on the Family and Society* (Prentice-Hall, 1964). A companion to the previous volume.

*W. J. Goode.—*World Revolution and Family Patterns* (Collier-Macmillan, 1963), especially Chapters 1, 2, and conclusion.

P. Halmos (ed.).—*The Sociological Review Monograph No. 8: The Development of Industrial Societies* (Keele, 1964), pp. 65–96. Examines the impact of industrialization on the structure, stability and functions of the family. Discusses the evidence and clarifies the issues.

J. Klein.—*Samples from English Culture*, Vols. 1 and 2 (Routledge, 1965). A summary of a number of monographs on the family together with an analysis of differences between middle and working class family life and culture, and socializing practices.

V. Klein.—*Britain's Married Women Workers* (Routledge, 1965).

*O. R. McGregor.—*Divorce in England* (Heinemann, 1957). Analyses the changing attitudes of the Christian churches to marriage and divorce, the statistics of divorce, and challenges the myths about the Victorian family.

D. G. McKinley.—*Social Class and Family Life* (Collier Macmillan, 1964). Empirical data on the relation between husband's occupation, family roles and socialization.

C. Rosser and C. Harris.—*The Family and Social Change* (Routledge, 1965).

*A. T. Welford, et al.—*Society* (Routledge, 1962), Chapters 21 and 24. A summary of data on population and the family.

*P. Willmott and M. Young.—*Family and Class in a London Suburb* (Routledge, 1960).

*M. Young and P. Willmott.—*Family and Kinship in East London* (Routledge, 1957). Two studies exploring the family in middle and working class suburbs.

Chapter 3

THE EDUCATIONAL SYSTEM

The crucial significance of *culture* for an understanding of social systems should now be beyond doubt. Shared beliefs, values, and norms ensure at least some measure of articulation between the behaviour of actors in a social system. On the first day at college, for example, both students and teachers enter with a set of shared expectations. Students attend to what the lecturer has to say and take notes, while despite differences in style, lecturers comply with well established conventions.

Every society is faced with the need to ensure adequate preservation and transmission of culture. In pre-literate societies, the cultural heritage is limited by what can be remembered and passed on from father to son, although even in such societies there may be some division of labour, and some individuals (priests, magicians) who specialize in the preservation and transmission of often esoteric knowledge. The invention of writing marks a major development since it permits cultural accumulation and preservation on a scale never before possible. And it necessitates the emergence of a class of learned men, either sacred or secular, who are the guardians and transmitters of knowledge.

Advanced industrial societies differ in other important respects even from early literate societies. Firstly, the rate of cultural innovation is greatly accelerated, due largely to the institutionalization of innovation with the growth of organized science research institutions, and a growing emphasis on the research function in the universities.[1] Secondly, they are characterized by universal literacy, which greatly extends the possibilities of cultural communication beyond a narrow class of literati. And thirdly, technological advances have made possible new and powerful cultural agencies in the form of radio, television and the cinema.

[1] D. S. L. Cardwell, *The Organisation of Science in England* (1957).

EDUCATION, CULTURE AND SOCIAL STRUCTURE

Schools and colleges are obviously major agencies of cultural preservation and transmission. But however important they may be in modifying the knowledge and beliefs, the norms, and the values of individuals, it would be somewhat arbitrary to limit discussion to such cultural agencies, and to ignore broadcasting, the Press, and the cinema. In this chapter, therefore, we shall be looking at all these agencies which are primarily concerned with cultural preservation, transmission, and innovation.[1] It will examine the way in which the main cultural agencies articulate with other major structural elements in society, notably the political and economic systems. Secondly, it will examine in particular schools and colleges as social systems and their performance, and any cultural transformations contributed by the mass media. In this analysis, we shall not be concerned with actual knowledge and belief systems, that is, with a study of the actual content of culture and its determinants. This is a subject for separate study in Chapter 6. But we must begin by noting that what is taught in schools involves selection from the sum total of culture. Indeed, the very word, 'culture' is ambiguous. We must turn first therefore, to an examination of the interaction between the educational system and culture.

Education and culture
Some years ago in his lecture on the 'Two Cultures'[2] C. P. Snow stimulated a debate which has continued to be a subject for keen controversy. He challenged the traditional notion of 'culture'[3] which excluded science and technology. He argued that this branch of knowledge was just as much a part of 'culture' as the arts and humanities. Our intellectual inheritance now includes a knowledge of the way in which man is achieving mastery over nature, as well as a knowledge of man's past and of his creative achievements in the field of art, literature and music.

This debate on the nature of culture raises an interesting question.

[1] Other agencies such as the family and churches are also involved in cultural transmission. But this chapter will concentrate on the systems of schools and colleges and those agencies such as the Press and broadcasting whose activities are closely articulated.

[2] *The Two Cultures and the Scientific Revolution* (1959).

[3] Throughout this chapter, wherever the meaning is ambiguous, the word *culture* in italics indicates that it is being used in a technical sociological sense; in quotation marks it indicates the use of the term to refer to valued intellectual products.

Why is the prevailing notion of culture being challenged at this particular time? It also provides an opportunity to clarify the difference between the technical meaning given to the word *culture* by sociologists and the social definition of 'culture' in any particular society. What Snow was really doing was to challenge the way in which society evaluates different kinds of knowledge. 'Culture' is the word which society uses to refer to certain kinds of intellectual products on which it places a high value. It is, that is to say, a prescriptive word; it tells us what kinds of knowledge we ought to value and acquire. Snow is saying that we ought to value and acquire knowledge of science and technology as well as literature and the arts, for these too are parts of 'culture'.

For the sociologist, this debate serves to illustrate the fact that societies attach more value to some kinds of knowledge than to others; and that this will have a profound effect on the activities of educational institutions whose task is to transmit and enlarge the body of 'culture', as society defines it. It also raises the very important question for the sociology of education: why do societies attach more value to some kinds of knowledge than to others?

To understand this, we must explore more fully the role which the men of knowledge and their organizations play in the social structure. Much early knowledge has grown out of the attempts to solve practical problems. Early knowledge of astronomy for example, grew from the problems of devising a calendar which was essential for the more detailed regulation of agriculture, and from navigation. Geometry, similarly, grew from the problems of architecture and building. Pythagoras's theorem provides us with a simple method for constructing a right angle, and π gives a formula for measuring the length of iron necessary to make a tyre for a wheel.[1]

Advances in technology made possible a more elaborate division of labour. But under the conditions in which early civilizations emerged, they also made possible a differentiation within society whereby a relatively leisured aristocracy was supported by the labours of a large subordinate stratum with varying degrees of slavery and freedom. It was this division of society which came to be reflected in the values attached to different kinds of knowledge. The leisured aristocracy in Greece, for example, speculated on politics and ethics, while mathematics became an intellectual activity divorced from its practical applications. Manufacture, agriculture and mining were carried on by slaves, and the knowledge related to such affairs came to be considered inferior ('banausic'—suitable for a

[1] See Chapter 6 for a more detailed analysis of the sociology of knowledge.

mere mechanic). Thus, the intellectual interests of the upper stratum have been related to their functions; to government, warfare and leisure. Politics, philosophy, literature and music have been valued by them and defined as 'culture', while technology has been excluded. Indeed, German universities refused to include technology in the nineteenth century, while English universities have in the past only acted as reluctant hosts.

The content of formal education then is socially determined. The curriculum reflects a society's evaluation of what it is important to teach. The 'Two Cultures' debate is related to the changing role of the scientist in society and his attempt to re-define 'culture' so that it reflects the importance of his role.

We have then a complex interrelation between *culture* and the social structure. What is defined as 'culture' will reflect the values of the dominant stratum, and these values in turn will be related to their role in the social structure. If the dominant stratum is a leisured aristocracy, they will tend to place high value on intellectual products related to their role. These will include creative intellectual products such as art and literature providing enjoyable leisure, while know-ledge of manufactures is only likely to be patronized if it contributes to warfare. This does not mean that science will be neglected, but it will be pursued as an intellectual activity rather than applied to practical affairs. Neither Greek nor Egyptian science was applied systematically to production.

Education and the economic system
The growth of knowledge (not only science and technology, but also of accounting, architecture, and the social and behavioural sciences) has been accompanied by its increasing application to production, administration and the provision of specialized services such as medicine. There has been increasing division of labour and the growth of a variety of intellectual occupations for the application of such specialized knowledge to practical affairs. These occupations include the 'professions' such as medicine, the law, engineering, accountancy, and a wide range of intellectual occupations such as radiographer, teacher, nurse, and technician. There are in fact nearly 200 occupations for which qualifications can be gained by passing the written examinations of qualifying associations.[1] In addition, there are a large number of occupations for which qualifications may be important for promotion, such as national certificates in engineering for draughtsmen and technicians or City and Guilds certificates for

[1] G. Millerson, *The Qualifying Associations* (1964).

operatives and craftsmen, but which are not awarded by qualifying associations. The implications for education are obvious. Educational qualifications have become increasingly important for occupational advancement. Some idea of the scale of vocational educational effort can be gained by the fact that there are something like one and a half million students enrolled in part-time (day and evening) vocational classes in technical colleges.[1] To this must be added the large numbers studying by correspondence courses, and those reading full-time for subjects such as medicine and engineering in universities and technical colleges.

We have a situation then where a considerable proportion of those in the elite educational institutions are reading subjects which have little relevance to practical affairs, while the bulk of the educational preparation for industry is by part-time study in technical colleges and by correspondence courses. The clue to this situation is to be found partly in the way in which society has defined culture and therefore influenced the activities of educational institutions. As we have seen, the prevailing notion of culture in the nineteenth century certainly excluded knowledge of manufacture. A second factor was the existence of traditional institutions for the transmission of knowledge of practical affairs. From the lawyer to the craftsman, apprenticeship had become the traditional vehicle for educating the novice. This had one advantage, among others, in that it allowed a profession to safeguard the 'secrets' of its practice and so strengthen its market situation against the entry of unauthorized parvenus. The rapid expansion of intellectual occupations in the nineteenth century occurred in this context, in which the idea of the university excluded vocational studies for business, and manufacture (but not the church and politics), and in which apprenticeship[2] was the traditional vehicle for vocational education and training.

As more and more professions introduced written examinations as a test of competence, the problem of providing the necessary education was solved in a variety of ways. The chartered accountants, for example, turned to correspondence courses, and have strongly resisted attempts to provide full-time courses in technical colleges.[3] Solicitors followed a similar practice, supplemented by short intensive cram-courses. Engineering drew some of its members from the universities, but between the wars, an increasing number had

[1] S. F. Cotgrove, *Technical Education and Social Change* (1958).

[2] G. Williams, *Recruitment to Skilled Trades* (1957). See also Chapter 4 for a discussion of apprenticeship as an occupational strategy.

[3] S. F. Cotgrove, *op. cit.* (1958), Chapter 11.

studied part-time at technical colleges. The technical colleges expanded rapidly after the 1880s to meet a growing demand for paper qualifications in a wide range of manufacturing and business studies. They were essentially a product of the nineteenth century with its deeply rooted belief that practical experience was the best teacher for practical affairs and that educational institutions could contribute little. The demand came from ambitious students anxious to acquire a paper qualification which they could use as a lever for promotion. It is from this that we have inherited the 'night-school' tradition of part-time study to supplement practical experience. As knowledge has grown, this situation has been increasingly challenged. Rapid advances in electronics, for example, have made it more and more difficult for the engineer to acquire the necessary knowledge by part-time study. Moreover, as the demand for qualified manpower has exceeded the supply in many fields, traditional part-time methods have been under pressure to change.[1]

One important function of examinations[2] is to confer a licence to practise. In medicine, for example, examinations test the fact that the doctor has the knowledge necessary for competent practice. But in many such occupations, it is believed that various personal qualities are also necessary. Where the examination confers a licence to practise, it will be important to try to select first for personal qualities those who are to be accepted for education and training. Social work students are a further example. Where qualification is not a licence to practise, selection can take place afterwards and not all who qualify are admitted to the occupation. A degree in history, for example, does not by itself confer a licence to teach. Recognition by the Department of Education and Science is also necessary after a probationary period.

The impact of the economic system on education has led not only to the emergence of new institutions for vocational education. The occupational significance of education has also influenced the structure and content of secondary education. The growing demand for grammar-school places over the last fifty years reflects the recognition not only by middle-class, but increasingly by working-class parents that the grammar-school provides the key to entry to the coveted, secure, black-coated and professional occupations. The occupational significance of the grammar school is confirmed by the large scale research into social mobility carried out by the London

[1] *Ibid.*
[2] For a detailed analysis of the various functions of examinations, see S. Wiseman (ed.), *Examinations and English Education* (1961).

School of Economics after the Second World War.[1] This concludes that a grammar school education is strongly associated with the achievement of higher status occupations. Dr Banks has also shown that the occupational significance of secondary education has influenced the school curriculum where attempts in the inter-war years to establish a technical curriculum orientated towards careers in industry failed because of the relatively lower status and poorer chances of upward mobility associated with technical jobs. It also accounts for the failure of the secondary modern school to achieve parity of estec

The grammar school borrows prestige from the occupations for which it prepares,[2] and buildings and equipment alone cannot earn parity of esteem in the eyes of society for schools which lead to the lower rungs of the occupational ladder.

Pressures from the economic system can distort educational processes in other ways. If the emphasis shifts from studying for examinations as a means of improving one's performance in a job to seeking qualification as a means of achieving promotion, there may come to be little relation between the content of the curriculum and the occupation for which it is ostensibly intended. Studies of the craft examinations of the City & Guilds illustrate this process. An analysis of the content of craft courses in the mid-1950s[3] brought to light a rather surprising finding, that a high proportion of these so-called 'craft' courses were pitched at technician level. A possible hypothesis is that this situation has resulted from the fact that such courses have functioned in the past as a basis for selecting technicians rather than training craftsmen. It has already been noted that the growth of technical education has been due mainly to the demand by ambitious men for a qualification that can earn them promotion. If an examination performs a selective function, this could explain the fact that high rates of failure had been tolerated in such examinations. Moreover, the curriculum can be related to future function rather than present occupation; hence the technician rather than craft level of the course. In order to test this hypothesis, a follow-up study was made of men who had sat a City & Guilds examination some years earlier. It was found, as predicted, that the majority of those who had passed had left the bench and become technicians, while most of those who failed remained craftsmen.[4] Further re-

[1] D. V. Glass (ed.), *Social Mobility in Britain* (1954).

[2] O. Banks, *Parity and Prestige in English Secondary Education* (1955).

[3] S. F. Cotgrove, 'Technicians and the City and Guilds', *Technology* (Dec. 1958).

[4] Incidentally, this research brought to light an unexpected finding. Those who

search may show that other occupational qualifications function as a basis for selection rather than as a vehicle for the transmission of occupationally relevant knowledge.[1]

Education and the political system

In Britain, the relations between education and the political system have attracted little attention from sociologists,[2] who have been mainly preoccupied with exploring educational opportunity. The state has itself been primarily responsible for determining educational opportunity, since it is the political system which allocates researches to education, and determines who shall be educated. The series of education acts are all examples of state intervention, mainly to extend the provision of various forms of education to wider classes of individuals. In doing so, the political system has responded to a variety of pressures, including the demand from more and more individuals for an extended education, partly because this is defined as good in itself and should therefore be available to all, but more important because of the growing recognition of the value of education for social advancement.[3]

Apart from its role in the provision of educational opportunity, the state in Britain has allowed a considerable degree of autonomy to the educational system. This situation is itself largely the result of historical forces which shaped the relations between the educational and political systems during the formative years of the state system in the nineteenth century, and the struggle for control between the religious denominations and the state. The growth of new knowledge after the Renaissance was in any case a challenge to the religious

had passed no longer thought of themselves as being simply craftsmen; passing the examination had modified their identities. They felt that they were worth a better job than those who had failed or never even studied, and this had motivated them to seek promotion from the bench.

[1] City and Guilds courses have now been revised, and the multifunctional courses which functioned to promote those who passed, and to provide some relevant knowledge for those who failed have been replaced by separate courses more closely geared to the occupational needs of craftsmen and technicians. But in the light of the above evidence, it can be predicted that unless the majority of craftsmen are expected to have passed exams, those who have qualified will continue to seek promotion and may well be lost to the ranks of craftsmen.

[2] The trend report by J. Floud and A. H. Halsey, 'The Sociology of Education' (*Current Sociology*, No. 3, 1958), does not include any systematic discussion of the relations between education and politics.

[3] See M. Ginsberg (ed.), *Law and Opinion in the Twentieth Century*, pp. 319–46, chapter by D. V. Glass, for an account of the extension of educational opportunity.

monopoly of culture in the middle ages. But the struggle between the Anglicans and the non-conformists delayed the establishment of a state system of education for half a century. The free churches feared that a state system might lead to the imposition of Anglicanism.[1] Consequently, Anglicans, non-conformists, and Roman Catholics all provided their own schools and their own teacher-training colleges, lest their rivals should extend their influence over the minds of the young.[2] When state education was finally introduced, the system of control first by school boards, and then by local education authorities of local government gave a maximum of local autonomy, reflecting not only the fears of the non-conformists of state dominance, but also the prevailing *laissez-faire* ideology. Indeed, the first board schools were seen as an extension of the poor law, intended only for the children of manual workers, and not for the middle-classes who could afford to provide for the education of their own children.[3]

The trend, however, is to strengthen the powers of the government. The 1902 Act was largely permissive. It empowered local authorities to provide education. The 1944 Act established a Minister for Education, with the duty to promote education and to ensure the execution of a national policy under his control and direction. This reflects the increasing role of the government in an industrial society to mobilize human and material resources and to allocate them to socially desired goals. It reflects too, the increasing demand for educational opportunity from below.[4] But the local authorities still retain some autonomy in deciding on the extent and nature of provision and the form which the organization of local education may take. However, even here, there has been growing pressure from the Labour government for reorganization along comprehensive lines, and the possibility of some action to integrate the public schools.

The measure of autonomy of the education authorities from central government control does not, of course, mean that teachers enjoy autonomy in the classroom. On the contrary, pressures from the

[1] The Anglicans for long refused a licence to teach to non-Anglicans: while at Oxford and Cambridge, those who were not members of the Church of England were excluded until 1871. See W. O. Lester Smith, *Education* (1957), for a brief account.

[2] For a more detailed analysis of the relations between religion and education, see N. Hans, *Comparative Education* (1949).

[3] For an account of the extension of elemertary instruction, see G. A. N. Lowndes, *The Silent Social Revolution* (1937).

[4] W. O. Lester Smith, *op. cit.* (1957).

universities at the upper levels of secondary education largely determine the curriculum, while the influence of central government inspectors, has probably been considerable. A major source of control over the teacher, however, especially at the lower levels, comes from his selection, education and training in, until recently, mainly single sex institutions, segregated from other forms of post-secondary education for other professions. The teacher's role in socialization and the inculcation of values make his work the object of anxious scrutiny. The close association between the churches and teacher training exemplifies the concern of society with the role of the teacher who is expected to transmit culture without challenging prevailing moral standards and religious beliefs.[1]

MASS MEDIA AND THE SOCIAL STRUCTURE

The relations between the mass-media and the social structure are generally very different from those of schools and colleges. The Press, for example, is mainly privately owned and controlled. And it is this which is at the root of much of the anxiety which has given rise to two royal commissions on the Press.[2] A major fear underlying these inquiries is that there may be a growing concentration of ownership, which would reduce the range of opinion. The 1949 report concluded that there was nothing approaching a monopoly in the Press, and that the largest single aggregation of newspapers under one ownership (Kemsley Newspapers Ltd) accounted for 17 per cent of the total of daily and Sunday papers. But by 1962, the commission reported a marked increase in concentration. Seventeen daily or Sunday papers had ceased production since 1949 and only four new ones had started.[3] The 1962 commission concluded that there is still a considerable range of choice, but it would be better if there were more.

Advertising constitutes a substantial proportion of the revenue of the Press. This is the key for understanding relations between the Press and the economic system. The ability of a publication to compete for advertising depends not only on the size of its readership,

[1] Community control over teachers especially in rural areas in the United States penetrated far into their private lives in the recent past. See L. A. Cook, *Community Backgrounds of Education* (1935).

[2] *Royal Commission on the Press*, 1947–1949 (1949); *Royal Commission on the Press*, 1961–1962 (1962). For a historical account of the Press and its place in society, see F. Williams, *The Dangerous Estate* (1959), and R. Williams, *The Long Revolution* (1961).

[3] 1962 report, p. 112.

but also on its character. 'Quality' papers, for example, have a smaller circulation, but they are read by the higher income groups and by those in positions which enable them to control substantial expenditure. Such papers therefore are able to charge much higher rates. Such dependence on advertising revenue has inevitably raised the question of the possibility that advertisers may seek to influence the expression of opinion. The 1949 commission had some evidence of such attempts, though it considered them to be infrequent and largely unsuccessful. The main aim of a paper is to increase its circulation. It is more likely, therefore, to be influenced in what it prints by the interests of its readers than of its advertisers. Nevertheless, the 1949 commission considered that a paper will 'probably avoid taking a line detrimental to advertisers' interests unless by so doing it can increase its interest to the public'.[1]

There are two main keys to the content of the Press. Firstly there is the influence of the proprietors. Most papers are consistent adherents of a particular political party. Partisanship occurs in all papers to some degree. 'The Press is part of our political machinery, which is essentially partisan.'[2] Although proprietors will seldom exercise day to day control over their editors, they will choose men whose views coincide with the policy which the proprietors wish to pursue.[3] But the distortions of truth and excessive bias were not confined to any one form of ownership. The 1949 report concluded that all the popular papers and some of the quality papers fell short of the standard achieved by the best through excessive partisanship or distortion in the interest of news value.[4] The second main influence is the pursuit of large circulation, the main root of the second major criticism of the Press—its triviality and sensationalism. Neither of these shortcomings was peculiar to newspapers with any particular form of ownership, and occurred in papers owned by co-operative societies, as well as those where political control is formally divorced from commercial policy.

THE EDUCATIONAL SYSTEM

So far we have examined the articulation between the educational system and other elements of the social structure. We turn now to an

[1] Op. cit., p. 143.
[2] Report 1949, p. 151.
[3] For a more detailed discussion of the Press and politics, see F. Williams, op. cit. (1959).
[4] Op. cit., p. 151.

examination of the interaction between the sub-systems within the educational system itself. A full treatment would require an analysis not only of the various educational and cultural structures such as schools, colleges, universities, newspapers, broadcasting companies, but also the interaction between them; between, for example, universities and grammar schools, television companies and schools.

Relatively little sociological inquiry of this kind has, in fact, been carried out. Indeed, it is only comparatively recently that attention has been focused on schools and colleges as social systems. The main emphasis here has been on the interaction between student sub-cultures and the academic process, and quite recently, attempts have been made to look at the school as an organization and to study the teacher's role in the organization and in society. These latter aspects are more appropriately discussed within the context of the study of organizations in Chapter 8 and the analysis of occupations in Chapter 4.

In examining schools and colleges as social systems, a major focus of interest is to obtain some kind of measure of their functioning. It is in the classroom and lecture hall, at the grassroots of the system, that the function of the cultural transformation of students and pupils takes place. Fortunately, we have such measures, crude though they may be, in the shape of statistics on examinations and other indices of educational performance. These provide us with some measure of the result of the interaction process between child and teacher, student and lecturer. And it is important to stress that in order to understand this interaction process, we need to explore the characteristics not only of pupils, in terms of their potential for learning, their attitudes and motives, but also the characteristics of the teachers with whom they interact in the classroom, and the total school environment. Moreover, as the child also interacts with his family and neighbourhood as well as with the school, the educational process cannot be understood without taking account of the family and neighbourhood influence.[1]

The school as a social system

As we have seen the functions of education are the development of personal qualities including the inculcation of values and norms and

[1] The educability of the child 'depends as much on the assumptions, values and aims embodied in the school organization into which he is supposed to assimilate himself, as on those he brings with him from his home'. Jean Floud and A. H. Halsey, 'The Sociology of Education' (*Current Sociology*, Vol. VII, No. 3, 1958: Blackwell), p. 184.

the transmission of knowledge. These are two primary goals which society expects the schools to achieve. They constitute the *charter* of the educational system. To these must be added a third. Attendance at school is compulsory up to the statutory school-leaving age. The schools have, therefore, to ensure attendance and to perform a custodial function.

Schools may attach varying degrees of importance to these goals. In other words, we can conceptualize the culture of the school as being predominantly 'academic', 'missionary' or 'custodial', according to the emphasis it places on academic achievement, developing the personal qualities of the child (child-centred) or simply maintaining order and discipline. The culture of the school will reflect not only the expectations of society but will also be influenced by its interaction with its environment. Academic goals are the main objective of many schools, particularly grammar schools in middle-class areas. Such schools will be characterized by a predominantly academic sub-culture, shared by staff and pupils. By contrast, a secondary modern school in a working-class area will find it extremely difficult to pursue academic goals. Its pupils have been defined by the selection process as unacademic, and the values of working-class culture compared with middle-class culture do not place the same premium on academic achievement. Two dominant goals seem to be adopted by such schools. Firstly, they may adopt a custodial role, aimed primarily at keeping the children in order. Alternatively, they may stress the socializing function of the school and pursue a primarily missionary role.[1]

A second major element in the school system will be the allocation and definition of roles. The teacher's role is in part defined by society and the educational system. But the goals of the school will also generate role expectations to which the teacher will be under pressure to conform. In the 'custodial' school, his role will be what Webb[2] has conceptualized as the 'drill-sergeant', with its emphasis on discipline, punishment and routine. In this way, the goals of the school will influence the strategies which are developed both inside and outside the classroom, and the responses of the pupils. Drill-sergeant techniques for example, are likely to generate high levels of aggression which spill over into delinquency after school. Such a school is likely to exhibit the characteristics of a 'blackboard jungle', requiring even more stern repressive measures and the further domi-

[1] M. Carter, *Home, School and Work* (1962), Chapter 3, describes a number of schools which could be fitted into these categories.

[2] J. Webb, 'The Sociology of a School', *B.J.S.* (Sept. 1962).

nance of custodial functions. It will exhibit a strongly developed delinquent subculture.[1]

A grammar-school in a working class area is less likely to abdicate academic goals. One way in which it may solve its problems is by adopting rigorous streaming, and by sponsoring selected pupils to ensure that some, at least, achieve the academic goals which are the criteria for success of the grammar school.

Two factors will modify this over-simplified picture. Firstly, the personal qualities of teachers will influence the 'style' with which they play their roles. A teacher with considerable flair, may be able to play a custodial role in a way which is compatible with the pursuit of academic or missionary goals. Secondly, a process of selection and self-selection may occur. 'Academic' teachers who find themselves in 'missionary' schools will be under pressure to change, but it is un-likely that all teachers even in a long-established school will adopt the same goals.

A third subculture has been described by students of American high schools which may also be applicable in Britain. Researches indicate the existence of a 'fun' subculture in addition to the 'aca-demic' and 'delinquent' subcultures already discussed. The fun sub-culture attaches value to good personality, being friendly, good reputation, being an athlete, good grades and being smart—although the latter accounts for only 12 per cent of the response. Indeed, the competition for recognition and status in such a subculture does not include academic success. The prevailing norms are against working too hard.[2] Thus, although the fun subculture may be sup-ported by the school with its emphasis on athletics as a means of achieving identification and integration, its also functions to inhibit the pursuit of academic goals.

Studies of American college life have similarly brought to light the existence of four comparable student subcultures, differing in the importance attached to collegiate life and to involvement with ideas.[3] The 'collegiate' subculture involves strong attachment to college life, to sports, college societies and other extra-curricular activities. It is however, resistant to excessive involvement in studies or ideas beyond what is necessary to pass examinations. Its most

[1] See Burton R. Clark, *Educating the Expert Society* (1962), for a more detailed account.
[2] James S. Coleman, 'Academic Achievement and the Structure of Competi-tion', *Harvard Educational Review*, Vol. 29, 1959 (summarized in Burton R. Clark, *Educating the Expert Society* (1962)).
[3] Burton R. Clark, *op. cit.* (1962).

active supporters come from the upper and upper-middle classes, and it flourishes only in residential colleges. The 'vocational' subculture sees the college courses as leading to diplomas and degrees and the better jobs which these can command. It is resistant to intellectual demands beyond those necessary for passing examinations and to active involvement in college life. Its supporters are usually students from lower-middle or working class homes. The 'academic' sub-culture identifies with the value of the academic staff. Knowledge and ideas are intrinsically valuable and the excitement of intellectual study is the main motivation. The 'non-conformist' subculture is critical of the 'establishment' and detached from the college. Such students may be deeply involved with the ideas of the classroom, and even more with current issues in literature, politics, or art. They are often seeking identity and are likely to adopt distinctive styles of dress.

With the increasing proportion of boys from lower-middle class homes, the collegiate subculture is declining and the vocational becoming dominant. The problem facing the colleges now is not whether students will study or play, but whether they will concern themselves with narrow studies for a job. Student peer-group cultures have been shown to exert a powerful influence on the activities and interests of students and to enable them to resist the influence of faculty members.[1] This raises an interesting question. One result of encouraging the development of a strong student community by residential accommodation may be to reduce the impact of the intellectual challenge of college life.

It must be stressed that in looking at schools and colleges as sub-systems, we can only understand the changes taking place by relating them to the external educational and social system. The changes in student subcultures, for example, are functions of the changing social origins of students and of the changing relations between education and occupation. Similarly, the adoption of particular teaching strategies such as streaming is only possible in some societies where they are congruent with the mobility system and its supporting ideology. Streaming is not practised at all, for example, in the USSR where the culture is strongly equalitarian and opposed to the notion of the inherent superiority of some individuals. Similarly, the gradual eroding of aristocratic values and the shift to a more equalitarian ethos in British society may be a factor contributing to the modification of a sponsored system of education[2] with a decline in streaming

---

[1] J. H. Bushnell, 'Student Culture at Vassar', in N. Sanford (ed.), *The American College* (1962), Chapter 14.
[2] This is discussed later in this chapter.

and educational segregation at the secondary stage.

This discussion of the existence of high-school and college sub-culture raises the more general question of the extent to which these articulate with a more pervasive youth culture. It is to this to which we now turn.

AGE GROUPS AND YOUTH CULTURE

Although the family and the school are major agencies for the socialization of the young, there are a number of ways in which they fail to bridge the gap between childhood and adult status, particularly in modern complex societies.[1] Such societies are characterized by a great variety and complexity of youth groups which function to help bridge this gap.[2] In these societies, status is largely achieved and judged by universalistic criteria, mainly performance. In the family, by contrast, status is ascribed and relations are charged with strong emotional ties. There is, that is to say, a sharp discontinuity between the emotionally secure world of children and the impersonal world of adults. The school, however, does little to bridge this gap. It reflects rather the achievement oriented, universalistic, affectively neutral values of adult society. The emphasis is on the instrumental activities of mastering educational skills. Moreover, the great difference in power and authority between teacher and pupil still further emphasises the discontinuities between the world of the child and that of the adult.[3] Further more, the extension of education delays social maturity until well beyond the attainment of sexual and physiological maturity, generating fresh problems for the older adolescent.

It is under such conditions that young people develop a need to join youth groups. Here the emphasis is on solidarity, on belonging to a group, in which status is ascribed. The criterion for acceptance is age. The emphasis is on expressive activities (sports, dancing, wearing fashionable 'gear', special language) participation in which symbolizes membership and solidarity. There is strong emphasis

[1] For an early and readable discussion of this view, see M. Mead, *Coming of Age in Samoa.*

[2] S. N. Eisenstadt, *From Generation to Generation* (1956) (esp. pp. 159–85).

[3] M. P. Carter, *Home, School and Work* (1962), documents the strong resentment against the authority relations of the classroom, where adolescents are treated like children and contrasts this with the adult status of the young worker in the factory. These considerations raise serious doubts about the recommendations of the Newsom report to extend the school day.

on common experience, and mutual identification.[1] The age group functions, that is to say, to help the adolescent to achieve an identity, with an accepted status in a group, in a society in which he has not yet achieved an adult status, and in which his ascribed family status is no longer adequate. The very insecurity of his status in the changing peer group emphasizes the need for conformity and the intolerance of non-conformity.[2] It is the discontinuities between childhood and adulthood which explain the adolescents' need for the membership of an age group.

The existence of age-groups does not necessarily justify the conclusion that these are also characterized by distinctive subcultures. There is, in fact, some terminological confusion as to the precise meaning to be attached to the notion of a youth culture. Hess argues, that if we mean by this 'a set of values that are independent of the values of adult society, and .. are transmitted from one generation to another,'[3] then it would be difficult to argue that youth culture in this sense exists. More usually, however, the term is used to indicate patterns of behaviour among young people which differ from, and are sometimes in conflict with, those of their parents. Parsons, for example, characterizes youth culture as emphasizing athletic prowess, and evaluating individuals by non-utilitarian qualities such as glamour and irresponsibility.[4] It is important to establish that such subcultural differences are not, in fact, a reflection of differing adult subcultures; that is, that they reflect class subcultures. Moreover, the degree of difference may be relatively mild. Where the differences involve marked conflict with adult values, Yinger suggests the term contra-culture.[5]

Empirical researches in America, however, have failed to find support for the existence of a contra-culture.[6] A recent study of political attitudes among young voters in Britain[7] also fails to find any distinctive characteristics. Moreover, a study of the aspirations of school-leavers found that in their beliefs about the place of hard

---

[1] S. N. Eisenstadt, op. cit. (1957), p. 184. This is also the conclusion of a study by Ralph Turner, The Social Context of Ambition (1964).

[2] Ralph Turner, op. cit. (1964).

[3] D. Gottlieb and J. Reeves, Adolescent Behaviour in Urban Areas (1963).

[4] T. Parsons, Essays in Sociological Theory (1954), Chapter V.

[5] J. M. Yinger, 'Contraculture and Subculture', A.S.R.. Oct. 25, 1960, pp. 625–35. See also D. M. Downes, The Delinquent Solution (1966), Chapter 1, for a discussion of the concept of delinquent subculture.

[6] Ralph Turner, op. cit.

[7] P. Abrams and A. Little, 'The Young Voter in British Politics', B.J.S., June 1965.

work in getting-on, and in their ambitions, 'young people do seem to be remarkably like us'.[1]

Turner provides a clue when he stresses the segmental and ritualistic character of youth culture.[2] It does not embrace a set of values and beliefs about all the major areas of life, but is primarily related to peer group activities. Moreover, its symbolic function as a means of expressing solidarity gives it a ritualistic flavour: it may be subscribed to without any inner conviction or internalization. It follows that youth culture does not necessarily involve the devaluation of academic and occupational achievement. In particular, it does not necessarily eradicate differences in attitudes towards education and occupation derived from class backgrounds, and has less of an equalizing effect than might be supposed. Turner found in fact, from a study of 2,800 children in ten American high schools (senior classes, twelfth grade) that the ambitious were more likely to be favoured by their peers, and that academic success was no bar to popularity. The only exceptions emerged when Turner distinguished between neighbourhoods. Here, the schools which drew predominantly from lower middle-class backgrounds did provide some support for the hypothesis that there is antagonism between youth culture and ambition. A study of English grammar school boys indicates similar conclusions. Criteria for choosing friends included among favoured characteristics putting homework first, reading and talking about books, and a preference for those who spend half rather than most of their time in playing games. There were, however, significant differences in the preferences of working class boys, indicating the persistence of subcultural differences in the grammar school, with middle-class boys showing a higher regard for scholastic attainments and greater willingness to postpone gratifications.[3]

If this view is correct, it suggests that the role of the mass media in determining youth culture is less crucial than is often supposed. The teenager has certainly become an industry. His substantially increased earnings have attracted the interests of the mass media advertising and the entertainments industry.[4] These have provided him with the symbols which he needs—'pop' music, 'pop' art, 'gear' as expressions of peer-group identity and symbolic ritual activities. But in doing so they are meeting needs generated by the ambiguous

[1] T. Veness, *School Leavers* (1961), p. 165.

[2] *Op. cit.*, p. 144–6.

[3] A. N. Oppenheim, 'Social status among grammar school boys', *B.J.S.*, Sept. 1955.

[4] M. Abrams, *Teenage Consumer Spending in 1959* (1961).

status of the adolescent in society, and the discontinuities between childhood and adult status which the family fails to meet, and the extended schooling exacerbates.

EDUCATION AS SOCIAL PROCESS

Schools function as systems, bringing together in an interaction process teachers and pupils with various characteristics, and achieving varying degrees of cultural transformation in the pupils, in their knowledge, beliefs, values, norms.[1] There is now a considerable amount of empirical data to enable us to measure the outputs of the system and to isolate the variables which contribute to these outputs.

Scholastic attainments

As a starting point, we can observe that there are considerable differences in the output of children with differing social backgrounds from various sectors of the educational system. A much higher proportion of the children of non-manual workers have attended grammar schools, and gone on to university. (Table 3.1) Moreover, the children of unskilled workers are not only under-represented on entry to grammar school, (Table 3.2) but gradually fall farther behind in their educational achievements, (Table 3.3).

Such differences in output may reflect either qualitative or quantitative differences in input. Before 1944, children from working-class homes were certainly hindered by financial barriers from attending grammar-schools. But the abolition of fees has not resulted in the levelling-up in educational achievements that was expected. As can be seen from Table 3.1, the chances of the son of a manual worker reaching university are very small compared with sons of professionals and managers. Educational opportunities have greatly increased, but the class differences in opportunity remain. Indeed, although there was some narrowing of differentials in the inter-war and early post-war period, they may have widened slightly rather than narrowed in more recent years, with the declining importance of standardized ability tests in selection at eleven-plus.[2]

In the nineteenth century, it was widely assumed that the lack of achievements of some strata in society were due mainly to their

[1] The interaction process also has consequences for the teachers, including the experience of strain and conflict. This will be discussed in the next chapter.

[2] A. Little and J. Westgaard, 'The Trend in Class Differentials in Educational Opportunity in England and Wales', *B.J.S.* (Dec. 1964).

inferior genetic endowment. Galton, for example, attributed the high levels of achievement of some outstanding families to their inherited genius. The development of intelligence tests offered a promising line of inquiry, but it became increasingly apparent that these were not, in fact, measuring a genetic factor uninfluenced by environment. Attempts to unravel the relative importance of 'Nature and nurture' and the influence of other non-genetic factors such as

TABLE 3.1*

PROPORTION IN DIFFERENT CLASSES OBTAINING GRAMMAR SCHOOL AND UNIVERSITY EDUCATION (BOYS)

		1910–19 %	Born 1920–29 %	Late 1930s %
Prof./Managerial:†	Gram.	44	54	62
	Univ.	8½		19
Skilled manual and other non-manual:	Gram.	13	15	20
	Univ.	3½		3½
Semi/unskilled:	Gram.	4	9	10
	Univ.	1		1

* For grammar schools, these occupational categories refer to Hall-Jones 1–3, 4–5 and 6–7 pre-1929, and to Crowther Report groups post-1930. For universities, the pre-1929 are Hall-Jones 1–4, 5, 6–7 and post-1930 Registrar General's Classes I and II, III, and IV and V.

† Compiled from A. Little and J. Westergaard, *op. cit.* (1964). This study drew on data from A. H. Halsey, *Ability and Educational Opportunity* (1961), the Crowther Report, and R. K. Kelsall, *Report on an Enquiry into Applications for Admissions to British Universities* (1957).

TABLE 3.2*

OCCUPATIONAL BACKGROUND OF PUPILS AT MAINTAINED AND DIRECT GRANT SCHOOLS

	Professional & managerial %	Clerical %	Father's occupation Skilled %	Semi-skilled %	Unskilled %	
All schools	15·0	4·0	51·0	18·0	12·0	100
Grammar	25·0	10·3	43·7	15·3	5·6	100
Sixth forms	43·7	12·0	37·0	5·8	1·5	100

* Central Advisory Council, *Early Leaving* (1954), Table J.

TABLE 3.3*

BOYS IN SELECTION GROUP 1 ACHIEVING TWO 'A' LEVELS OR
FOUR 'O' LEVELS (A) AND PERCENTAGE GOING ON TO FULL-TIME FURTHER
EDUCATION (B) ACCORDING TO FATHER'S OCCUPATION

	(a) %	(b) %
Professional, managerial	80·4	25·1
Clerical	61·8	19·1
Skilled	62·6	9·6
Semi-skilled	48·3	10·7
Unskilled	26·7	3·3
Total	51·6	14·5

* From Early Leaving Report (1954), Tables 7 and 11.

motivation in the determination of measured intelligence have proved only partially successful.

In recent years, the attack has shifted to a study of those environmental factors which influence educational achievement. There is little doubt that the relatively inferior educational achievements of children from working-class homes are due to factors other than ability. Floud, Halsey and Martin[1] found that entry to the grammar school was determined entirely by measured ability. But more recent researches by Douglas indicate that fewer working-class boys are admitted to the grammar-school than middle-class boys in the same groups of measured ability. The difference is particularly marked for those with test scores of 54 or less, where the percentage declines from 40 per cent of the upper middle-class to 7.9 per cent from lower working-class homes.[2] At the grammar-school, the achievements of working-class children fall steadily behind middle-class children who were in the same ability groups when they were admitted to the school (Table 3.2). It can be seen that children whose fathers are semi- or unskilled are all below the average in achievement while those whose fathers are skilled, black-coated, or professional are over-achievers. Moreover, nearly eight times the proportion of sons of professional fathers go on to further education compared with the sons of unskilled fathers from the same achievement groups.

These findings are reinforced by the Crowther Report. A survey of national service recruits found that 42 per cent in the top ability group (out of six) did not attempt the sixth form course to advanced level. The percentage was significantly higher for the sons of manual

[1] Social Class and Educational Opportunity (1956).
[2] The Home and the School (1964).

workers at 63 per cent.[1] Similar results are quoted in the Robbins Report. Of those in the top ability group (IQ 130-plus) who are the sons of non-manual workers, 37 per cent went on to degree level courses, compared with 18 per cent of the sons of manual workers.[2]

This association between educational achievement and social background does not tell us which are the causal factors. Although fees have been abolished, this does not rule out the operation of financial considerations. Family allowances, for example, cease at age sixteen. The Early Leaving Report considers that shortage of money affects 11 per cent of the boys and 18 per cent of the girls who leave early. There is little doubt 'that poverty affects the decision to leave in an appreciable number of cases'. The Crowther Report found that 34 per cent of the boys and 43 per cent of the girls who wanted to stay on at school left because they needed or wanted to earn money.[3] There was also a strong association between parent's income and early-leaving. Seventy-three per cent of the boys whose fathers earned less than £10 per week left grammar and technical schools by age sixteen, compared with 53 per cent of those whose fathers earned more than £16.

Two main variables affect both measured intelligence and educational achievement; the home and the school. The influence of the home includes both material conditions, and more complex characteristics such as parental attitudes and encouragement. A study in Merseyside concluded that in summer, 27 per cent and in winter 44 per cent of children had to do homework under definitely bad conditions.[4] Parental interest not only has a marked effect on the child's attitude towards school and willingness to work hard, but even brings about an improvement in intelligence test scores between age eight and eleven. The professional's son is more likely to plan a career for which an extended education is essential. The combined effect of future careers and parental attitudes is seen in a particularly marked way in the very different academic achievements of boys compared with girls coming from skilled and semi-skilled workers' homes. Such differences certainly cannot be explained in terms of differential ability.

Recent studies have begun to probe in more detail the intervening variables between family background and educational achievement. It has long been known that children from lower working-class

[1] *15 to 18* (1960), Table 4.
[2] *Higher Education* (1963), Appendix One, Table 5, p. 43.
[3] *15 to 18* (1960) (Vol. 11, Table 10).
[4] *Early Leaving*, p. 36.

homes score significantly lower on verbal tests of intelligence, compared with their performance on non-verbal tests. Researches by Bernstein[1] demonstrate some of the ways in which the linguistic deprivation of working-class children may account for this discrepancy. Not only do such children learn a very much restricted vocabulary, but the sentence construction and thought processes to which they are exposed are also very different from those of middle-class children. What he calls the 'public' language characterized by lower working-class speech consists of short, grammatically simple, often unfinished sentences, with rigid syntax. It is a mode of speech in which there are only restricted possibilities for clarifying and making explicit a variety of meanings. The grammatically complex sentence construction of 'formal' language, by contrast, can convey much more complex meaning, and makes possible more complex thought processes. Thus the working class child has not only to extend his vocabulary, but to learn how to learn, by acquiring the more complex grammatical forms on which much learning and thinking depend.

Such language forms, Bernstein argues, are sociological phenomena, since they arise out of different social structures and differing relations between mother and child in working-class and middle-class families. Although the analysis is too complex to be treated here, a simple example will illustrate the basic approach. Husbands and wives who have been married for a length of time may develop a more restricted public language in which meanings are implicit rather than explicit, against a backcloth of shared experiences. There is no need to verbalize fully: an expressive movement of hand or head may suffice to convey meaning. Language, that is to say, is a function of a social relationship.

The second main group of variables in educational achievement are the school and the interaction between the child and the school. In the Douglas inquiry, schools were classified according to their past record in academic achievement. Those with a good record improved the test scores of all but the top ability group, while in the poor schools, the top and most of the intermediate ability groups decline, although the lowest ability group shows a gain. Even controlling for parental interest and related variables, by age eleven, the school is second only to parents' interest in its effects on ability scores and good teaching can make up for parental indifference.[2]

[1] B. Bernstein, 'Social Structure, Language and Learning', *Educational Research*, June 1961.

[2] J. W. B. Douglas, *op. cit.* (1964), Chapter XIV.

If the task of the school is to achieve cultural transmission, we could expect its functioning to be hindered by any marked discontinuities between its attitudes and values and those of the home. A study of eighty working-class grammar school boys[1] suggests that the conflict between the culture of home and school can, in fact, exert a very powerful influence on educational achievement. The working-class boy will find many of the values and attitudes of the grammar school differ sharply from those of the home. Faced with the need to choose, he frequently rejects the values of the school, withdraws from involvement in its activities, and seeks support by identification with a peer group of boys with similar backgrounds. So strong is this conflict that Jackson and Marsden found that the only working-class boys who successfully completed the grammar-school course were those with middle-class connections—a mother, for example, who came from a middle-class home. There is also evidence to suggest that parental indifference and hostility hinders the entry of working-class boys into universities.[2]

Educational achievement is influenced too by the way in which the school is organized and the techniques of teaching adopted. These are sociological variables, since they reflect the culture of society and the schools—the knowledge, and more important, the assumptions which a society has about the educational process, and the value which it attaches to various goals. In a 'sponsored' system, for example, ability streaming is a device which enables resources to be concentrated in an attempt to maximize the achievement of the most able children.

Evidence on the effects of ability streaming on achievement is somewhat scanty, but in general it supports the conclusion that streaming functions as a self-fulfilling prophecy.[3] Those who are defined as less able in fact achieve less. In streamed schools, the lower streams score progressively lower in a variety of tests, and the gap between the lowest and highest streams widens.[4] Douglas found an increase in the measured ability of those in upper streams from age eight to eleven, which was particularly marked for the lower ability groups. A corresponding decline in the scores of those in lower streams was most marked for the upper ability groups.[5] There

[1] Jackson and Marsden, *Education and the Working Class* (1962).
[2] C. T. Sandford, M. Couper and S. Griffin, 'Class Influences in Higher Education', *Brit. J. Educ. Psych.*, June 1965.
[3] See Merton, *op. cit.*, for a discussion of this concept and examples.
[4] B. Jackson, *Streaming: an education system in miniature* (1964).
[5] J. W. B. Douglas, *op. cit.* (1964), p. 115.

is, however, a possibility that boys from working-class homes are more likely to complete a grammar school course if they are streamed.[1] Division into grammar and modern streams has comparable results. In all ability groups, there are increases in the measured ability between the ages of eleven and fifteen of those attending grammar schools and a decline in those at modern schools. This is particularly marked for the children of manual workers in the top ability group (scores 60–58) attending modern schools whose score drops four points.[2]

Evidence on the educational consequences of comprehensive secondary education is equally scanty. On theoretical grounds, great differences would not be expected. Most comprehensive schools practise ability streaming. Transfer between grammar and non-grammar streams, is of course, theoretically easier than between schools, but less frequent in fact than teachers believe to be the case. Since an increasing proportion of modern-schools have grammar-school streams, and are likely to concentrate their resources on these, the advantages of comprehensive schools for purely educational achievement may not be great,[3] although Dr Pedley's evidence suggests that 14 per cent of pupils achieve good GCE results in areas organized on comprehensive lines, compared with 10 per cent where the tripartite system operates.[4] More are entered for GCE but more fail. There is, however, a net gain.

The organization and administration of examinations is a further factor contributing to success or failure. Studies of university pass rates show that these vary widely between faculties in the same university, and between the same faculties in different universities. Venables[5] has shown that many technical college examinations have built-in failure rates. A high level of failure results when students are not allowed to proceed to the next year of a course until they have passed sessional examinations. Moreover, there is evidence to suggest that a relatively stable failure rate is applied from year to year in spite of the varying merit of examination scripts.

Attitudes and values
The effect of the school on other aspects of behaviour is less well demonstrated. There is, however, data which suggests that such

[1] Verbal communication from D. Young.
[2] *Higher Education*, Appendix One, p. 50.
[3] We are not here arguing the case for or against the comprehensive school, although the issue being analysed is very relevant.
[4] R. Pedley, *The Comprehensive School* (1963), Chapter 3.
[5] E. Venables, *The Young Worker at College* (1966).

consequences differ considerably according to type of school and the ability stream experienced. Allocation to grammar or modern school has a considerable effect on vocational aspirations.[1] Modern schoolboys are more likely to want good wages and are less likely to stress instrinsic rewards such as interest and autonomy.[2] Secondary grammar school boys see their future status as being mainly achieved through work and dependent on their own exertions. Few secondary modern boys see efforts at work as the determinant of future status, while a substantial proportion have fantasies in which future status is achieved in the field of sport or entertainment. The success through effort pattern is more marked in the A than in the B streams of both grammar and modern schools.[3] There is some evidence too that assignment to a low status in school affects the pupil's self-esteem and generates a sense of inferiority, contributing to the under-utilization of mental abilities which has been discussed earlier.[4] Moreover, working-class boys with a grammar school background are more likely than those attending modern school to vote Conservative. Ex-modern schoolboys were also more likely to be politically apathetic, and less likely to believe that 'Big Business', the 'House of Commons' and similar institutions were working well.[5] Elder concludes: 'A large number of modern school attenders, regardless of their occupational status, seem to be somewhat alienated from the economic and political life of the country. Frustration of the achievement needs of these youths may result in the search for meaning and satisfaction in delinquent, sexual, and religious activities.'[6]

The Mass Media

To measure the functioning of broadcasting, the radio or Press in terms of behavioural consequences presents much more difficult problems. The close link between the mass media and entertainment makes their output much more difficult to measure. A play on television may for example, have a 'message', and result in some reorganization in the way in which listeners perceive or evaluate some issue, for example race relations. On the other hand, it may function to release tensions built up during the working day, by

[1] H. T. Himmelweit, A. H. Halsey and A. N. Oppenheim, 'The Views of Adolescents on Some Aspects of the Class Structure', *B.J.S.*, June 1952. Factors affecting achievement motivation will be analysed in more detail in Chapter 7.

[2] Gallup Survey, quoted in Glen H. Elder, Jr, 'Life Opportunity and Personality: Some Consequences of Stratified Secondary Education in Great Britain', *Soc. of Educ.*, Spring 1965.

[3] *Ibid.* [4] Gallup Survey, quoted in Elder, *op. cit.*

[5] T. Veness, *School Leavers* (1962). [6] *Op. cit.*, p. 199.

establishing an emotional identification between the viewer and one of the characters. Its effects, that is to say, may be cognitive, normative, or cathartic.

But even if we could estimate the impact of, for example, the Press on an election campaign, this would still leave us to discover the variables associated with the effectiveness of the communication. We find in fact, that the situation is analogous to the interaction process between teacher and pupils. We have to take account of the characteristics of both the communicator and the recipient. Researches suggest that the response of the recipient can only be understood if we see him not as an isolated individual, but as a member of a variety of groups. Most important is his primary-group membership. Studies of propaganda in the Second World War for example, showed that the affective ties between soldiers and other members of their combat units protected them from the effects of propaganda.[1] It was this camaraderie which maintained the cohesion of army units rather than any commitment to official ideology. Hence, propaganda aimed at discrediting political and ideological beliefs was ineffective. Similarly studies of election campaigns suggest that the perception and interpretation of communications are structured by the recipient's membership of groups, which lead him to interpret the communication in a way which makes it congruent with the norms and beliefs of his reference groups.[2] In other words, communications must always be seen as a part of a total pattern of interaction between individuals and groups.

The importance of taking account of the social structures within which communications flow has been underlined by the studies of Lazarsfield and his associates.[3] Such studies have brought to light the existence of a communication network of interconnected individuals. This is in contrast to the concept of a mass of disconnected individuals, each in direct contact with the media. Of key importance here are the opinion leaders, who are particularly exposed to mass media, and who act as intermediaries.[4]

A number of empirical studies have attempted to assess the impact

[1] E. Shils, 'Primordial, Personal, Sacred and Civil Ties', *B.J.S.*, June 1957; E. Shils and M. Janowitz, 'Cohesion and Disintegration in the Wehrmacht in World War II', *Pub. Op. Quart.*, Vol. 12, 1948.

[2] J. W. and M. Riley, 'Mass Communication and the Social System', in R. K. Merton, L. Broom and L. S. Cottrell, *Sociology Today* (1965).

[3] P. F. Lazarsfield, *et al.*, *The People's Choice* (1948). For a summary of related researches, see J. W. and M. W. Riley, *op. cit.* (1965).

[4] See Cauter and Downham, *The Communication of Ideas* (1954), for comparable English material on communication structures.

of the mass media. A substantial volume of research has concentrated on the effects of television. It is clear from this that both the consumption of television and its impact is heavily patterned, and that 'the level and direction of consumption varies sharply with age, sex, intelligence, education, social class, parental habits and social relations. The effect of television depends on these variables. We must get away from the habit of thinking in terms of what television does to people and substitute for it the idea of what people do with television.'[1] The impact of television on leisure, for example, depends to a considerable extent on what people did with their time before they had TV. Himmelweit[2] has noted what she calls a 'displacement effect'; television viewing replaces comparable activities such as reading comics, cinema visits and radio listening. On the other hand, it has little effect on reading books, and sports activities.

Such researches have been stimulated largely by a growing public anxiety about the effect of the mass media and especially television which penetrates the home with an immediacy and potential power far greater than other forms. Lazarsfield and Merton have identified four main kinds of anxiety.[3] Firstly, there is alarm at the potency of the media to manipulate the individual and his powerlessness in the face of such a threat. Secondly, there is the fear that economic interest groups may use the media to minimize social criticism and ensure conformity to the economic status quo. Thirdly, there is anxiety lest a desire to attract mass audiences causes a deterioration in cultural standards. And finally, there is the fear that the media are producing passivity, dependency and escapism.

The evidence is somewhat complex. Many individuals with anxiety tendencies do seek fantasy and escape, and for these, television meets a need, and probably reinforces their escapist tendencies. Himmelweit, Oppenheim and Vince have not found evidence that TV makes children passive. But Belson discovered that television reduced the activities and initiative of viewers. Lazarsfield and Merton in America, however, argue that television does have a narcotic effect, and that 'the commercially-sponsored mass media indirectly but effectively restrain the cogent development of a genuinely critical outlook'.[4] There is little doubt that violence on TV does not have the

[1] J. D. Halloran, *The Effects of Mass Communication with Special Reference to Television* (1964), p. 20.

[2] H. Himmelweit, *et al.*, *Television and the Child* (1958). In the USA, television does appear to have reduced the time spent in reading books and magazines.

[3] Summarized in J. D. Halloran, *op. cit.* (1964).

[4] *Mass Communication, Popular Taste and Organised Social Action, 1948*; quoted in J. D. Halloran, *op. cit.*, 1964, p. 23.

cathartic effect frequently claimed for it by reducing aggression vicariously. On the contrary, such material would appear to be especially dangerous for delinquents for whom such characters have been found to provide heroes, and models for action, while heavy exposure to violence on the screen heightens the possibility that someone will behave aggressively.[1]

The long-term effect on tastes and interests is more difficult to discover. Himmelweit found that when there was only one channel, television did extend tastes, but with the opportunity for selective viewing offered by a second channel, there was a marked narrowing of tastes and preferences. American studies have similarly found evidence for a hardening of taste at a level which reflects its own search for a common denominator of taste. Himmelweit found that it widened tastes only for the bright ten and eleven years old, and for the average thirteen and fourteen years old.[2]

The effects of television, though significant and important, do not appear to be dramatic. But it is difficult to come to any firm conclusions from the available evidence of its cumulative and long-term effects. The fact that the impact of television in a three-week election campaign is slight[3] does not rule out the possibility that it may have more marked effects on political attitudes over a greater length of time. More research will be needed before this can be judged with any degree of certainty.

The influence of the Press is difficult to assess on the available evidence. The reports of 1949 and 1962 concluded that the popular press and on occasion, the quality press, fell short of the highest standards and were guilty of excessive partisanship, distortion, triviality and sensationalism. But the complex nature of the communication process does not enable conclusions to be drawn based simply on the content of communication. However, the 1949 report concluded that with few exceptions, newspapers 'fail to supply the electorate with adequate materials for sound political judgment.'[4] The fact that collectively the Press represents the whole spectrum of political opinion does little to help the average reader who is not in a position to perform the very complex task of comparing a number of partial and distorted accounts in order to extract an unbiased conclusion. The most probable result is that in those areas where the reader has direct experience, the Press is unlikely to have a major

[1] J. D. Halloran, *op. cit.* (1964).
[2] *Op. cit.* (1958).
[3] J. Trenaman and D. McQuail, *Television and the Political Image* (1961).
[4] *Op. cit.*, p. 154.

influence. But where he relies almost entirely on the Press, its distortions could have more significant effect.

THE SOCIAL FUNCTIONS OF EDUCATION

A major function of the educational system is to contribute to the socialization process by the transmission of the culture of a society. But the variety of roles for which men must be socialized increases with the growth of division of labour and social differentiation. And the same formal education is not appropriate for all. Throughout most of human history formal education has been received by only a small section of society. Indeed, knowledge has often been seen as a source of power and influence, and on these grounds jealously preserved and guarded by a small elite. Priest and scholar have usually been closely related roles. It is only in the last hundred years that industrial societies have extended education to other sections of society until universal literacy has become the rule in the more industrially advanced societies.

The extension of education raises new problems of content. What is appropriate for the administrator or landowner is not fitting for the artisan and labourer. The spread of education in the nineteenth century went side by side with a growing differentiation of structure and content. But in order to understand the structure of education in the nineteenth century, we must first explore more fully the relations between education and social roles.

It will be helpful to begin by thinking of two polar types of education. On the one hand, education may seek to impart specialized expert training, as for example, the education of doctors or engineers. On the other hand, some systems of education aim at cultivating personal qualities. An example is education to awaken what Max Weber called 'charisma', that is to say, heroic qualities or magical gifts. The Chinese Literati, for example, did not acquire a knowledge of administration, but the literary and stylistic education which they received was believed to confer on the mandarins special qualities and authority which were essential in an administrator.[1] These two extreme types are what Weber called *ideal types*. That is to say, they are concepts of possible polar types, although in practice, actual systems of education include elements of both. Nevertheless, the distinction proves useful; it is, that is to say, a 'heuristic' device, useful for analytical purposes.

[1] H. H. Gerth and C. W. Mills, *From Max Weber, Essays in Sociology* (1947).

Socialization

If we now look at education in the nineteenth century it can be seen that a major aim of the extension of education to the labouring classes was socialization to cultivate personal qualities, to 'gentle the masses'. The early bible classes of the Non-Conformists aimed at teaching reading simply as a means of bible study. The denominational societies later extended their provision by setting up day-schools, and the influence of the churches was strengthened by the fact that the colleges to train teachers for the labouring classes were also denominational. In the words of one of the speakers in a parliamentary debate in 1820, every poor man 'ought to be made sensible that there is an attainable good in this life superior to animal gratification, . . . and that a life of faith and obedience affords hope of a happy immortality. Of this every poor man in the nation should be made sensible and for this purpose the humble schools prepared for him are sufficient; for I believe they never neglect reading the scriptures, catechetical instruction, and daily supplication.'[1]

At another social level, a major emphasis of the rapidly expanding public schools was on devising educational regimes which would develop qualities of character and leadership in the children of the emerging middle class. Even in the relatively undeveloped field of vocational education, there was a major emphasis on the colleges and schools producing 'intelligent workmen' who would 'understand the principle underlying their trade'. Specialized knowledge, it was argued, would be learnt on the job, not in the educational institutions.[2] Similarly, the reform of recruitment to the civil service reflected the same approach. The administrative grade took men with good honours, not because the knowledge acquired could be applied to administration but because, like the Mandarins of China, their diplomas were indications of qualities of mind.

If the educational system was to perform the function of socializing for a variety of social roles, differention of structure was essential. The structural differences reflected of course, social, rather than educational criteria such as ability. Indeed, the Schools Inquiry Commission of 1868 proposed that there should be three distinct types of secondary education, and that the differences would be grounded in social distinctions. The third grade, for example, was to be for the sons of middle-class parents of straightened means, destined for careers in business, leaving at fourteen, and receiving a more practical education than that intended for the sons of the

[1] Quoted in J. W. Adamson, *English Education 1789–1902* (1930), p. 54.
[2] S. F. Cotgrove, *op. cit.* (1958).

well-to-do who would leave at eighteen for the university. There was no question of secondary education for the children of the labouring classes. It was during the nineteenth century too, that the public schools became the preserves of the middle and upper classes. They had originally been established and endowed with funds to provide poor scholars with an education which would enable them to enter the church. As the rising industrial middle class became increasingly dissatisfied with the education provided by the local endowed schools, a number of such schools gradually emerged as pre-eminent, attracting boarding scholars from farther afield, while the local foundationers became a diminishing element in such schools.[1]

The educational system of the nineteenth century then was closely related to the class-structure, both by the source from which the various types of schools drew their pupils and by the curriculum. The efforts of the two-year trained elementary school teachers to raise their status and the level of education in the working-class schools were effectively hindered by administrative action, notably by Low's system of payment by results in 1861 shich ensured that only reading, writing and reckoning should be taught.[2] Even the achievement of literacy was hindered by the sterility of the curriculum forced on the elementary schools. It was feared that too much education would make working class children unfit for their station in life. But even this limited intellectual diet was thought to be too literary, producing clerks and not artisans, and was consequently extended to include manual instruction for training the co-ordination of hand and eye following the recommendations of the Cross Commission of 1888. Even subjects such as political economy were used as vehicles for moral education. The syllabus for Social Economy of the London School Board for 1871 included such topics as 'thrift, temperance, and economy and their bearing on general wages. Honesty, trustworthiness and fore-thought and their influence on the wealth of the community . . .'[3] What the elementary schools did then was to cultivate personal qualities essential for workers in an industrial society with an emphasis on punctuality, regularity, obedience, and habits of industry.

Although the schools are no longer so explicitly oriented towards 'gentling the masses', they continue to perform important socializing functions. In Britain, religious instruction is the only item in the

[1] *The Public Schools and the General Educational System* (Flemming Report), HMSO, 1944.

[2] A. Tropp, *The School Teachers* (1957), Chapters 5 and 6.

[3] From the *Report of the School Board for London*, 1904.

curriculum which is mandatory. In the USSR, instruction in Marxist-Leninist philosophy is an integral part of education. School history books in all countries tend to be written from an ethno-centric viewpoint, and to inculcate nationalistic attitudes. Unesco is currently engaged in trying to get such texts re-written from a world view point. The recent increase in delinquency and illegitimacy among young people has prompted the Newsom Report to propose extending the operations of the school into leisure times, thus taking over from the family and extending the school's socializing influence.

The socializing function of the primary school is particularly important. It is here, for example, that the child is exposed to social norms and values beyond those which are available for learning in the family. In the family, individuals are judged by what Parsons calls particularistic standards in which feelings predominate, while in the school the child is expected to conform to universalistic standards which are applied impartially to all. Furthermore, while in the family, ascriptive roles based on age and sex predominate; that is to say, the child is expected to behave according to the norms for his age and sex. School, however, reflects the orientation of the wider society, in which roles are allocated on the basis of achievement. The emphasis placed on achievement legitimizes selection and reduces the strains imposed by differentiation.[1]

The school, argues Parsons, plays an important role in developing the achievement orientation necessary to generate the high levels of motivation required by an industrial society.[2] But a latent function of such pressure to achieve may be to produce a youth-culture which includes anti-intellectual elements. In particular, high ability low status children are likely to rebel against a situation in which the stakes are high, and to express their protest against the adult world by rejecting the intellectual values which they are being pressured to achieve.[3]

The socializing function however, does raise problems. It assumes a measure of agreement on what personal qualities society wishes to cultivate. Rapid social change makes these less certain. But it also suggests a major objective for education for the future—to fit the future generation to adjust to social change. There is certainly pressure to introduce a more occupationally and socially relevant curriculum in the schools. Newsom proposes that 'the final year

[1] T. Parsons, 'The School Class as a Social System and some of its Functions', Halsey, Floud and Anderson, op. cit., Chapter 31.

[2] Achievement motivation is examined more fully in Chapter 7.

[3] T. Parsons, op. cit.

ought to be deliberately outgoing—an initiation into the adult world of work and leisure', and the fourth and fifth years should include 'a range of courses broadly related to occupational interests . . .' F. Musgrove[1] however, has warned against a curriculum for the grammar school which is too closely geared to the needs of the locality. The grammar school boy is occupationally and geographically mobile, and needs an education which will extend his horizons and experiences.

Selection and mobility promotion

If education functioned in the nineteenth century mainly to socialize the children of the various social strata for their station in life, this is no longer an adequate explanation of the structure and function of education. In the nineteenth century status was predominantly ascribed. The sons of artisans were expected to become artisans, and were educated accordingly. By a series of steps, society has moved to a position where achievement plays a very much larger part. The growth of knowledge and its application to the performance of increasingly specialized roles means that talent is largely replacing kinship as the basis for recruitment. As certificates and diplomas are more and more the means of entry to the better paid, more secure, higher status jobs, education becomes increasingly important as a basis for occupational achievement and upward social mobility. The emphasis has shifted from socialization to selection.

However, despite its changing functions the English educational system has retained many of its nineteenth century features. We have kept distinct types of school educating for distinct levels in the social system. The grammar school leads to white collar, professional and managerial posts, while the secondary modern leads mainly to manual work. But we have modified the method of selection and recruitment to such schools. The Act of 1944 abolished fees for secondary education and rounded off the process of change whereby selection by ability to profit has gradually replaced selection by ability to pay.

It must not be concluded that the selective functions of the schools have determined the particular structure of education which we have in this country. Rather, an essentially aristocratic structure has been modified so that schools which once educated a social elite now educate an intellectual elite. Much the same can be said of other elements in the educational system, such as the universities which have similarly come to be places for the education of an

[1] *The Migratory Elite* (1963).

intellectual elite. But the structures have been largely inherited from the past. It is the sources and methods of recruitment to elites which have been modified.

By comparison, other societies such as America, have evolved somewhat different systems of mobility, and the contrast enables us to see the ways in which other elements in the educational system are related. Turner[1] suggests that there are two polar types of mobility systems, which he calls sponsored and contest mobility, each of which is related to characteristic types of education. In a sponsored system, potential recruits to elite positions are selected and allocated as early as possible to elite educational institutions so that they may be exposed to the lengthy socialization necessary to develop elite qualities. The system may be likened to a series of escalators. The most able are placed on the bottom step of a long and fast moving escalator which carries them up and drops them off at the top. The selection process also goes on within the school with the allocation of the most able to higher 'streams' (ability groups) where once again they are carried along at a faster pace.

The contest system is exemplified by the American system. This, by contrast with the sponsored system, can be likened to a race in which everything is done to give the outsider a fair chance. The race is not won until the winner passes the post, so everyone must be allowed to stay in the race. There is no question of selection. To change the metaphor, the educational system is comparable to a broad ladder up which anyone can climb and carry on climbing until he decides to give up. In America, for example, there is no early selection of the likely winners. All go to common schools. And whereas in a sponsored system, much research effort is devoted to devising the most efficient selection procedure, in a contest system the problem is to motivate the student to keep trying, since his achievement will depend heavily on his own efforts. He is not carried along by the educational escalator which in the sponsored system is constantly buttressing and reinforcing his efforts by defining him as successful and expecting high levels of achievement (unless he is in a C or D stream).

The system has consequences too for the curriculum. In the sponsored system of Britain the elite has opened its doors to the recruitment of the carefully selected and socialized parvenu. In order to preserve its status it fosters an elite culture, which stresses correct

[1] R. Turner, 'Modes of Ascent through Education', in A. H. Halsey, *et al.*, *op. cit.* (1961). For a critique of Turner, see A. H. Halsey, *A.S.R.*, June 1961, pp. 454–6.

syntax, distinctive speech styles and the acquisition of non-utilitarian knowledge, all of which require a lengthy socialization process. By this technique, the elite stratum can preserve its distinctive characteristics. In the contest system of America, there is no such distinctive elite culture. The door must be left open to the outsider, and early selection and special socialization is not possible. Consequently, there is less stress on the status value of non-utilitarian knowledge, and the way is open for educational institutions to foster the growth of studies related to practical affairs. The much larger number of vocational courses in American universities, and particularly the large numbers of engineering students contrast with the small proportion in English universities. Once again we see that the character of the elite influences the concept of 'culture', and therefore the activities of educational institutions.

If education is to function to promote upward social mobility, it will be necessary for those born into the lower status groups to have access to mobility-promoting educational institutions, and the chance to win the certificates and diplomas which are the mark of educational achievement. This as we have seen is far from being the case. It is, however, important to emphasize that education is only one of a number of factors which determine the achievement of higher status occupations. There are other means of upward mobility apart from the educational ladder, and high educational achievement will not by itself determine recruitment to elite positions. This will be examined more fully in Chapter 7.

EDUCATION AND SOCIAL CHANGE

It is clear that in an industrial society, the links between education and occupation become increasingly important. The functions of the educational system shift from conferring charisma on priests or mandarins, to an emphasis on socializing the masses during the early unsettled phase of industrialization, and then to preparing an increasing range of specialists for their occupational roles and so selecting for upward mobility. Concomitant with these changes in function there are changes in the structure of the educational system with the growth of secondary schools, technical and teacher-training colleges and universities, and the changes in the curriculum as the notion of culture is slowly modified with the increasing importance of science, technology and practical knowledge and the accompanying increase in the influence and status of scientists and technologists.

The relations between the educational system and the social

structure are very complex and not yet fully understood. We can certainly see some ways in which changes in the social structure exert pressures for change on the educational system. The growth of political democracy, for example, leads to the demand for greater equality of opportunity. This demand in turn, springs in part from the increasing importance of education for occupation, and reflects changes in the economic system of production which increasingly applies specialized knowledge, making the possession of diplomas more rewarding in economic terms.

The present pressure towards a comprehensive 'contest' system of education is a further example of change in the educational system in response to forces largely external to the system, and to some extent resisted by parts of the educational system. It has already been explained that the tripartite system of grammar, modern and technical schools which emerged as a result of the 1944 Act[1] was a continuation of the essentially aristocratic system of the nineteenth century. The main change was in the more democratic method of recruitment which substituted ability to profit for ability to pay. This change however, gave rise to mounting criticisms of tripartism focused on the methods of selection used to allocate children to the coveted grammar-school places. This system excluded many middle-class children who would previously have attended as fee-payers having passed the less-rigorous selection test imposed on those not dependent on a free-place. Moreover, there was the growing evidence that many admitted were failing to complete the grammar-school course, while the chances of admission to a grammar-school varied considerably according to locality, with ratios varying from under 10 per cent to over 50 per cent.

The occupational significance of a grammar-school education was alone enough to generate great anxiety in the middle-class parents at the possibility of failure at the '11-plus'. Reinforced by the evidence of the weakness in selection procedure, social pressure has led to a widespread acceptance of the desirability of 'ending the 11-plus'. But since some form of selection is essential if separate types of secondary school remain, such a policy can only lead to the introduction of some form of 'comprehensive' education, in which the common school catering for all ranges of ability continues in some form at the secondary stage. Furthermore, the

[1] The act did not specify the form which secondary education should take, but tripartism was strongly supported by the Ministry of Education and by many LEA's. The Minister, in fact, has intervened on occasions to prevent the abolition of some grammar schools.

rigid distinctions of tripartism have been eroded in recent years by the marked increase in GCE courses in secondary-modern schools and the development of a variety of school-leaving examinations. Again, social pressures deriving from the occupational significance of educational qualifications eventually overcame the persistent refusal of successive Ministers to introduce leaving examinations in the modern schools.[1]

Changes in the economic system which increasingly applies specialized knowledge to production have led to a growth in the demand for qualified manpower. As a result, the possession of diplomas has become more economically rewarding and therefore more highly sought, thus still further increasing the demand for educational places. It is this mechanism which underlies the educational explosion in the advanced industrial societies.

But this 'feed-back' from the economic system to the educational system does not necessarily produce an equilibrium between the demand for qualified manpower and the supply. Other elements in the social system exert an influence. For example, the inferior status of technology and its limited acceptance as a part of culture have hindered the growth of technological studies in Britain.[2] The newly industrializing societies of Africa and India are faced with especially difficult problems. High status occupations such as politics attract large numbers of students to the study of law, while there are serious shortages of engineers and technicians. In India, the high status of education plus the keen competition for jobs resulting from the shortage of appropriate occupations meant that a university degree came to be a qualification for clerical work, thus producing an even greater demand for graduate qualifications. The over-production of graduates in many European countries similarly produced a discontented intellectual proletariat who tended to support extremist political movements.[3]

The precise relationship between economic development and the expansion of education is only partially understood. There are two main possibilities. The expansion of educational opportunity may reflect mainly the growing consumer-demand for education by individuals for a variety of reasons, particularly the value of education for social mobility. It may, on the other hand, be due to the growing demand for qualified manpower from the labour-market

[1] W. Taylor, *The Secondary Modern School* (1963).

[2] D. W. Hutchings, *Technology and the Sixth Form Boy* (1963), and S. F. Cotgrove, *op. cit.* (1958).

[3] W. M. Kotschnig, *Unemployment in the Learned Professions* (1937).

reflecting the rising level of expertees required by modern industry.[1] Available data suggest that both factors have been at work, although there is some evidence that the supply of education has in some occupations outstripped the demand. Analysing data for the United States, Folger and Nam conclude that 'the evidence favours the hypothesis that within-occupation rises in education exceed in magnitude the shifts in educational requirements resulting from shifts in occupational structure.'[2] Although the expanding occupations are those requiring higher educational levels, the evidence suggests that the educational up-grading of occupations is greater than shifts in the occupational structure in a direction requiring higher educational levels. This conclusion would not necessarily apply of course, to Britain where the median length of education is less than that in the USA. But even here, the evidence suggests that the expansion, at least until recently, has been due to consumer-demand rather than to industrial pressures affecting the labour market.[3] There is also some evidence to suggest that it is such an increase in the supply of educated personnel which was acted as a stimulus to economic growth, rather than the reverse relationship. The growth of an educational system supplying qualified scientists would appear to have played a major role in the expansion of scientific industries in Germany in the nineteenth century. By contrast, England lacked a class of professional scientists, and failed to respond to the challenges in the dyestuffs and electrical engineering industries in the nineteenth century.[4] Technological advances in industry depend on prior developments in the educational system. The presence of scientifically qualified men in key posts in industry is essential if industry is to be in a position to apply science to production. And a class of scientists is the product of the educational system. A somewhat analogous situation exists today in the social sciences. The Heyworth Committee[5] for example, has had some trenchant things to say about the utilization of social science research findings. The Treasury, which is responsible for the efficient running of the machinery of government, employed (at the date of the inquiry) no social scientists other than economists to advise on the techniques of management. Industry similarly fails to employ social scientists in a professional

[1] J. K. Folger and C. B. Nam, 'Trends in Education in Relation to the Occupational Structure', *Soc. of Educ.*, Vol. 38, No. 1.
[2] Comment, *Soc. of Educ.*, Vol. 38, No. 2, 1965.
[3] S. F. Cotgrove, *op. cit.* (1958).
[4] D. S. L. Cardwell, *op. cit.* (1957).
[5] *Report of the Committee on Social Studies* (1965).

capacity where they could identify problems and feed in research knowledge where appropriate. The growth of the social sciences owes little to the demands of industry and government for their services in these fields.[1]

It would appear then that the educational system does not perform a purely passive role, responding more or less slowly to societal pressures. New knowledge is itself a function of the educational system. And it is this which has contributed so much to the transformation of society. As the rate of growth of new knowledge increases, universities and research institutes become increasingly influential as generators of new ideas. Technological needs have certainly played an important part in the growth of science in the past,[2] but with the institutionalization of science and the growth of science as a profession,[3] new knowledge is generated by relatively autonomous educational institutions, with all the repercussions of nuclear fission and electronics on the social structure and international relations. In fact, so important are developments in knowledge as agents of social change that Popper argues it is impossible to predict long-term social change, because we can never know what new knowledge we will discover.[4] What we can say with reasonable certainty is that the rate of social change brought about by new knowledge will increase, because the rate of growth of knowledge corresponds to a geometric rather than an arithmetic progression.

This shift in the role of the universities[5] from cultural preservation to innovation faces them with new problems. Once institutions are established, they are resistant to change. Their practices will generally be legitimized by beliefs that they are morally right. A suggestion that the universities should concern themselves more with practical affairs and with the after-careers of their students brought the reply from one group of dons 'To have such a solemn, humourless, Benthamite pawing with the basic moral assumptions of university life fills one with horror.'[6]

---

[1] The factors underlying the growth in science will be examined in Chapter 6.

[2] R. K. Merton, *Essays in Social Theory and Social Structure* (1957).

[3] D. S. L. Cardwell, *The Organisation of Science in England* (1957). Promotion depends increasingly on publication. The academic market-place motivates academics to higher levels of research effort. Caplow and McGee, *The Academic Market Place* (1961).

[4] K. Popper, *The Poverty of Historicism* (1957).

[5] A. H. Halsey, 'The Changing Functions of Universities', in A. H. Halsey, *et al., op. cit.* (1961).

[6] *Observer*, March 5, 1961. See S. F. Cotgrove, 'Education and Occupation', *B.J.S.*, March 1962.

Much will depend on the degree of autonomy whch academic institutions enjoy. In stable democracies such as Britain, education is highly autonomous, and less sensitive to pressure to change. In dictatorships, educational institutions can be more easily directed towards the achievement of political objectives. As we have seen, the relatively autonomous educational institutions of Britain have been slow to respond to the needs of industry for scientists and technologists. There has, in fact, been relatively little discussion of the implications for the universities of their changing functions in society. The Robbins report,[1] for example, states the functions of the universities in four paragraphs; to provide a vocationally relevant education, to train the mind, to advance the frontiers of knowledge, and to produce cultured persons. There is no indication in the report of the enormous complexities of some of these functions. Educating to produce 'cultured' persons raises sociological issues of substantial magnitude. What kinds of capacities are needed for performing the increasingly complex roles of contemporary societies? And what kinds of personal qualities do they require? What kind of men and women do we want our schools and universities to produce? There is no consensus on such questions, and little research to guide us. One major difficulty as we shall see later in Chapter 4 is that it may prove difficult to produce individuals adequately socialized to perform some occupational roles, who also possess other qualities considered desirable by society. For example, a worker who is trained to carry out a routine efficiently may not also be capable of active participation in the democratic process, or of active creative leisure.

SUMMARY AND CONCLUSIONS

Education is the socialization of individuals by the transmission of culture. Every society must ensure the adequate socialization of its members, and is in this sense an educative society. The family, peer groups, schools and colleges, apprenticeship—all of these may contribute to the educative process.

The emergence of specialized educational institutions raises two issues. What part of culture will they transmit? To whom will they teach it? They are, in fact, interrelated questions. Both the social origins of students and their probable future social roles will be related to what they are taught and equally important, what they assimilate.

The education of elite strata of priests, mandarins, or ruling

[1] *Higher Education*, 1963, pp. 6–7.

aristocracies, will be shaped by the values of the elite; will aim to cultivate those personal qualities necessary for the style of life approved by the high status groups and to legitimize their authority. This in turn will be related to their social function, whether praying, fighting, ruling, or, in more settled times, the cultivation of leisure. In pre-industrial societies then, formal education is mainly socialization for a style of life appropriate to one's station. It performs, that is to say, a symbolic function.

Industrialization is accompanied by a demand for mass instruction. The social disruption of early industrialization places on education the task of contributing to social control by 'gentling the masses', and developing those personal qualities of industry, regularity, subordination to routine, and obedience to rules required by an industrial society. At the same time, the public schools emerged with quite distinctive educational regimes aimed at developing qualities of character and leadership in the middle and upper classes.

As the division of labour demands more specialized knowledge, education becomes increasingly closely linked with occupational recruitment and educational institutions become major selective agencies. The educational system becomes oriented to the selection of talent, and able children are 'sponsored' for the higher rungs of the occupational ladder, by selection and allocation to secondary grammar schools. The hierarchical structure of the educational system is retained, reflecting the hierarchical structure of society, but the method of recruitment is changed. The selective function of education does not however, necessarily demand a hierarchical school system. In America, for example, there is no selection and all go to common schools. But occupation remains closely linked to length of schooling and to educational achievement.

The association between education and occupation has resulted in the proliferation of qualifying associations conferring certificates and diplomas sought for their career value. The educational values of the nineteenth century plus the existence of apprenticeship as the traditional mode of occupational training has meant that most vocational education has taken place outside the schools and universities. The institutions relating education to occupation have by no means ensured their effective co-ordination. The regulatory functions of apprenticeship for example, have hindered its effective functioning as a vehicle for vocational education and training. The selective function of occupational qualifications has also contributed to high failure rates and to a lack of close association between the content of courses and the future occupational roles of students. The political system plays an important role in allocating resources to education and in determining who shall be educated. Although the state has allowed a considerable measure of autonomy to local education authorities to shape local provision, the freedom of teachers in the classroom is limited by pressures from the universities which play a large part in shaping the curriculum. Moreover, they are subject to influences from central government inspectors. Public anxiety about their key role in socializing the young is reflected in their careful selection, and close association between the churches and the training of teachers in segregated colleges.

Unlike schools and colleges, the mass media such as the Press and commercial television are closely articulated with the economic system and the political system. The content of the Press is largely shaped by its search for increased circulation, while its partisanship on a variety of issues reflects its connexion with party politics through the influence of proprietors.

Schools can be viewed as a sub-system, related to the educational and social systems. The educational strategies each adopts are likely to be related to the dominant goals which it pursues, whether 'custodial', 'missionary', or 'academic', and the teacher's role. Studies of college student cultures suggest that these may sometimes conflict with academic values and inhibit the student's response to the intellectual challenge of college life. The existence of a distinctive 'youth culture' and the extent to which this functions as a socializing agency, is a matter of current researches. The need for youth groups seems to be the result of significant discontinuities between childhood and adult status. Youth culture appears to be peripheral, symbolizing age-group membership and solidarity. Its ritualistic and segmental character suggests that it does not modify class subcultural beliefs and values about major areas such as occupation and marriage.

Studies of the educational process demonstrate marked differences in the achievements of children from different social backgrounds. The evidence shows that these cannot be attributed to differences in ability but reflect the interaction between home and school. Parental income, and interest, together with the experience of linguistic deprivation and discontinuities between the attitudes and values of home and school have all been demonstrated to influence achievement. The influence of school experience on political and social attitudes also appears to be marked.

Researches into the influence of the mass media demonstrate the complexity of the process. Communications flow through group structures and are not received passively by isolated individuals. Moreover, there are marked differences in the consumption of television and its impact varies considerably between types of viewer. For some, it simply displaces similar activities. For others, it provides an escape and with the opportunities for selective viewing, narrows the range of interests.

The relation between education and social change appears to be two-way. The schools have certainly changed both in structure and function with the process of industrialization, and in this sense appear as passive respondents to changes in the political and economic systems, shifting in emphasis from socialization to selective functions, and more recently moving from a sponsored towards a contest system. But such pressures by no means ensure equilibrium between education and the social system. The educational system can fail to produce either the numbers or the type of persons needed for the effective functioning of the social system. There is one important way in which education can be seen as an active agent of social change. Colleges are not only the custodians of culture; they are increasingly power houses for the generation of new knowledge and innovation. And the application of such knowledge to production, and the techniques of persuasion, communication and management, have transformed social life. In this way, universities are likely to become increasingly important as agents of social change. But neither they, nor their intellectual products, are autonomous, being in turn functionally related to the social system. The model which seems most useful for describing the relations between education and society is of two systems each of which is functionally related to the other by feed-back mechanisms.

QUESTIONS AND EXERCISES

1. 'The prevailing definition of "culture" will largely determine the content of education.' Explain and discuss.
2. Examine the influence of the economic system on education.
3. How would you account for the increasingly close connexion between education and occupation in the last hundred years?
4. What are some of the problems which face the educational system today which result from its closer association with occupations?
5. In what ways have economic and technological changes influenced the educational system?
6. Examine the influence of the political system on education.
7. 'The mass media can best be understood if we examine their articulation with the economic system.' Discuss.

8. How far has the aim of equality of educational opportunity been achieved?
9. 'The organization of any particular school is related to the culture of society, its place in the educational system, and the problems derived from its immediate environment.' Discuss.
10. Examine the evidence for the existence and influence of a 'youth culture'.
11. Examine systematically the differences between a 'custodial' school and an 'academic' school.
12. What social factors influence educational achievement?
13. How far has the aim of equality of educational opportunity been achieved?
14. 'The influence of the mass media has been exaggerated.' Discuss.
15. 'In recent years, the selective and mobility promoting function of education has become more important than its socializing function.' Do you agree?
16. How far do you think that Turner's notion of a sponsored system of mobility can be applied to English education?
17. 'The main function of education in the nineteenth century was socialization.' How far does the historical evidence support or refute this view?
18. In what ways was the structure of the educational system in the nineteenth century shaped by its functions?
19. 'The gradual shift away from tripartism illustrates the response of the educational system to the pressures of the social system.' Explain.
20. 'The relations between education and society can most usefully be described as that between two systems, each functionally related to the other by feedback mechanism.' Discuss.

READING

O. Banks.—*Parity and Prestige in English Secondary Education* (Routledge, 1955). Stresses the crucial role which the selective function of the grammar schools has played in determining their curricula and prestige.

*M. Carter.—*Home, School and Work* (Pergamon Press, 1962), Chapters 3 and 4. Descriptive accounts of a number of schools in Sheffield and of the children's attitudes towards school.

*B. R. Clark.—*Educating the Expert Society* (Chandler Pub. Co., 1962), Chapters 1, 2, and 5–8. Useful chapters on the school as an organization and student cultures.

S. F. Cotgrove.—*Technical Education and Social Change* (Allen & Unwin, 1957). Examines the response of the educational system to the needs of industrial society for trained manpower and the social factors which have shaped the system of technical education.

S. F. Cotgrove.—'Education and Occupation' (*B.J.S.*, March 1962). Examines the problem of vocationalism in education and the relations between education and occupation.

*J. W. B. Douglas.—*The Home and the School* (MacGibbon & Kee, 1964). Explores the factors influencing educational achievement in the primary school.

S. N. Eisenstadt.—*From Generation to Generation* (Free Press, 1956). A comparative study of age groups.

*D. Gottlieb and J. Reeves.—*Adolescent Behaviour in Urban Areas* (Collier Macmillan, 1963), Part II, 'Some Comments on Adolescent Subcultures'.

*J. D. Halloran.—*The Effects of Mass Communication with Special Reference to Television* (Leicester University Press, 1964). A summary of researches.

A. H. Halsey, J. Floud and C. A. Anderson.—*Education, Economy and Society: a Reader in the Sociology of Education*. See especially introduction and chapters 9, 12, 15, 24, 26, 28, 31, 32, 39, 41.

B. Jackson and D. Marsden.—*Education and the Working Class* (Routledge, 1962).

B. Jackson.—*Streaming: an education system in miniature* (Routledge, 1964).

*K. Liepmann.—*Apprenticeship* (Routledge and Kegan Paul, 1960), especially chapter IX. Examines the regulatory functions of apprenticeship in protecting the market and work situation and their conflict with training functions.

J. B. Mays.—*Education and the Urban Child* (Liverpool University Press, 1962).

W. Taylor.—*The Secondary Modern School* (London, 1963). Examines the way in which the selective function of education has influenced the modern school.

A. Tropp.—*The School Teachers* (Heinemann, 1957), chapters 5 and 6. An analysis of policies adopted to restrict the development of working class education in the nineteenth century.

R. Turner.—*The Social Context of Ambition* (Chandler, 1964). Includes an analysis of youth culture tested with empirical data.

J. Webb.—'The Sociology of a School', *B.J.S.* (Sept. 1962).

G. Williams.—*Recruitment to Skilled Trades* (Routledge, 1957). An influential study which first established authoritatively the inadequacy of apprenticeship as a training institution.

B. R. Wilson.—'The Teacher's Role' (*B.J.S.*, March 1962).

R. Williams.—*The Long Revolution* (Chatto, 1961).

S. Wiseman.—*Education and Environment* (Manchester UP, 1964). A summary of the data on social factors influencing achievement.

Royal Commission on the Press, 1947–1949 (HMSO, 1949).

Royal Commission on the Press, 1961–1962 (HMSO, 1962).

Chapter 4

THE ECONOMIC SYSTEM
AND OCCUPATIONS

=====

WORK AND NON-WORK

If we meet a stranger, at a party perhaps, or a new neighbour moves in, one of the first questions we are likely to ask is 'What does he do? What's his job?' This information will give us a clue to his income, and his social standing. But much more than this, it will give us hints about his likely attitudes on political questions, and his interests and outlook. Indeed, some occupations profoundly influence the *identity* of the individual, so that if we are told that someone is a lawyer, or scientist, or doctor, or teacher, we feel that we already know quite a lot about the kind of person he is. Why is this? Do occupations attract particular types of persons? Or does the occupation imprint its influence on the individual? Researches suggest that both factors must be taken into account. Furthermore, they support the view that the kind of work that a man does has a profound influence on non-work areas of life, on family life (as we saw in Chapter 2), on leisure, and on class and political attitudes.

This relation between work and non-work is scarcely surprising. Industrialization has been so conspicuously successful in increasing wealth precisely because it has mobilized armies of workers by hand and brain to regular and systematic work, so that work has become a dominant influence in the life of the individual, taking up the major part of his energies five or more days a week, for most of the year, and for most of his life. It is probable that at no previous time in history have so many worked so hard and for so long as in nineteenth-century Britain. And the more recent reduction in the demands of work from the seventy or more hours fifty-two weeks in the year of the nineteenth-century factory worker, to a forty-four hour week in most industrial societies still compares unfavourably with the working hours of the urban artisan in pre-industrial society.

According to Wilensky[1] the skilled artisan in the thirteenth century worked as little as 194 days a year. Moreover, professionals and administrators today certainly work considerably longer than in pre-industrial society.

But it is not simply a question of the changing distribution of time between work and non-work. The nature of work itself has undergone profound changes. The mechanization of work has resulted in its concentration in factories. The majority of occupations now involve working in large scale organizations, and this has produced complex problems of the relations between individuals and organizations. Moreover, growing division of labour and the application of science to production has changed work tasks so that we have a decline in old skills and the disappearance of the traditional craftsman, raising questions about the impact of mass production on the life of the worker. On the other hand, we have a growing demand for highly trained mathematicians and scientists and this in turn generates new problems. For example, researches suggest that the outlook and values of scientists may differ from those of the administrators and the organizations for which they work. Such conflicts, it is believed, may hinder the intellectual creativity of scientists and in this way threaten the efficient growth of scientific knowledge.[2]

In this chapter we shall examine work from a particular perspective. We will be looking at types of work roles in the social system; that is to say, at the typical roles which individuals occupy in the processes of production, distribution and exchange. We will, moreover, be concentrating here on the individual, on his experiences, the meaning which these have for him, and the consequences of these work experiences for non-work behaviour. But this does not mean that we have shifted from a sociological to a psychological perspective. Our interest is not in individuals as such, but in types of work roles which exist in particular societies. That is to say, we are interested in specifically social facts.

But what is work? At the outset there is the problem of definition. If we talk to some writers, artists, scientists, and other professionals, we may find that they have difficulty in saying where their working day begins and ends. They may say, 'Well, I don't consider what I

[1] H. L. Wilensky, 'The Uneven Distribution of Leisure: The Impact of Economic Growth on Free Time', in E. O. Smigel (ed.), *Work and Leisure* (1963).

[2] Although occupations cannot be understood except in an organizational setting, this Chapter will concentrate on their study from the perspective of the individual, while Chapter 8 will take up the theme of the operation of organizations.

do is really work. I thoroughly enjoy it; it's what I want to do.' This suggests one important dimension of work-roles—the element of compulsion which characterizes them. But to exclude the scientists from our study because he has freely chosen to do his job would clearly be unsatisfactory. A second dimension of work roles is the fact that we are paid for what we do. Does this mean that when the scientist papers the living-room at the weekend this is not work? He is much more likely to define this as work than his activities in the laboratory. Moreover, it is an economic activity just as much as his laboratory work, for he is earning money in the sense that he would otherwise have to pay someone else to do the job.[1] Similarly, the housewife 'works' even though she is not paid by an employer.

This discussion reminds us of the difficulty already encountered, that sociology uses an existing vocabulary which frequently emerges as unsatisfactory for scientific analysis. We have to arrive at an 'operational' definition, which clearly identifies the phenomena for study. For this purpose we can define work as any activity which is directed towards the production of goods and services which typically have a value in exchange and which are carried out for a valuable consideration. Moreover, although the degree of compulsion which enters into such activities varies widely, we cannot define work simply as compulsory activities. In practice, we can largely avoid these problems of definition by studying 'occupations', that is to say those roles which determine a man's *market situation*: his ability to command goods and services for a consideration (monetary or otherwise).

The following table indicates the possible combinations between the variables and locates leisure activities in relaton to (a) market situation (b) the nature of involvement in the activity, whether it is undertaken for purely 'instrumental' reasons or whether it is an 'expressive' activity which is intrinsically satisfying.

FIGURE 4.1

WORK AND NON-WORK

	Market	Non-market
Expressive	After-hours reading of scientist	Hobby—e.g. painting (Leisure)
Instrumental	Form-filling	Helping with wash up (Non-work obligations)

[1] N. Anderson, *Work and Leisure* (1961), suggests the term 'non-work obligations' for such activities.

THE ECONOMY AND THE SOCIAL SYSTEM

Every society has to solve the problem of getting work done. This involves socializing individuals in order to produce the skills, capacities and motivation necessary. It also requires machinery for the selection and allocation of individuals to work roles, and for organizing the relations of production distribution and exchange. In simple terms, the basic problem which societies have to solve is 'How do we ensure that people work?'

Work, the economy and the political system
One extreme solution to the production problem is the use of coercion in slave systems. Here the monopoly of coercive means in the hands of the politically and economically dominant stratum is used to enforce the maximum exploitation of servile labour, as in the chattel slavery of the Southern states of America until the mid-nineteenth century. But even in the early phases of industrialization, the power of the employer to extract a maximum effort was strongly reinforced by the political system which conferred on the employer a variety of legally (coercively) enforceable rights, while at the same time, limiting the protective measures which could be taken by workers, by limiting their rights of assembly, and organization.

A major variable in the relations between the political system and the economy is the extent to which governments allow autonomy to economic units. A maximum of autonomy existed under *laissez-faire* capitalism[1] in nineteenth-century Britain. Here, the means of production were privately owned, and the property laws conferred extensive powers on property owners. Property rights can most simply be conceived as a bundle of legally enforceable claims to use and control things. In the last analysis, property rights depend on the extent to which the state is prepared to use its monopoly of coercive means to enforce such claims. Property laws therefore, provide the main mechanism for the control of both ownership, production and distribution. In the nineteenth century, the rights of property gave almost unlimited powers of use and control. And since most were dependent on the property of others (such as factory and land-owners), for access to the means of earning a livelihood, the powers of property include the control over persons through things. Factory owners had almost unlimited powers to hire and fire whom they chose. In the face of such powers, workers were individually weak, but

[1] The word is used here in a strictly descriptive sense to refer to an economic system in which the private ownership of the means of production predominates.

were prevented from taking collective action by the Combination Acts. Thus, even in a *laissez-faire* economy, the state intervened in a decisive way to determine the relations between employers and employees.

The growth of industrialization has been accompanied by the gradual extension of political protection to the worker. The right to form trade unions, the right to strike, industrial legislation and arbitration courts, factory legislation, redundancy agreements, unemployment benefits, severance pay, have all increased his relative bargaining power and restricted the economic and physical demands that can be made on the worker.[1] Although there is still a coercive element in work for most, this now derives from the fact that the individual needs to sell his labours to earn an income. But political action is still significant in shaping the relative bargaining power of the two sides. The state determines the framework within which the power-struggle over the amount and conditions of work and its rewards takes place. The 'distribution of economic, or purchasing power is one aspect of the distribution of social power'.[2] Much of the literature on industrial relations is, in fact, a description of the collective bargaining machinery which has been set up and of the roles of government, employers associations and trade unions.[3]

The key significance of property laws in determining the exercise of control in the economy can be seen by a more detailed study of one particular form of property—the joint stock company which is now the dominant form of productive property. This was an invention of the nineteenth century to make possible the mobilization of capital in more permanent forms for large scale enterprises. The joint stock company is a legal person in whom is vested the property of the company. The powers of the company are exercised on its behalf by its legally appointed officers. The shareholders own shares in the company, not the walls and machinery of the factory. A share carries with it a right to distributed profits, and (with the exception of non-voting shares) the right to determine the risk-taking policy of the company through a vote at shareholders meetings, including the election of the board of directors. The control of the affairs of the company therefore is, in theory, in the hands of the shareholders

[1] For a detailed analysis of changes in property laws, see W. Freidmann, *Law in a Changing Society* (1964).

[2] D. Lockwood, 'Arbitration and Industrial Conflict', *B.J.S.*, Dec. 1955.

[3] For a brief account, see I. C. McGivering, *et al.*, *Management in Britain* (1960), Chapter 3. Industrial relations at plant level will be examined in more detail later in this chapter in the discussion of occupational strategies, and in Chapter 8 as an illustration of the processes of organizations.

meeting and the board of directors.

It can be seen that the various rights of control which ownership confers are distributed in a complex way. Only the board of directors and the officials of the company whom they appoint can exercise the powers of control As a result, it has been argued, the major consequence of the dominance of the joint stock company has been to divorce ownership from control.[1] Moreover, by devices such as holding companies and interlocking directorates, it is argued, a relatively small number of individuals owning only a fraction of the total share capital, can control vast industrial empires. In other words, a few individuals can control that which they do not own.[2]

A modification of this theory put forward by J. Burnham[3] argues that the running of giant corporations is an increasingly complex business requiring specialized knowledge. Moreover, with the increasing public ownership of the means of production, control is passing into the hands of the expert managers on whose know-how production is more and more dependent.

The complex issues can, to some extent, be clarified by empirical data on shareholding. There are three main possibilities. Firstly, an individual or family can own the majority of shares. There are very few cases of such individual or family ownership. Secondly, financial control is possible for an individual or small group of individuals to own between them a sufficiently large block of shares to be able to achieve a majority vote at a shareholders meeting. In practice, the number of votes necessary could be quite small if most of the voting shares are widely dispersed. The number of shareholders may be over 100,000—only a few of whom ever attend a shareholders' meeting. Thirdly, shareholding may be so dispersed that no one or group of shareholders can exercise stable financial control. Under such circumstances, managerial control by the top executives is probable, with little intrusion of financial interests into managerial policy. The actual centre of control cannot, of course, be deduced with any certainty from such statistics. But they do support the general thesis that the majority of the shareholders are unlikely to have any very effective voice in the control of company affairs. This conclusion is strengthened by the observation that few shareholders have either

---

[1] This is a further example of the division of labour and specialization of roles which characterizes industrial societies.

[2] A. A. Berle and G. C. Means, *The Modern Corporation and Private Property* (1932).

[3] *The Managerial Revolution* (1941).

the time or the knowledge to participate, while the high turnover in stocks indicates only a transient interest by many in the affairs of the company.

A study of ninety-two very large companies in Britain[1] shows that in thirteen companies the largest twenty shareholders own more than 30 per cent of the shares and that more than 10 per cent of the shares are owned by the board. That is to say, in these companies only, there is substantial concentration of ownership on the board. These companies include those controlling Press and cinema such as Ranks and Kemsley and brewery firms, together with a chemical firm, and an aircraft firm. In another twenty-one firms, there is a substantial share concentration (the largest twenty shareholders owning more than 30 per cent, but the board own less than 10 per cent). In over one third of the large companies, share distribution makes possible ownership control.

No firm conclusion can be drawn from such data. Some have argued that the evidence indicates the separation of management and control from ownership, and the emergence of an influential class of professional managers whose interests do not coincide with those of either the shareholders or labour. In one half of the large companies, for example, the directors own less than 2 per cent of all shares. On the other hand, it can be argued, that the fact remains that most directors are substantial shareholders, that one quarter of the directors are among the twenty largest shareholders, and this together with the various emoluments which directors enjoy results in substantial congruence between their interests and those of the shareholders. There is, in fact, no divorce between the ownership of property and the management of industry. On the contrary, relatively small amounts of property give control over great concentrations of economic power.

The broad trend seems to be towards a decline in the concentration of shareholding. In 1951, in thirty-two of the ninety-two companies, the largest twenty shareholders owned more than 20 per cent of the voting shares compared with forty-five in 1936. On the other hand, institutional shareholding is increasing. The Prudential is now among the largest twenty shareholders in forty-seven out of the ninety-eight companies. This may simply mean that by means of mergers, nominee holdings, and interlocking directorates, the influence of a few corporate rich has been maintained or extended. Moreover, the growth of proxy voting has probably increased the power of the directors in office.

[1] P. S. Florence, *Ownership, Control and Success of Large Companies* (1961).

It is possible to argue that what has happened in recent years is the separation of control over access to the means of production (which is increasingly in the hands of career managers), from control over preferential distribution of the proceeds from production (which is exercised by large-shareholders, directors, and financiers).[1] Whether this will mean that the control over distribution will eventually shift to the managers as Burnham has argued, remains a matter of controversy. But it must be stressed that in the last analysis, it is the political system, by its property legislation, which determines the exercise of economic power.[2]

The extension of the political control of the economy is not only reflected in the decline in the rights of private property, the regulation over investment, the location of industry, and labour relations, but also by the growth of the public sector of the economy through nationalization.[3] One-third of all assets of companies are now in the hands of public corporations. In socialist societies, the public ownership and control of the means of production has been carried much further, so that in the USSR, the party machinery effectively controls the entire production process. But most industrial societies have substantially reduced the autonomy of the economic system, and the traditional labels of 'capitalist' and 'socialist' are no longer particularly useful for characterizing such economies.[4] Moreover, political control is not limited simply to regulating production and ownership. Distribution also takes place within the framework of a legal system regulating relations between buyers and sellers, controlling currency and weights and measures, and more recently, seeking to protect the consumer by indicating standards of quality. Furthermore, much government action takes the form of co-ordinating or stimulating economic action, rather than regulating or controlling it in a restricted sense.

So far, some of the ways in which the political system structures the economic system have been examined. There are also a num-

[1] I. C. McGivering, op. cit. (1960).

[2] The problem of whether the political elite is dominated by men of property will be examined in Chapter 5. See also R. Dahrendorf, Class and Class Conflict in Industrial Societies (1959), for a statement of the view that property derives from power.

[3] It is important to avoid confusion between capitalism and industrialization. Much of the early literature on the determinants and consequences of industrialization failed to make such a distinction. See J. W. Sombart, 'Capitalism', Encyclopedia of the Social Sciences.

[4] The control of the nationalized sector may still remain substantially in the hands of those who also control the private sector. See C. Jenkins, Power at the Top (1959).

ber of ways in which the economic system influences the political system. Both employers and employees form pressure groups to exert influence on the government, and more recently consumers have formed similar pressure groups. But this aspect of the interaction between the economy and the policy will be examined within the context of analysing the political system in Chapter 5.

Work, the economy and the cultural system

Even the most coercive system of production will have difficulty in relying on coercion alone. Apart from the practical difficulties of getting hard work out of slaves, a slave society is faced with the problem of justifying its actions and salving its conscience. It will be necessary for there to be a set of shared beliefs and values which legitimize the practices of slavery. Where the slaves constituted a distinct ethnic group, such as the negroes in the Southern States of America, it was possible to develop a rigid out-group morality and to believe that they did not possess the same qualities as whites. The 'Sambo' personality of servility and dependence was believed to be essentially inborn. Moreover, it was possible to find scriptural justification for slavery and for the churches to lend their support to its practice.[1]

In the early stages of industrialization, there was still a substantial coercive element in work. But in a relatively more free society, it was necessary to attempt to reinforce the drive to work with moral (normative) pressures. According to Max Weber,[2] the cultural imperatives necessary for the emergence of industrial capitalism were generated by the puritan sects of the sixteenth century. These stressed the connexion between hard work, thrift, and abstinence and religious salvation, and hence made an essential contribution to the growth of the 'capitalist spirit'. We do not necessarily need to agree with Weber that it was the protestant sects which generated this new ethos of capitalism. But there is no doubt that religion served to legitimize the values of a capitalist society and helped to socialize workers to play their roles in the new machine economy. Unlike the traditional Christian condemnation of wealth, the new ethic saw riches as the reward of a life of diligence, thrift, and sobriety. Poverty on the other hand, was viewed as indicating a weakness of moral fibre rather than as a concommitant of holiness. Furthermore, the ideas of Social Darwinism with its doctrine of the survival of the fittest in the competitive social struggle legitmized the authority of

[1] S. M. Elkins, *Slavery* (1959).
[2] M. Weber, *The Protestant Ethic and the Spirit of Capitalism* (1930).

the captains of industry. The mere fact of their success was sufficient evidence of their fitness to govern industrial empires and to demand the obedience of their workers.[1]

The crucial significance of private property for maintaining the control of production and distribution in private hands was also legitimized and supported by an elaborate ideology. Private property was justified by the philosophers as the basis for freedom and for the development of personality, and defended as a natural and inalienable right.[2]

In the more developed economies of the later nineteenth and twentieth centuries, the organization of production undergoes structural changes. Large-scale corporations dominate the economic system, and account for the bulk of production. The growth in scale gives rise to new problems, particularly those of co-ordinating the activities of large numbers of workers and maximizing their output. Industry employs an increasing number of specialists, and as a consequence, there has been a marked increase in the numbers, prestige, and power of managers,[3] who now occupy the key roles in the economy and have displaced the entrepreneur of early capitalism. But the qualities which ensure success for the organization man are very different from those necessary for survival in the early stages of capitalism. The manager needs to be a good committee man, skilled in inter-personal relations, and a good company man, loyal to the corporation and willing to pursue its goals with single-minded enthusiasm. It is this social ethic of conformity to the corporation which Whyte[4] argues is becoming dominant, replacing the rugged individualism of the protestant ethic. These 'other directed' men of the giant corporations are in sharp contrast with the 'inner directed' industrialists of early captalism.[5]

Bendix has documented in considerable detail the subtle changes by which the 'entrepreneurial ideology' of the nineteenth century has gradually become transformed into a 'managerial ideology', which has functioned to legitimize the managerial exercise of control in

---

[1] See R. Bendix, *Work and Authority in Industry* (1956), for a detailed analysis of economic ideologies and their metamorphoses in Britain, America and Russia.

[2] See, for example, the works of John Locke and Bishop Gore, and the Papal encyclical, *Rerum Novarum* (1891).

[3] I. C. McGivering, *et al.*, *op. cit.* (1960). Comparisons between the composition of the American business elite born in 1801-30 and 1891-1920 show an increase in the percentage of managers from 16 to 48 per cent and a decline in entrepreneurs from 68 to 18 per cent. R. Bendix, *op. cit.* (1956), p. 229.

[4] W. H. Whyte, *Organisation Man* (1957).

[5] D. Rieseman, *The Lonely Crowd* (1950).

large scale organizations. The scientific management movement inspired by Frederick Taylor in the 1920s stressed the need for a more empirical approach to discover the conditions which would maximize the productive efficiency of the worker, by removing the sources of fatigue and dissatisfaction. The 'human relations' movement in the 1930s stressed even more strongly the possibility of harmonious co-operation between management and men if only management would learn and exercise the appropriate skills in meeting the human needs of workers for recognition, and would remove the misunderstandings which led to a faulty perception of conflicting interests by improved communications.

Bendix argues that the main stimulus to the emergence of the new managerial ideology in America was the bureaucratization of industry plus the growing challenge of the trade union movement. In Britain it has been pointed out[1] that the new ideology was associated mainly with the capital-intensive industries, notably chemicals and iron and steel. Here, labour disputes might lead to expensive shutdowns of large amounts of valuable plant. Sir Alfred Mond, chairman of ICI was an insistent proponent in the 1920s of a new approach to labour questions. Industry was no longer dominated by a few, but was now run by managers, he argued, whose task it was to act as arbitrators between the claims of capitalist, labour, and the public. All in industry are employees, even the directors, and their interests coincide. The task of management is to educate the workers into identifying their interests with those of management, and to win their willing co-operation and loyalty by such schemes as profit-sharing and co-partnership.

In addition to their role in legitimizing ownership and managerial control, ideologies also play an important part in regulating the process of distribution. Social philosphers[2] have long sought to arrive at a satisfactory set of principles for distributive justice. And such ideas enter into all discussions on the problem of fair wages. But although most agree in contemporary society on the desirability of pursuing the goal of distributive justice, there is little consensus on the relative importance to be attached to human need, skill effort, achievement, comparability, and what industry can afford. It is the lack of such consensus which underlies much industrial conflict and inhibits the achievement of incomes policies.[3]

[1] I. C. McGivering, *op. cit.*, pp. 91–101.
[2] See, for example, S. I. Benn and R. Peters, *Social Principles in the Democratic State* (1959).
[3] D. Lockwood, *op. cit.* (1955). Industrial conflict will be examined in Chapter 9.

The interaction between culture and the economic system is, of course, more complex than has so far been indicated. Culture serves on the one hand to provide individuals with motives and to legitimize their actions in the economic sphere. We believe, for example, that we ought to work for a living, and that refrigerators and cars are goods which we have a right to enjoy. Ideologies serve too, to enable individuals to adjust to situations of strain.[1] Studies of automobile workers in America show how they adjust to the prevailing culture imperative to 'get ahead' in the face of limited opportunities for advancement by redefining 'getting ahead' to mean ambitions for their children.[2] On the other hand, changes in the economic system result in the obsolescence of old values and beliefs and their inappropriateness for new situations. For example, the growing opportunities for the employment of women, coupled with labour shortages, are gradually modifying the traditional cultural belief that the place of women is in the home, thus leading more and more women to seek paid employment. Or again, the affluent society is faced with problems of consumption rather than of capital accumulation and production. Thrift and abstinence are no longer virtues. The mass media urge us instead to spend, while manufacturers build in 'planned obsolescence' to maintain demand at a high level. Furthermore, it is obviously an over-simplification to speak as though all levels in the economic system required the same perspectives. Indeed, it will be argued later that different types of workroles generate different outlooks and values.[3] As work plays a steadily decreasing role in the lives of most in industrially advanced societies, the old values and beliefs about work will no longer serve. We may well find the emergence of new philosophies which stress rather the role of creative leisure activities and legitimize the reduction in work.

Our analysis so far has examined the relations between the economic system and other major subsystems. But in the last analysis, production distribution and exchange are activities carried out by individuals. And it is to the interaction between the individual and the economic system that we now turn. Or rather, it is to the study of types of economic roles, since it is social types and not individuals as such who are the subjects of sociological study. That is to say, we are especially interested in occupational roles, such as skilled-workers, managers, scientists, teachers.

[1] N. J. Smelser, The Sociology of Economic Life (1963).
[2] E. Chinoy, Automobile Workers and the American Dream (1955).
[3] See also Chapter 7 for a discussion of class consciousness.

OCCUPATIONS AND THE ECONOMY

Of all the roles which the individual occupies, as husband, father, friend, member of a sports club, or of a political party, his occupation is probably the most significant for understanding him—the kind of person he is, his political and social attitudes, his leisure pursuits, attitudes towards his children's education, and even his relations with his wife. Occupation is the main determinant of income and of status. It also determines the tasks and activities which will occupy one half of his waking hours for most of his life. In other words, an individual's occupation locates him in a market situation, a status situation and a work situation. It is these three main dimensions of occupational roles that will now be examined.

The work system
One of the most challenging views on the effects of industrialization on the worker derives from Karl Marx. Marx argued that increasing division of labour and the institutions of capitalist production would result in the increasing alienation of the worker.[1] Highly mechanized systems take the intelligence and skill out of work and build it into the machines. The worker is left with monotonous routine work which yields no personal satisfaction. Moreover, he loses control over the work process: his actions and the pace of work are all controlled by the machine. Work ceases to have any meaning for him, and he is robbed of a sense of purpose. The property relations of capitalist society also contribute to the process of alienation as they separate the worker from the product of his labour over which he has no control. The worker does not own what he produces: he has nothing to sell but his labour. And because the factory belongs to the capitalist and the profits do not benefit the worker, he feels isolated from the whole system of organized production.

There has been considerable debate over the precise meaning which Marx attached to alienation. This need not concern us here. The value of Marx's analysis is that it directs our attention to a problem which is capable of empirical investigation and indicates some of the relevant variables. It serves to illustrate too, an important concept for the analysis of work-situations—the notion of *sociotechnical systems*. Men and machines form complex systems of interaction. Technical factors influence the relations between men which are involved in the production process.

[1] T. B. Bottomore (ed.) and M. Rubel, *Karl Marx: Selected Writings in Sociology and Social Philosophy* (1963), pp. 175–85.

To argue, as Marx did, that industrialization involves the alienation of the worker is to overlook the variety of socio-technical
systems in modern industry. Marx's analysis is particularly relevant
to assembly-line systems, such as those involved in car manufacture.
But it would not necessarily apply to continuous-process systems,
such as those used in the chemical and oil industries. A study by
Blauner[1] provides a good illustration of the way in which a rather
imprecise concept such as alienation can be translated into specific
research variables which are capable of measurement.

Blauner identifies four dimensions of alienation. 1. 'Powerlessness'
he defines as the inability to control work, such as the inability to
influence management decisions, lack of control over conditions of
employment, and lack of control over immediate work processes.
2. 'Meaninglessness' is the inability of the worker to develop a sense
of purpose by seeing the relationship between his job and the
overall production process and is determined by the scope and span
of the work tasks. 3. 'Isolation' is lack of membership of industrial
communities and is reflected in impersonal administration and the
absence of informal groups. 4. 'Self-estrangement' is the failure to
become involved in work as a means of self-expression. It is reflected
in the isolation and separation of work from the totality of social
life, and in work being simply instrumental (a source of income)
rather than a source of intrinsic satisfaction.[2]

Conditions in modern industry vary widely in the extent to which
they contribute to the alienation of the worker in these ways. The
printing industry for example, is still predominantly based on craft
technology. The craft printer has substantial control over his work
situation, and can control the pace, quality and quantity of the
product. His work is not subdivided and he can enjoy an intrinsic
satisfaction in contributing to a product with which he can identify.
Moreover, in the small shops which are characteristic of the printing
industry, there is an absence of the sense of anonymity and isolation
which typifies large-scale mass-production industries.

By contrast, the assembly-line workers in car factories are the
polar-opposite. They completely lack control over their work tasks
and conditions of employment, the pace, quantity and quality of the
product is largely determined by the conveyor belt, while the extreme
division of labour results in work tasks which require little skill,
yield no intrinsic satisfaction, and make it extremely difficult for

[1] R. Blauner, *Alienation and Freedom: The Manual Worker in Industry* (1963).
[2] It does not follow that alienation in the work situation is accompanied by
'global' alienation from the individual's total social milieu.

the worker to see the relationhip between his task and the total product.

The two socio-technical systems investigated can be seen to have quite different alienating tendencies. The craft printers are not alienated in Blauner's sense of the term, while the assembly line workers were highly alienated. Moreover, while only 4 per cent of craft printers expressed dissatisfaction with their jobs, 61 per cent of car assembly-line workers were dissatisfied.

Other studies confirm that the socio-technical system effects the meaning which work has for the individual and the satisfaction he derives from it. Baldamus[1] shows that differences in skill and the length of the work cycle are responsible for enormous discrepancies in turnover rates. Enamellers, for example, who receive a two-week training and whose job-cycle is completed in five minutes, have a turnover rate of 96 per cent (that is, avoidable leavers in a year are 96 per cent of the total number employed). By contrast, pattern-makers with a training period of five years, and a job cycle of one to twelve weeks, have a turnover rate of only 4 per cent.

Among the more specific factors producing attachment to the job is 'line-traction', where the object passes through a series of operations carried out by different workers, with or without the help of a conveyor belt. 'Process-traction' is experienced where the tasks are determined by the chemical or physical nature of the production process, for example, pottery-throwing, welding, forging. 'Object-traction' derives from the mental picture of the work-object, and 'machine-traction' occurs where the worker feels drawn along by operations on machines which are constantly running. Each of the components of the task is determined by technology and organizational factors, and all produce varying degrees of physical and psychological strain reflected in turnover rates and other expressions of dissatisfaction.

One conclusion emerges strongly from recent studies of more conventional occupations. For the great mass of industrial workers, and for many white-collar workers too, work is not a significant area of life.[2] Dubin found in his study of several hundred American industrial workers that work was a central life interest for only a small minority. Lafitte interviewed three hundred factory workers in Melbourne, and came to the same conclusion; that the activities most

[1] W. Baldamus, 'Types of Work and Motivation', *B.J.S.*, March 1951.

[2] R. Dubin, 'Industrial Workers' Worlds: A Study of the "Central Life Interests" of Industrial Workers', in E. D. Smigel, *Work and Leisure* (1963), Chapter 3, and in A. M. Rose, *Human Behaviour and Social Processes* (1962).

valued are found chiefly outside work. The factory worker is seldom work-centred. Work for him is not something on which he centres his interest, his hopes and aspirations, nor even his worries. It is simply *instrumental* in providing him with an income. That is, the typical worker is neither alienated nor involved: rather he is dissociated and apathetic. Work is non-salient.

But not only do some kinds of work fail to involve the interest of the workers; some have argued that they are positively damaging in their effects. Harvey Swados, an American writer who has worked in factories, emphasizes the differences between manual and middle-- class non-manual work, despite their superficial similarities: 'there is one thing that the worker doesn't do like the middle class; he works like a worker . . . The worker's attitude towards his work is generally compounded of hatred, shame, and resignation . . . It is not simply status-hunger that makes a man hate work that is mindless, endless, stupefying, sweaty, filthy, noisy, exhausting, insecure in its prospects, and practically without hope of advancement . . .'[1] A study of assembly-line workers concluded that they viewed their jobs with a mixture of anger and resignation; complained bitterly of overwork, monotony and physical strain.[2]

C. Wright Mills[3] argues that the alienating conditions of modern work now extend to the salaried employee. The breaking down of jobs into small, repetitive, and uninteresting parts decreases skill, and destroys the autonomy and craftsmanship of work in office as well as factory. The office-worker is as chained to the commuting timetable as the factory worker is to clocking-on. For such men too, work is significant only as a source of income or prestige. But just as not all manual-work is alienating, so some forms of white-collar work yield substantial intrinsic satisfactions. Many scientists, for example, find research activities intrinsically satisfying. Indeed, it is precisely be- cause they positively enjoy pursuing solutions to scientific problems that they may find themselves faced with problems of a different kind. Their research interests, for example, may not coincide with the problems that the firm which employs them wishes to solve, and the scientist may find himself under pressure to research into prob- lems which are not of his own choosing.[4]

[1] See M. R. Stein, *et al.*, *Identity and Anxiety* (1960).
[2] L. Lipitz, 'Work Life and Political Attitudes: a Study of Manual Workers', *Am. Pol. Sc. Rev.*, Dec. 1964, p. 953.
[3] *White Collar* (1951).
[4] W. Kornhauser and W. D. Hagstrom, *Scientists in Industry* (1962).

The market system and occupations

The occupation of an individual enables us to locate him in the market—a sub-system of the economic system. The market is the mechanism which regulates the supply and demand of economic goods, including labour and skills. The manual labourer who offers his skills for sale in the labour market receives a wage which is determined by a complex of forces which include the extent to which his occupation is organized and its effectiveness in bargaining, the economic strength of the industry, and the scarcity of his skill. But it will also be influenced by more specifically sociological factors such as the customary notions as to what constitutes a fair wage; what he is morally entitled to. Thus in general, non-manual workers think that they ought to be paid more than manual workers, even though the job they are doing may require less skill.

Although economists have specialized in the study of market behaviour, we may observe here that it is not in fact possible to isolate the market from the social system in which it functions, except perhaps in the very short run, when all the non-economic factors are constant. The rights to organize and to strike which are confirmed and safeguarded by legislation clearly effect the bargaining position of workers in the market. The economic system is related to the political system in a number of ways which effect the market situation of the worker, that is to say his ability to command goods and services.

A major distinction can be made between those who derive an income from the ownership and control of productive resources and those who sell their labours for a wage or salary. This was, of course, the basic dichotomy drawn by Marx between the bourgeoisie and the proletariat. It is certainly an important determinant of class and political attitudes as we shall see in Chapter 7. But it cannot explain all the variables in which we are interested. Craft printers and assembly-line workers are equally members of the proletariat in the Marxian sense, but as we have seen, the differences between them are very considerable.

The market situation involves not only the size of income, but also its security. Moreover, income includes non-monetary rewards such as sick benefits and welfare facilities. Work, in fact, carries with it the right to rewards which can differ in both size and security of enjoyment. The complexity of the differences can be simplified somewhat if we use the language of the property market. Property consists of the enjoyment of recognized rights. The tenant, for example, has strictly limited rights of enjoyment. He cannot alter the fabric of his tenement, while his tenancy is terminable at relatively short notice. By contrast, the freeholder enjoys a much more extensive range of rights and almost complete security. He can be dispossessed, but only after lengthy legal process and with safeguards for adequate compensation.

Jobs are property in much the same sense.[1] The factory owner, or the independent professional is a freeholder, while the factory worker is a tenant. But the tendency in the more advanced societies is for more and more jobs to shift to the intermediate position of leaseholder.[2] Salaried jobs like teachers and employed accountants enjoy considerable security of tenure, while firms are extending the range of rewards to which office-holders are entitled, with a variety of welfare benefits, and even paying fees for the sons of executives to attend public schools. Similarly, the extension of the machinery of protection to manual workers, with increasing rights of severance pay as compensation means that more and more workers are moving from vulnerable tenancies to more secure leasehold occupancy of jobs. Careers, as distinct from jobs, are characterized by leasehold rights. A career offers a reasonably secure expectation of continued employment, with regular promotions according to formal criteria and with predictable salaries at each stage.

Occupations and the status system
Society attaches different values to different occupations. Manual work, for example, carries low prestige, while non-manual work is highly esteemed. Social status is the social evaluation of roles. And occupational roles are the main determinants of the social status of the individual.

Empirical studies show that there is considerable social consensus on the relative standing of occupations. Ranked in order of prestige, we have medical officer of health, company director, school teacher, insurance agent, policeman, carpenter, bricklayer, railway porter, agricultural labourer, road sweeper.[3] Moreover, there is considerable agreement on the prestige ranking of occupations in all industrial societies. Power, influence, wealth and moral worth are all criteria which contribute to the formation of the complex judgments of social

---

[1] I am indebted to Douglas Young for this notion.
[2] This reflects the strategy increasingly adopted by employers to win the loyalty and co-operation of workers (see R. Bendix, *op. cit.*, 1956) as well as the efforts of trade unions to gain security for their members.
[3] C. A. Moser and J. R. Hall, 'The Social Grading of Occupations', in D. V. Glass (ed.), *Social Mobility* (London, 1954), Chapter 2.

standing. Income alone is not enough. It does not lead to the acceptance on an equal footing of well-paid manual workers by black-coated workers who may earn less. Moreover, service occupations such as teachers and clergymen enjoy a relatively high standing in society, compared with their relatively low incomes. One very important factor in the social evaluation of an occupation is the position which it occupies in the authority structure of industry. The inferior status of the manual worker to the clerk, despite his often superior income, probably derives from his inferior position and lack of autonomy in the work situation. His subordinate role on the job spills over and influences his off-the-job standing.[1]

There are, however, important sub-cultural differences in prestige rankings. Young and Willmott found in their inquiries in Bethnal Green that a substantial minority of lower status workers rejected the more general prestige rankings and adopted the criterion of usefulness to society which resulted in a dustman, for example, ranking his occupation on equal terms with a medical officer of health. Company directors were demoted to an inferior position on the same grounds.[2]

Socialization, selection and occupational choice
Satisfaction from work and the significance attached to it will depend not only on the nature of the work but also on the expectations which the individual brings to his job. These, in turn, will be the result of complex processes of selection and socialization, which begin at 11-plus with entry to the grammar or modern school, each of which carries its stream of children on to broad groups of occupations.

Carter's[3] recent study of school leavers provides a striking demonstration of this socializing process. For the less able child in the lower forms of the modern school, the dominant picture that emerges is one of school as a source of boredom and frustration. In many schools the imposition of dull, mechanical tasks, which lack any apparent significance or relevance to the life of the child, effectively train him to accept the routine demands of industry. The transition from school to work involves little more than a change of routine. Many expect little from work and are satisfied with what

[1] J. H. Goldthorpe and D. Lockwood, 'Affluence and British Class Structure', *Soc. Rev.*, Vol. 11, July 1963. The question of status and status consistency will be explored in more detail in Chapter 7.

[2] M. Young and P. Willmott, 'Social Grading by Manual Workers', *B.J.S.*, Dec. 1956.

[3] M. Carter, *op. cit.*

they find, even though the work is repetitive and makes few demands. The secondary modern boy leaving school at fifteen has received early training in dissociating himself from the demands which 'they' make upon him. He simply doesn't care It is not surprising that psychologists have discovered that many are content to carry out routine tasks. Dissatisfaction is a measure of the gap between aspiration and achievement. For many, no such gap exists—their expectations and aspirations are centred on the world outside the factory.

The same socializing and selection mechanism can be seen very clearly in the recruitment of Hull fishermen. Most of the boys who become fishermen originate from the lower stream of the modern school near the docks. Here the boys have learned to see themselves as future unskilled workers, and the teacher as the prototype of the white-collar world which oppresses the manual worker. Whether they go straight from school, or after a variety of unskilled jobs, fishing is seen as an escape into a world of virile men with money in their pockets. 'One reason why these boys want to go on trawlers . . . is that they are trying to say "No" to their inferior position in the class system. On a trawler . . . there are none of the wider distinctions of accent, vocabulary, social distance.'[1] During his first years, the young fisherman learns to be tough, to drink, to spend freely. He lacks education and position. But his job gives him manhood and money. By twenty-three, 'he has indelibly printed on him certain habits, reflexes, patterns of spending, attitudes to life . . . he cannot go back.'

Socialization can also influence the expectations which the individual brings to the job and the satisfaction which he gains from it. Technicians who have qualified by taking examinations, or have simply attended courses are much more likely than those who have not studied to expect and to enjoy intrinsic satisfactions, such as an interesting job, and a chance to use abilities to the full.[2] Other studies show that professionals, who have undergone an extended education, are more identified with and satisfied with their work.[3]

Where an occupation requires particular personal qualities, we can expect a considerable amount of attention to be paid to socialization and selection. Military academies, for example, not only pay great attention to the social background of recruits, but they also

[1] J. Tunstall, *The Fishermen* (1962).
[2] S. Cotgrove, 'The Relations between Work and Non-work among Technicians', *Soc. Rev.*, July 1965.
[3] Morris Rosenburg, *Occupation and Values* (1957).

subject him to a rigorous education and training designed to develop military qualities of honour and loyalty, which includes detailed regulation of the recruits' daily routines, and indoctrination in military traditions and in professional etiquette.[1]

Some degree of socialization may also occur during employment. If the characteristics of the individual do not match up entirely with the demands of the job, he may adjust to the situation by changing his own values or norms. Merton[2] discusses the tendency in bureaucracies for officials to become over-conformist, to adhere rigidly to the rules and regulations for their own sake. A major structural pressure to behave in this way stems from the fact that the official's life is planned for him in terms of a graded career. The rewards for conformity are promotion, security and eventually a pension. These pressures to conform induce timidity, and conservativism. Moreover, strict conformity to the rules protects the individual against criticism, and may be a device sought by the timid. The result is that importance comes to be displaced from ends to means; from organizational goals to rules. How far this process is the result of the resocialization of the official and how far it is due to a tendency for bureaucracies to attract less adventurous types of personality cannot be determined in the light of present knowledge.

Not only then do employers select employees: there is also self-selection by workers. Their choice of job will be influenced by two main variables; their awareness of the needs and satisfactions which they expect a job to meet, and secondly, their perception of the extent to which different employment conditions are likely to meet their expectations. Science students, for example, differ in the extent to which they attach value to scientific needs such as freedom to choose research projects, freedom to publish, and material needs such as income. They agree, however, that employment in industry is likely to be better paid, while the universities allow more freedom to research and publish. Inquiries have shown that science students attaching more value to pay, in fact, choose to work in industry, while those valuing scientific freedom more highly prefer to work in universities or teaching.[3]

[1] For a detailed account of American military academies, and the discontinuities between professional education and the realities of military life, see M. Janowitz, *The Professional Soldier*, 1960, pp. 127–45. On the socialization of doctors, see R. K. Merton, *et al.*, *The Student Physician* (1957).

[2] R. K. Merton, 'Bureaucratic Structure and Personality', in *Social Theory and Social Structure* (1957).

[3] S. Box and S. Cotgrove, 'Scientific Identity, Occupational Selection and Role Strain', *B.J.S.*, March 1966.

Occupational roles, role strain and role conflict
Most individuals are employed in organizations,[1] and many in large
scale organizations. It is the organization which defines and spells
out the daily activities of the individual. In some occupations, the
individual is also subject to more general social pressures. Teachers,
and clergymen, and other occupations which involve contact with
the general public, for example, are expected to behave in specific
ways and to conform to social pressures.

The concept of *role* is particularly useful for examining the relations between the individual and organizations or other aspects of
the social structure. We have used it before to talk about the role
of the husband or wife when we wanted to stress the fact that being a
husband was in many ways like acting a part in a play which someone else has written. Being a nurse in a hospital or a teacher in a
school, a scientist in a research laboratory or a prison-officer—
all involve playing a part, which in this case, has been written by
the organization. The rules of the organization provide us with the
script, define our tasks and the goals we are expected to pursue.

The script gives us our part. But the actor determines how he will
play it. Each actor has his own *role style*. The way he plays the part
will be shaped by his own characteristics. It will depend on how he
perceives the role, as well as the skills and capacities he has for
carrying out the tasks which the role requires.[2]

Teachers
It has already been pointed out in Chapter 3 that there are differences among teachers in the importance which they attach to the
various functions of education. Academic teachers stress the pursuit
of knowledge, while on the other hand, there are those who place
more emphasis on the development of the child and can be conceptualized as child-centred. We could expect such differences to
reflect differential socialization and selection.[3] University graduates,
for example, will have become attached to an academic subject
before deciding to become a teacher and being exposed to professional training. Moreover, graduate teachers more often come from
middle-class homes, and a considerable proportion enter teaching
only as a second choice. They are anxious to maintain their middle-

[1] These issues are also discussed in Chapter 8, 'Organization'.
[2] D. J. Levinson, 'Role, Personality and Social Structure in the Organizational
Setting', in N. J. Smelser and W. T. Smelser, *Personality and Social Systems* (1963).
[3] J. Kob, 'Definition of the Teacher's Role', in Halsey, Floud and Anderson,
op. cit., 1958.

class status and will cling to their connexion with the university. Such teachers are more frequently subject-centred. By contrast, teachers from training colleges more often come from a working-class home, have chosen teaching as a means of achieving higher status, and have been educated in a professionally oriented course. Such teachers are more frequently child-centred. But in spite of such differences in the way in which teachers define their role, there do not appear to be any distinctive personality characteristics which differentiate teachers from other occupational types.[1]

In carrying out his role, the teacher is subjected to a number of (sometimes conflicting) pressures. The teacher's *role-set*,[2] that is to say, the complex of other roles which his own role interacts, includes school governors, the local authority, inspectors, and parents. Parents, for example, may seek to increase their influence over the teachers by the formation of parent-teachers associations. Some parents may have strong views on the adoption of progressive teaching methods and many would seek to reverse a decision to demote a child to a lower stream.

Wilson[3] has drawn attention to a number of other role-conflicts and sources of strain. There are those, for example, which derive from the diffuse nature of the teacher's role, the absence of any clear boundary whereby he can know when he had done his job. The task of socialization cannot be measured in the way that a doctor's or solicitor's role performance can be measured. The teacher must continually ask himself whether he has fully discharged his obligations and there is a tendency to over-extend himself. The socializing role also requires an affective relationship with his pupils. But his custodial role as a disciplinary agent may be jeopardized if he becomes too friendly.

Other strains arise out of conflicting commitments to role and career. If he is to 'get on', the teacher needs to be on the move, seeking promotion or moving to a more congenial school. Yet his commitment to the values of teaching may pull him towards staying in a tough school and certainly staying long enough to really know his pupils.

Scientists
There is no necessary fit between the demands of the organization

[1] F. W. Musgrove, *The Sociology of Education* (1965), Chapter 16, 'The Role of the Teacher'.

[2] R. K. Merton, 'The Role-Set: Problems in Sociological Theory', *B.J.S.*, June 1955.

[3] B. R. Wilson, 'The Teacher's Role', *B.J.S.*, March 1962, pp. 15–32.

and the characteristics of the individual. One of the clearest examples of this arises out of the employment of scientists in industry. The scientist is a professional. That is to say, he attaches high value to knowledge and demands freedom to pursue the solution to scientific problems. Moreover, his reputation will depend on his standing in eyes of other scientists, and this in turn will be achieved by contributions to science through publications and papers read to learned society meetings. These activities will be particularly important to the scientist, for whereas doctors, architects and engineers are judged by their practical performance, scientists are judged by their contribution to knowledge.[1]

Such a scientist employed in an industrial laboratory may well find that the organization makes demands on him which conflict with his own values and needs. For example, a firm will be anxious to protect any discoveries by patents before it allows them to be published. Yet the scientist is keen to claim recognition for his contribution to knowledge and will be particularly anxious lest someone else should publish before he does. The firm and the scientist are also likely to differ in the importance they attach to a particular piece of research. The scientist may wish to pursue it because it is likely to result in a particularly important contribution to knowledge. But the firm may want to terminate the project because it is unlikely to be capable of development into a marketable product. The scientist may experience strain then on at least two counts; frustrations to his professional autonomy and hindrances to establishing a scientific reputation through publication.[2]

Strains, then, can be felt as a result of a lack of congruence between the needs which the individual brings to the organization and those which the organization can satisfy. But they can arise, too, when organizations make ambiguous or conflicting demands on individuals.[3]

Foremen
The case of the foreman in industry provides examples of role strain

[1] Their problems will be shared by other academics who have identified themselves with the world of knowledge and its values who are employed by organizations.
[2] W. Kornhauser, *et al.*, *Scientists in Industry* (1962). See also S. Box and S. Cotgrove, 'Scientists and Employers', *New Scientist*, Vol. 22, pp. 362–4 (1964), and S. Box and S. Cotgrove, *op. cit.*, *B.J.S.*, March 1966.
[3] The relations between individuals and organizations are discussed more fully in Chapter 8.

from such sources.[1] His position in the management structure subjects him to conflicting demands. The first line supervisor is at the base of the authority pyramid and hence is likely to experience the full force of any conflicts between management and men. His role has become ambiguous and his status threatened by the development of staff functions which have eroded many of the foreman's traditional functions. Hiring and firing has become a specialized task performed by the personnel department. The increasing application of science to production and the growth of specialized research and development departments have challenged the foreman's traditional role as the custodian of accumulated know how. Scientists and technicians are now taking the decisions he used to take.

The development of joint-consultation has been a further factor introducing an element of ambiguity into the foreman's role. Works committees in which higher management and workers meet face-to-face have weakened his position in the chain of communication. The growth of full-employment and the shop stewards movement have challenged and reduced his authority.

As a result of such changes, the foreman's position in the authority structure has become ambiguous, his powers weakened, and his functions eroded. It is no longer always as clear at it once was that he is part of management. Moreover, piece-work and overtime under conditions of full-employment have greatly reduced the income differentials which were once a mark of his superior status.[2] He is a 'marginal man', sharing something of the perspectives of both management and men.

OCCUPATIONAL STRATEGIES[3]

Members of occupations adopt a variety of devices to protect themselves against the strains and conflicts to which their work exposes them. Some of these adaptations involve compensatory activities outside work, such as creative leisure pursuits. These will be examined later in this Chapter. But they also adopt various strategies

[1] NIIP, *The Foreman in British Industry* (1951). C. Argyris, *op. cit.*, Chapter 5.

[2] These are only a few examples of the many strains and conflicts which result from the employment of individuals in occupational roles. For a perceptive study of the conflicts between the values of art and the pressures of the market, see Griff, 'The Commercial Artist', in M. R. Stein, *et al.*, *Identity and Anxiety* (1960).

[3] I am indebted to Noel Parry for many of the ideas expressed in this section. For a summary of strategies, see A. Tourraine, *et al.*, *Workers' Attitudes to Technical Change* (1965), pp. 109–13.

to exercise control over their work, market, and status situations. These include restrictive practices on the shop floor at one end of the spectrum, through collective bargaining, to an organized labour movement seeking to transform society at the other.

Strategies of independence[1]
A well-documented example is to be found in the famous Hawthorne investigations. Workers in the bank-wiring room (wiring banks of telephone terminals) had developed a strong informal organization which exercised control over the output of workers in the group, reinforced by a variety of sanctions including horseplay and mild physical violence. In this way, the group exercised some small measure of control over a largely management-determined working day, and offset to some extent the insecurity of their position which would be heightened if they worked themselves out of a job.[2] Absenteeism and some strikes are other examples of strategies to control the pressures of the work situation.[3]

Members of occupations share common interests which almost invariably leads to the formation of associations for their pursuit and promotion. Trade unions are familiar examples. They function to protect and improve both the work situation and the market situation of the manual worker. The strategies which they adopt are a function of their position in the economic and status systems. Since workers are freely interchangeable, they are individually virtually powerless. Only by collective action have they been able to achieve a stronger bargaining position with their employers. Lockwood's[4] study of clerks illustrates the ways in which differences in work, market and status situations influence the strategies of occupations.

Clerks and trade unions
It is in the work-situation and not in market-determined income, that Lockwood finds the main clue to understanding the strategies adopted by clerks. The typical clerk in industry is employed in a small office, and usually one in which his relationship to his employer

[1] This term is used by R. Bendix, *op. cit.* (1956). See also C. Argyris, *Integrating the Individual and the Organization* (1964), Chapter 4.

[2] F. J. Roethlisberger and W. J. Dickson, *Management and the Worker* (1939).

[3] F. W. Musgrave, *op. cit.* (1965), suggests that teachers seek to protect themselves against parental pressures by not encouraging the formation of parent-teacher associations. See also H. S. Becker, 'The Teacher in the authority system of the public school', in A. Etzioni, *Complex Organizations—A Reader*.

[4] *The Blackcoated Worker* (1958).

is paternalistic. His functions, remuneration, promotion and pension will be determined by a personal relation with his employer. Such conditions do not promote a sense of common identity of interest amongst clerks essential for collective action. Moreover, clerical work is typically a stepping-stone to executive and managerial posts. The clerk will therefore tend to see his future dependent on his own efforts and the impression he can make on his employer. Collective bargaining is hardly likely to earn promotion.[1] He will be conscious too of the fact that membership of a trade union is inconsistent with middle-class status and values. Such clerks, therefore, have not been highly unionized. Moreover, where they have formed occupational organizations, such as in banking, they have in the past refused to affiliate to the TUC or to adopt strike action. By contrast, bureaucratic organizations establish uniform working conditions regulated by impersonal rules, which exclude all forms of personal consideration between employer and clerk. It is, in fact, in the bureaucratically organized civil service and local government service that clerical unions have flourished, whereas the unions catering for industrial clerks have hitherto made relatively little progress. It is where the work situation of the clerk corresponds most closely with that of the factory worker that he is most likely to adopt the union strategies of collective bargaining and the threat of strike action to improve his market situation. In short then, whether clerks are prepared to adopt collective bargaining or whether they prefer to rely on individual efforts will depend on the organization of the work situations and on the strategies which are most likely to achieve an improvement in their market situation.

The recent increase in white-collar unionization can be explained in these terms. More and more clerks are employed in large open-planned offices; the salary and educational differentials with manual workers have declined and thus some of the most important bases of their claim to superior status have been threatened. Moreover, management and executive posts are being increasingly recruited from university graduates and the chances of internal promotion reduced. More clerks therefore are coming to see union organization as instrumental in improving their market and work situation.

Professions

Differing again from both clerks and manual workers are a group of

[1] A. J. M. Sykes, 'Some Differences in the Attitudes of Clerical and Manual Workers', *Soc. Rev.*, Nov. 1965, found that 92 per cent of a sample of clerks preferred to bargain individually, and 92 per cent disapproved of trade unions for clerks.

occupations which are referred to rather ambiguously as professions. There is no agreement as to precisely what are the characteristics of a profession.[1] There are no criteria which can be applied to all the occupations loosely included in this group. Their most general characteristic is the application of a body of knowledge to some practical occupation. Thus engineering, medicine, architecture, the law—all require the mastery of a body of knowledge, and most such occupations now insist on passing formal examinations as a condition of entry.

Professional occupations have generally formed associations of members, and one of the main functions of such associations has been to examine aspirants to practice and to confer qualifications necessary for entry. Furthermore, some have devised ethical codes to regulate the conduct of their members, as for example, medicine. The formation of associations conferring qualifications and regulating conduct then are features of this group of intellectual occupations.

Now although they have common features, there are also considerable differences in both the work and market situations of, for example, doctors and engineers. Teachers and engineers are mainly employees, while doctors and solicitors are usually in private practice, either as individuals or as partners. Architects and accountants may be either principals of private practices, or employees. It is not surprising therefore, to find that occupations which experience a variety of situations in the economic system differ in the strategies they adopt and defy all efforts to define them by a set of common characteristics.

The highest degree of control is achieved where the professional sells his skills direct to a client for a fee, determined by his own professional association, and where the profession obtains a monopoly of the market by 'closure'. This involves an act of parliament which restricts certain key professional activities, such as signing death certificates in medicine, to practitioners whose names are included on the register kept by members of the profession. Under such circumstances, the profession individually and collectively regulates every aspect of its market and work situation.

Where the professional is paid a salary rather than charging a fee, his market situation is weakened. With the introduction of the National Health Service, doctors' remuneration was fixed in relation to the number of patients on their books, the total amount available for distribution being fixed by the government. This has resulted in the BMA assuming trade-union functions in bargaining for higher

[1] G. Millerson, *The Qualifying Associations* (1964).

rates and threatening strike action. Doctors then, have retained a high degree of autonomy in the work situation, but with the decline in private practice, their market situation has come to depend increasingly on collective bargaining.

Professional codes of conduct, and the activities of professional bodies to improve their status and the 'public image' are similarly related to the market situation. Status is the prestige attached to an occupation and reflects the value placed upon it by society. High status serves to legitimize both the authority which the professional exercises and also his economic rewards. 'Unethical conduct' threatens the standing of the occupation and weakens its claim to be worth more in economic terms.

These relations can be illustrated by researches carried out among scientists and engineers.[1] It is hypothesized that professional status serves to legitimize the high pay and dominant position occupied by professionals in the authority structure of the work situation. Those who occupy subordinate positions therefore can be expected to support trade union associations in which collective bargaining is the appropriate strategy rather than professional associations, which will place more emphasis on maintaining the high standing of the occupation. A study of qualified scientists and engineers confirmed these hypotheses. It concluded that a major function of the engineering institutions was with reinforcing the status claims of those employed in positions of responsibility.

The success of occupations such as medicine and the law in achieving high rewards in terms of income and prestige has provided a model which others have sought to imitate. Wherever an occupation requires the acquisition of a specific body of knowledge for its practice, it offers possibilities for adopting strategies modelled on those of the older professions. With the growth of knowledge, specialization, and division of labour, an increasing number of occupations have found themselves in a position to set up associations, whose prime function is to examine and qualify members. Qualifications provide a means of limiting entry to the occupations, and a basis for negotiating salary structures related to qualification. Such associations, however, differ from the independent professions mainly in that they lack a code of conduct. Such a code would be largely functionless in an occupation whose conduct is governed mainly by the conditions of employment in organizations, and if devised could function only as a status symbol.

The term profession then has little descriptive value. It refers to a

[1] K. Prandy, *Professional Employees—A Study of Scientists and Engineers* (1965).

group of occupations whose practice involves the applications of specialized intellectual knowledge sufficiently extensive to warrant formal educational and examination procedures. Such occupations are more likely to enjoy autonomy in the work situation and to be intrinsically involved. Moreover, their desire for public recognition and esteem and the frequently fiduciary element in their relations with clients will lead them to stress the element of service rather than income. However, since income and status are closely linked, they will seek to promote the pursuit of both by strategies which include the use of qualifications to control entry and to provide a basis for differential incomes. The strategies open to them will depend on their market and work situations. It is doubtful, in fact, whether the professions represent a different type of occupation,[1] oriented to service rather than to profit, as has been argued by Carr-Saunders & Wilson and by T. H. Marshall. This view has been challenged by Parsons[2] who sees the typical professional attitude with its emphasis on understanding and disinterested service and ethical conduct towards the client as functionally necessary requirements to maintain the delicate relationship between the professional and his client. Economists and political scientists have stressed the dysfunctional consequences of professional organizations, criticizing them for their monopolistic practices. Kessel has shown that the practices of the American Medical Association including the opposition to advertising 'are essentially similar to measures adopted by monopolies (and cartels) and serve the same purpose'[3]—functioning as a means of raising the price of professional services.

Skilled workers and apprenticeship

Just as intellectual occupations use qualifications as a lever for improving their position, so skilled trades will seek to protect their skills and the bargaining strength which this confers. And the institution of apprenticeship plays a key role in this process. Investigations in the 1950s into the working of apprenticeship[4] brought to light the fact that it was largely failing as an institution for education and training. On the industrial side, only a minority of apprentices received systematic training, most being left to pick it up by the

[1] See, for example, A. Carr-Saunders and Wilson, *The Professions* (1933), and T. H. Marshall, *Citizenship and Social Class* (1950).

[2] 'The Professions and Social Structure', in *Essays in Sociological Theory* (1958).

[3] J. Ben-David, 'Professions in the class system of present-day societies', *Current Sociology*, Vol. XII, No. 3, 1963–64. This article includes a summary of the literature on the professions.

[4] G. Williams, *Recruitment to Skilled Trades* (1957).

time-honoured method of 'sitting by Nellie'. On the college side, only about one in ten of those who began courses were successfully qualifying. Moreover, recognition as a skilled craftsman is not in any way dependent on passing examinatons or on providing proof of competent and systematic training. If the 'charter' of apprenticeship is to train young people in industrial skills, and if in fact, it is not functioning successfully, how can we account for the support which it receives from industry? The clue is to be found in an intensive study of apprenticeship by Dr K. Liepmann.[1] It appears from this that apprenticeship is important for its regulatory functions rather than for its training functions. With the rise of the trade-unions, the institution has come to be used by them primarily as a strategy for protecting their market situation. It provides a basis for regulating entry into the occupation, for protecting jobs by demarcation lines between skills, as a cushion against unemployment by agreements to dismiss dilutees (non-apprenticed labour) before craftsmen, and as a basis for claims to differential wages. A latent (unintended and unrecognized) function of the Ministry's policy of linking education to a predominantly regulatory institution has been the virtual failure of its plans to increase the supply of effectively trained skilled workers.[2]

NON-WORK CORRELATES

Occupation is clearly a most important influence in the life of the individual. Yet the study of occupations and their influence is an area which has hitherto been largely ignored by sociologists. In Britain, in particular, researches have concentrated rather on social class as a variable. We have a number of studies of working-class life, particularly investigations of family life. Such studies provide us with a good deal of useful descriptive material. But they fail to discover the variables in the working-class situation which are interrelated. Hoggart,[3] for example, refers to some of the distinctive elements in working-class sub-culture, such as belief in fate, and the distinction between 'them' who decide and 'us' who passively carry out instructions. Such embracing descriptions of working-class life fail to take account of the very considerable differences in market, status, and work-situations which exist, and consequently provide

[1] *Apprenticeship* (1960).
[2] Industrial Training Boards have now been set up with powers to ensure absolute training.
[3] R. Hoggart, *The Uses of Literacy* (1957).

little insight into the significance of such differences in the lives of workers. In short, the term 'working-class' includes a very wide range of variables, and does not refer to a homogeneous group of individuals. What we now need are more rigorous studies which relate variables in the market, status and work-situations to non-work variables. What, for example, are the consequences for family life, leisure activities, and political attitudes of alienative work experiences?[1]

Studies of particular occupations as distinct from studies of class groups make it possible to see much more clearly the way in which the kind of work that a man does influences his pattern of life. Both Dennis, Henriques and Slaughter's[2] study of a mining community and Clancy Sigal's *Week-End in Dinlock* present a vivid picture of a type of work which makes a powerful impact on the life of the community. The face-worker is deeply involved in his work and enjoys relative autonomy at the coal face. But it is dangerous and damaging work, demanding the closest co-operation, where one man's mistake can cause the deaths of others. It is this dangerous man's world which makes its indelible imprint on life after work— the forgetfulness of alcohol in the long round of pub visits on Saturday and Sunday, wives left at home, the deep significance of the trade union. And to repair the damages exacted by his work the miner expects a wife who will feed and comfort him, making few demands in return.

Jeremy Tunstall[3] shows that the work of the distant-water fisherman spills over in a similar way to influence leisure and home life. As with the miners, men who are thrown closely together at work and whose homes are work-based, spend their leisure together. It is a world which generates conservatism and belief in fate. It is a world of virile men with money in their pockets, defying their inferior position in the class structure. While on shore, the fisherman can be 'king for a day, wearing new suits, riding in taxis, drinking whisky'. Within the family, the prolonged absences of men at sea for three weeks at a time further encourage husbands and wives to lead separate lives, and husbands to treat their wives as servants (see Chapter 2).

A comparison between the attitudes of assembly-line and skilled workers with comparable education and income showed considerable differences in attitudes towards politics and the unions.

---

[1] C. Argyris, *op. cit.*, 1964, pp. 73–92; summarizes American data.
[2] *Coal is Our Life* (1956).
[3] *Op. cit.* (1962).

Assembly-line workers were found to be the most radical, but were less favourable towards unions, and gave no indication of a sense of participation or solidarity. The line workers who were conscious of having less control over their work were also more likely to adopt fatalistic attitudes and to view the world as unalterable.[1]

But the less exotic occupations of clerk and executive also leave their imprint. W. H. Whyte's impressionistic study, *Organization Man*, shows the man with a career looking forward to a succession of jobs, each carrying higher rewards in terms of income, prestige, and the perquisites of office. His working life is broadly predictable. Success for the organization man depends on conformity, being 'other-directed', being a good company man. Career prospects encourage training, and the adoption of the long view.[2] Such men will be strongly committed to their careers, and will not draw any clear distinction between work and leisure, combining vacation trips with business and social life with business contacts.

The relations between family roles and occupation have already been explored in Chapter 2. Later chapters will examine in more detail the influence of occupation on political and social attitudes, and on voting behaviour. The relations between work and leisure however, are particularly close. Leisure therefore, will now be explored more fully as an example of the influence of work on non-work.

Leisure

It is to be expected that occupation has a marked influence on leisure. A man's job determines in the first place the amount of free time he has left over for non-work activities. His market situation is a factor in the amount of money he has in his pocket for different leisure activities. His status situation may similarly influence free-time, by providing opportunities for achieving status in non-work activities which he cannot achieve through his occupation. Office in voluntary associations,[3] such as trade unions or political parties, success in the fields of sport or entertainment, provide possible alternative bases for status denied by occupation. Moreover, leisure

[1] L. Lipsitz, *op. cit.*

[2] Sykes found that 87 per cent of clerks compared with 9 per cent of workers expected promotion, while 94 per cent of clerks compared with 2 per cent of workers has attended night school (*op. cit.*, 1965).

[3] In practice, such associations function only to a limited extent as alternative avenues for status. Officers tend to be recruited mainly from the higher status groups. (D. V. Glass (ed.), *op. cit.*, Chapter 13.)

activities function as status symbols and are ways in which income can be spent in status-conferring ways.

The influence of the work-situation on leisure, however, is particularly marked. Parker[1] has suggested that there are three main types of association. The first, 'opposition' includes the leisure patterns of coal-miners, distant-water fishermen, and alienated workers in assembly-belt production. Here there is a sharp distinction between work and leisure. Work is not a central life interest, and yields only extrinsic satisfactions or may even generate hostility. In the words of C. Wright Mills,

'Each day, men sell little pieces of themselves in order to try to buy them back each night and weekend with the coin of fun.'

Or again, in the words of Arthur Seaton,

'If your machine was working well . . . You went off into pipe-dreams for the rest of the day. And in the evening, when admittedly you would be feeling as though your arms and legs had been stretched to breaking point on a torture-rack, you stepped out into a cosy world of pubs and noisy tarts that would one day provide you with the raw material for more pipe dreams as you stood at your lathe.'[2]

Withdrawal to home-centredness offers compensations of a different kind. Here, a man is boss of his own small world and can engage in meaningful tasks of his own choosing. Somewhat differently, the hard drinking of miners and distant-water fishermen is less a reaction against tedium than an attempt to escape from the world of work which is dangerous, damaging, and viewed with mixed feeling of attraction and dislike.

A second type of association between work and leisure identified by Parker is 'extension'. This relationship characterizes occupations in which work is intrinsically satisfying and for whom work is a central life interest. Parker found, for example, that youth employment officers and child care workers did not draw any sharp distinction between work and leisure, and work related activities frequently penetrate into leisure time. Gerstl[3] found that dentists tend to use their hands in jobs about the house, advertising men paint and write,

---

[1] S. Parker, 'Work and Non Work in Three Occupations', *Soc. Rev.*, Vol. 13, 1965.
[2] A. Sillitoe, *Saturday Night and Sunday Morning* (1958), p. 31.
[3] E. O. Smigel, *op. cit.*, ch. 8.

while professors read[1] and listen to music. Between these two types of association, there is a third—'complementarity'. Bank clerks, for example are neither so engrossed in their work that they want to carry it over into their spare time, nor does their work generate needs for which leisure time offers compensation. Their attitude towards work is rather one of indifference. Some indication that an element of apathy spills over into leisure can be seen in the relatively greater preference they express for relaxing and sleeping as a way of spending extra leisure time. Wilensky[2] suggests an alternative form of opposition where the influence of work may 'spill over' into leisure. Here, the exhaustion and tedium of work penetrate into non-work time. The worker collapses in his armchair, and twiddles the knobs on his TV set. The mental stultification produced by work permeates leisure: alienation from work becomes alienation from life.

SOCIAL CHANGE AND THE ECONOMY

To explore all the sociological aspects of economic growth would be a task of great complexity. We would need to know, for example, the social conditions such as the kinship and political systems which make possible and stimulate economic growth. We would also need to explore in detail the effects of economic change on the social system. Some aspects of these questions have been touched on, for example, the relations between changes in the economic system and culture, and the kinship system. We have also seen that economic change can be viewed in terms of changes within the economic system, such as changes in the composition of the labour force. The whole subject of economic growth, its conditions and consequences, will be re-examined in the final chapter on social change. Meanwhile, there are a few more limited issues that are relevant to an understanding of the probable trends in the next few decades.

It can be seen from the preceding analysis that the changes which are likely to be most sociologically significant are those which influence occupational roles, by changing the degree of autonomy and skill required and influencing the involvement and satisfaction of the worker by hand or brain. The broad pattern has been a shift from a predominance of primary extractive industry (hunting, fishing,

[1] If the professor's reading is connected with his lecturing or research, one would prefer to categorize this as work. See Table 4.1.

[2] H. L. Wilensky, 'Work, Careers and Social Integration', *International Soc. Sc. J.*, No. 4, 1960.

mining) to a secondary manufacturing industry, and now in the economically advanced societies to tertiary service industries (transport, education, retail trade). With this trend, has come a shift towards a higher proportion of non-manual workers in the labour force, the increasing employment of women, the growth of intellectual occupations, and a general rise in the levels of skill.[1] The growth of large-scale factory production and giant corporations means that the independent craftsmen and small *entrepreneur* has declined while an increasing proportion of the labour force is employed in organizations of varying size. Such changes offset the degree of economic autonomy of the individual. There are now fewer employers and a smaller proportion of employees are in managerial positions. Any extrapolation of existing trends inevitably involves considerable uncertainty. Bearing this in mind, it seems probable that technological change will bring about further changes in the occupational structure, a shift to non-manual occupations with increased skill and intellectual content.

The effects of such changes are still a matter for controversy and await further research. Automation certainly results in the re-integration of work. And in some cases this leads to increased worker satisfaction. It is important to remember that automation takes a variety of forms and these have different consequences. Although it reverses the trend towards the fragmentation of tasks, it may increase the isolation of the individual worker. However, not all forms of automation have this consequence. A study of automated electricity generating stations showed that work teams became more united.[2] Automation has also given rise to a good deal of optimism about the humanizing and up-grading of work.[3] Again the evidence is conflicting. Some studies have found identification and pride in automated machinery, while others have reported increasing estrangement from the productive processes.[4] A further possibility is that the increasing skills and knowledge will lead to the professionalization of work—a shift from jobs to careers.[5] Finally, the impact of automation may well be related to the characteristics

---

[1] For relevant statistics, see A. Carr-Saunders, C. Jones and C. Moser, *op. cit.*
[2] F. C. Mann and L. R. Hoffman, *Automation and the workers: a study of social change in power plants* (1960).
[3] D. Bell, *The End of Ideology* (1960), Chapter 11.
[4] W. A. Faunce, 'Automation and the automobile worker', in W. Galenson and S. K. Lipset, *Labour and trade-unionism, an interdisciplinary reader* (1960), pp. 37-9.
[5] For a summary of the effects of automation, see A. Tourraine, *et al.*, *Workers' Attitudes to Technical Changes* (1965), pp. 43-9.

which the worker brings to the job—especially his family life, previous education and work experience.

Such changes in socio-technical systems are accompanied by developments in occupational strategies. In highly automated systems, the worker can do little to affect production, and the link between production and wages is loosened. The level of wages comes to be determined more by comparison with other categories, and the emphasis shifts from a struggle on the shop floor to broader issues of wages and incomes policy. The various levels of labour strategy become more clearly differentiated, and collective bargaining shifts from preoccupation with resistance to change at plant level as the unions become increasingly involved in major social and economic decisions.[1]

On balance, it would appear that automation increases work satisfaction. This may well be accompanied by a decline in the demand for purely recuperative leisure activities in the increased leisure time available, although this will be unevenly spread, with scientists and other intellectual occupations continuing to work long hours. Such conditions are likely to be accompanied by associated changes in social and political attitudes.

One conclusion seems reasonably certain. Occupation is a key variable, functionally related to family life, leisure, social and political attitudes. Significant aspects of occupations are, in turn, related to changes in the economic system. The rate of change in the economic system is faster than at any previous time in history, and we can expect, therefore, that the rate of social change which it stimulates will also increase.

SUMMARY AND CONCLUSIONS

An individual's occupation in an industrial society is a crucial role among the many that he occupies. It provides a key to his income, social standing, social and political attitudes, interests, family life, and leisure. The occupations available depend in turn on developments in the economic system.

At one extreme (slavery), coercion may be used to ensure that individuals perform their roles in the economic system. Under industrialization, the political system at first exerts considerable coercion to extract a maximum effort out of the worker. But attempts

[1] A. Tourraine, *op. cit.*, pp. 110–11. Tourraine also emphasizes that different types of industrial society will evolve different labour strategies which can only be understood in the context of economic and political systems.

are also made to reinforce political and economic sanctions by normative pressures, stressing the moral obligation to work and save, the legitimacy of riches and the sanctity of private property, condemning idleness and pleasure seeking. Developments in the economic system are accompanied by a decline in the protestant 'work' ethic, while political sanctions are replaced by economic sanctions. Most industrial and clerical workers are instrumentally involved in the occupations, working simply to earn an income with which to buy non-work satisfactions.

But empirical studies of the work-situation do not support Marx's view that industrialization necessarily involves the alienation of the worker. Production takes place in a variety of socio-technical systems which differ considerably in the skills they require and the autonomy they permit. At the one extreme, the assembly-line worker experiences extreme alienation but craft-printers and process workers in fully automated plants do not. Moreover, professional occupations such as scientists are more likely to find work intrinsically satisfying. Technical changes, in fact, are tending to reduce alienating work-situations and to increase the skill and responsibility of work. But the typical situation is still apathy rather than involvement.

Occupations differ too, in the amount and security of their incomes and in the prestige in which they are held. Work, market and status situations are, in fact, interrelated in complex ways. The high pay of many manual workers, for example, is not enough to ensure an equal status with non-manual workers, earning no more or even less. It is probable that the subordinate position of the manual worker in the work situations spills over and contributes to his 'inferior' position in the social system outside the factory gates. High status, on the other hand, serves to legitimize authority and high pay.

Most occupations demand some kind of adjustment between the individual and his market, work, and status situations. To some extent, occupational selection and socialization ensures a measure of congruence between the characteristics of the individual and the demands of his occupation but some measure of role-strain exists in most occupations, whether it is the commercial artist experiencing the conflicting pulls of art and the market or the industrial scientist torn between the pursuit of knowledge and the need to contribute to marketable commodities, or the teacher treading delicately between an affective relationship and maintaining discipline.

Occupations adopt a variety of strategies to improve their market, work, and status positions. A characteristic feature of one group of occupations which includes those recognized as professions is that their practice depends on the acquisition of a specialized body of knowledge. This enables them to exercise varying degrees of control over their market situation by setting up associations to examine and qualify members, and to maintain and enhance professional status. Ethical codes appear to function to legitimize the claims of professions to high rewards in terms of income and prestige. Similarly, among black-coated workers, the strategies they adopt will depend on their situation. Those who work in the small industrial offices in which promotion depends on winning approval from a superior with whom one is in a personal relationship are unlikely to support trade unions, but in the large impersonal bureaucratically organized offices of central and local government, there is substantial support for trade unions. Similarly, craft unions use apprenticeship to regulate their work and market situations.

A characteristic feature of many industrial and non-industrial workers is that work for them is mainly a source of income rather than of satisfaction from the performance of tasks. They are not work-centred, and are likely to seek satisfaction in non-work areas. Under certain conditions, such men may become home-centred, or turn to leisure for meaningful and satisfying activities. Leisure can be shown to be functionally related to work in a variety of ways— as a compensation for monotony, as an extension of work for those who gain intrinsic satisfactions from their occupation, or boredom may simply spill over into apathetic and passive leisure. One trend is reasonably certain automation is likely both to increase leisure for some and to decrease apathy and alienation. There will probably be fewer whose work is so damaging that it stultifies leisure. But against this, there is the danger that those for whose limited skills society has little use, may face chronic under-employment, and yet possess few intellectual or personal resources to make use of the leisure with which technology has endowed them. Moreover, the need to both motivate the skilled to high levels of effort, while legitimizing the lack of work and enforced leisure for the unskilled will tax society with a crisis of values. The very significant role which occupation plays in the life of the individual suggests that the effect of economic developments on socio-technical systems may well be a crucial area for the study of social change.

QUESTIONS AND EXERCISES

1. How would you distinguish between work and non-work?
2. 'Even in a laissez-faire economy, the state intervenes in decisive ways in the economic system.' Discuss.

3. 'The divorce between ownership and control.' Explain and discuss.
4. Examine the ways in which political action has influenced industrial relations.
5. Examine critically the 'managerial revolution' thesis.
6. In what ways have economic ideologies evolved with changes in the organization of production?
7. In what ways have recent studies of socio-technical systems modified Marx's theory that industrialization would lead to the increasing alienation of the worker?
8. 'Economic analysis, by separating the market from the social system, cannot adequately explain the market situation of an occupation.' Discuss.
9. 'Work behaviour can only be understood if we take account of the mechanisms of occupational socialization and selection.' Discuss.
10. What is meant by role-strain? Illustrate by reference to studies of any one occupation.
11. Discuss the factors which influence occupational strategies.
12. How would you account for the differing degrees of support for trade unions among clerical workers?
13. 'The term "profession" has little descriptive value.' Explain and discuss the characteristic features of 'professions'.
14. How does apprenticeship function as an occupational strategy?
15. Examine some of the ways in which an individual's occupation influences his non-work behaviour.
16. What do you think will be some of the major social consequences of automation?
17. 'Stultifying work stultifies leisure.' Does it?

READING

R. Bendix.—*Work and Authority in Industry* (Harper, 1956). A study of changing managerial ideologies in the USA, Britain and the USSR.
A. A. Berle and G. C. Means.—*The Modern Corporation and Private Property* (Macmillan, 1937).
R. Blauner.—*Alienation and Freedom: the Manual Worker in Industry* (University of Chicago, 1964).
*L. Broom and P. Selznick.—*Sociology* (New York, 1955), Chapter 16. Includes discussions on religion and capitalism, alienation and socio-technical systems, and the labour force.
A. M. Carr-Saunders, D. C. Jones and C. Moser.—*Social Conditions in England and Wales* (Oxford, 1958). Chapters 7 and 8 give a summary of statistics on the changing composition of the labour force.
N. Dennis, F. Henriques and C. Slaughter.—*Coal is Our Life* (London, 1956). A study of work, family and trade union activities in the life of a mining community.

*R. Dubin.—'Industrial Workers Worlds. A Study of the "Central Life Interests" of Industrial Workers' (in E. O. Smigel, *op. cit.*, and A. M. Rose, *Human Behaviour and Social Processes*) (Routledge, 1962).

P. S. Florence.—*Ownership, Control and Success of Large Companies* (Sweet, 1961).

D. V. Glass (ed.).—*Social Mobility in Britain* (Routledge & Kegan Paul, 1954), Chapter 2, 'The Social Grading of Occupations'.

W. Kornhauser and W. D. Hagstrom.—*Scientists in Industry* (University of California, 1962). Role strain, conflict and accommodation among industrial scientists.

D. Lockwood.—*The Blackcoated Worker* (Allen & Unwin, 1958). Analyses the changing market, status and work situation of clerks, and relates these to class-consciousness and trade union activities.

*I. C. McGivering, *et al.*—*Management in Britain* (Liverpool University Press, 1960).

S. Nosow and W. H. Form (eds.).—*Man, Work and Society: A Reader in the Sociology of Occupations* (New York, 1962). A source book containing a large number of contributions by specialists on all aspects of the sociology of occupations. Contains many of the key articles by writers like Merton, Wilensky, etc.

K. Prandy.—*Professional Employees: A Study of Scientists and Engineers* (Faber, 1965). Illustrates the relation between occupational strategies and position in the work situation among scientists and engineers.

*N. J. Smelser.—*The Sociology of Economic Life* (Prentice-Hall, 1963), Chapters 3, 4, 5. Analyses the economy as a sub-system of society.

*E. O. Smigel.—*Work and Leisure* (College and University Press Services, 1963). Adopts a functionalist approach to the study of the relations between occupations and leisure. ('Social Problems, 1961' includes four of the articles reproduced in Smigel.)

A. Tourraine, *et al.*—*Workers' attitudes to technical change* (OECD, Paris, 1965). An analysis of available studies on the worker in industry with special reference to the impact of technical change.

J. Tunstall.—*The Fishermen* (MacGibbon, 1962). A largely descriptive study of the distant-water fishermen of Hull.

A. T. Welford (ed.).—*Society* (Routledge, 1962), Chapter 11, T. Burns, is an excellent summary of the scope and literature of industrial sociology.

W. H. Whyte.—*The Organization Man* (Cape, 1957). An impressionistic study of the life of the company executive in the large corporations of America.

*F. Zweig.—*The British Worker* (Penguin, 1952). An impressionistic but insightful study.

F. Zweig.—*The Worker in an Affluent Society* (Heinemann, 1961). A largely descriptive study of highly paid workers in four industries.

Chapter 5

THE POLITICAL SYSTEM[1]

========

We come now to the last of the main structural elements in the social system. The study of the political system presents very considerable difficulties. It is a subject which has long been the preserve of political philosophers who have been preoccupied with attempts to define the nature of the state and its relations with society and to answer problems concerning the legitimacy of government and the obligation to obey its commands. The Marxist focus on the notion of a ruling class has led to attempts to identify the personnel of the governing class and to explain their functions as expressions of economic interests. More recently, there have been studies of political parties and pressure groups, voting behaviour and the electoral system. Political science has emerged from this as a more systematic and empirical approach. And more recently still, there has been a growing convergence between the perspectives of political scientists and sociologists with attempts to explore the functional relations between the political system and the social system. The very complexity of this relationship defies any simple analysis and faces us with a variety of differing models. Some theories, such as that of C. Wright Mills, argue that a power élite comprising the top military, politicians, and corporation men dominate the political scene, while the pluralist model argues that no one interest dominates, but rather than the government acts as honest broker, seeking to coordinate a variety of interest and that no single group can be identified as the determiners of political decisions. What follows must therefore of necessity be even more tentative than the models used as frameworks for relating empirical data in previous chapters.

[1] I am much indebted to Anthony Taylor and Penri Griffiths for valuable discussion and suggestions for this Chapter. Any weaknesses are, of course, my own.

THE POLITICAL SYSTEM AND THE SOCIAL SYSTEM

A major difficulty confronts us at the outset. What precisely are the boundaries of the political system? It's by no means easy to arrive at any agreement on what exactly politics is about. We found no great difficulties in delineating the economic system or the kinship system sufficiently clearly to examine a rough working model. But the sphere of politics is more ambiguous. If we argue, for example, that politics refers to the exercise of power, then political behaviour penetrates all segments of society. Power and influence are exercised within the family, in schools, offices, factories and universities.[1] Such an approach blurs the boundaries between the political and social system and is not very helpful in delineating the political system as a cluster of distinct structures performing political functions. A somewhat similar approach is adopted by David Easton[2] who defines the political system as the authoritative allocation of values. The fact that policies or commands are authoritative, that is, defined as legitimate and promulgated by a legally constituted authority characterizes the policies of churches, universities, and other agencies and does not by itself clearly demarcate the political system. Moreover, there are some political systems which enjoy little legitimacy, and rely substantially on naked coercion. The degrees and type of legitimacy is, in fact, one of the variables which differentiates between political systems.[3] The threat of physical compulsion is clearly an essential element in politics. But it is not enough to identify the political system with the state; that is, with the apparatus which maintains order by the use or threat or use of more or less legitimate force. This would exclude the role of parties, and pressure groups, and would exclude the study of political systems in underdeveloped societies which have not yet evolved a distinct apparatus of state government. Almond[4] attempts to integrate these two elements of legitimacy and coercion in his definition: '. . . the political system is that system of interactions to be found in all independent societies which performs the functions of integration and adaptation (both

[1] P. Worsley suggests that we differentiate between governmental and non-governmental power as politics I and politics II. Sociological Review Monograph No. 8.

[2] *The Political System: An Inquiry into the State of Political Science* (1953).

[3] This will be discussed more fully in the section on the political system and culture.

[4] Gabriel A. Almond and James S. Coleman, *The Politics of Developing Areas* (1960). This Chapter draws heavily on the introduction by G. A. Almond for its theoretical framework.

internally and vis-à-vis other societies) by means of the employment, or threat of employment, of more or less legitimate physical compulsion.'[1]

The distinguishing feature of the political system which emerges from both Easton's and Almond's approaches is that politics is the most generalized system for the allocation of values and the maintenance of order in the social system. We can then identify two main elements in the political system. Firstly, there is the apparatus for decision making and the execution and enforcement of policies. In Britain, this includes Parliament as the rule-making machinery; the civil service and local government, backed by the police and the army apply the decisions and execute the policies of the government; while the judiciary and the courts adjudicate and contribute to rule enforcement as part of the machinery for applying the coercive sanctions of fines and imprisonment. The distribution of functions is not, of course, as clear cut as this. The judiciary, for example, make law as well as adjudicating it, while the civil service have limited rule-making functions.

But in arriving at decisions and policies, governments do not operate in a vacuum. They have to take account of various interests and pressures, and a variety of structures exist in modern industrial societies which feed demands into the political system and provide it with support.[2] Among the most important of the structures which serve to articulate demands and exert pressures are pressure groups, which are organized interest groups seeking to influence political decisions by devices such as lobbying and propaganda. They are not governmental structures, but arise as associations within other sub-systems of society. Within the economic system, for example, there are a variety of associations of manufacturers and employers which include pressure-group functions among their activities. They man the boundary between the political system and the economic system, performing the very important role of providing machinery for the articulation of the economic system with the political system. Similarly, the churches may seek to influence political decisions and in so doing, function as pressure groups. Some associations exist only as pressure groups, such as The Abortion Law Reform Society or the Lord's Day Observance Society. These are parts of the educational system in so far as they exist to change public opinion. Whenever the activities of an organization or association seek to bring

[1] *Op. cit.*, p. 7.
[2] David Easton, 'An Approach to the Analysis of Political Systems', in S. M. Lipset and N. J. Smelser, *Sociology: the Progress of a Decade* (1961), pp. 421–32.

pressures to bear on the political process, they function as pressure groups and their activities become a part of the political system.[1]

Unlike pressure groups political parties are an integral part of the political system. Their emergence in the nineteenth century in the form in which we now know them was a direct result of the extension of the franchise.[2] It was this which made necessary the establishment of machinery to organize popular support. They function as vote-getting agencies. As such, political party organizations are located within the political system. But they are not a part of the machinery of government, and like pressure groups, are located at the boundary of the political system serving primarily to link the parliamentary parties (which *are* part of the machinery of government), with the electorate.

There are several different types of parties in modern democracies. To understand such differences, it is necessary to look briefly at the varying circumstances underlying their origins.[3] Parties are relatively recent arrivals on the political scene. In 1850 there were no parties as we know them today. The pattern of their genesis is fairly general. Firstly, there is the emergence of parliamentary groups, followed by the appearance of electoral committees. Finally a permanent connexion is established between these two elements. Parliamentary groups have generally antedated universal suffrage. In eighteenth-century Britain, for example, English ministers ensured substantial majorities by buying the votes of MPs. Members received the price of their vote at the desk of the 'Patronage Secretary', who kept an eye on their votes and speeches, functioning also as the 'whip' to maintain discipline. In this way, the organization of the group and authority of the 'whip' emerged before the extension of the franchise, and constituted a rudimentary parliamentary group.

The extension of the franchise of 1832 lead to the rapid growth of registration societies to facilitate and encourage the procedure of registration. As the societies grew, they concerned themselves with the nomination of candidates. It was a short step to establishing regular connexions between parliamentary groups and electoral committees.

Extra-parliamentary factors have also operated in the genesis of parties. The British Labour Party is a clear example, resulting from a

[1] Gabriel A. Almond, *et al.*, *op. cit.* (1960), p. 8. For an account of the variety and functioning of pressure groups in Britain, see J. D. Stewart, *British Pressure Groups* (1958).

[2] R. T. McKenzie, *British Political Parties* (1964), p. 6.

[3] See M. Duverger, *Political Parties* (1959), 'Introduction'.

decision of the Trade Union Congress in 1899 to establish an electoral and parliamentary organization by a federation of trade unions and socialist societies to secure the election of working-class representatives to parliament. Parties which originate in this way outside parliament are more centralized, coherent and disciplined, than those arising within parliament. Moreover, the influence of the parliamentary group tends to be greater in parties with parliamentary or electoral origin.[1] It was natural that Labour MPs and the Parliamentary Labour Party were considered to be servants of the movement.[2] The Labour Party has traditionally claimed that the Party Conference is the parliament for the party and 'lays down the policy of the party and issues instructions which must be carried out by . . . (Labour) representatives in Parliament and on local authorities.'[3] If this were so, then the party caucus would rule, and would usurp the functions of Parliament. Robert McKenzie argues, however, that in the major political parties, effective decision-making authority 'resides with the leadership groups thrown up by the parliamentary parties (of whom much the most important individual is the party leader).'[4] In neither case, has the mass organization achieved the dominance over the parliamentary parties which Ostrogorski feared was the trend at the end of the nineteenth century. 'While the Leader of any party is Prime Minister, and his principal colleagues constitute a cabinet, there can be no debate as to where, in principle, final authority in the party lies.'[5]

Duverger differentiates several types of party-structures. The first is exemplified by the French Socialist party, in which individuals sign a membership form and pay a monthly subscription. This entails the setting up of an extensive organization, with a growing number of permanent officials, a complex structure of committees and powerful oligarchic tendencies. A second type survives in the shape of the Conservative and Liberal parties, and in America. These are based on caucuses, narrowly recruited, and aim to recruit outstanding people. Leadership is in the hands of parliamentary representatives

[1] *Ibid.*, p. xxxiv ff.
[2] R. T. McKenzie, *British Political Parties* (1964), p. 13.
[3] Lord Attlee quoted by R. T. McKenzie, *op. cit.* (1964), p. 12.
[4] *Ibid.*, Chapter XI, p. 635.
[5] *Ibid.*, p. 638. Dr McKenzie also examines Michels 'iron law of oligarchy' which argues that the leadership of organizations becomes stable and irremoveable. Similar tendencies could be argued to exist in trade unions. Such issues, however, are more appropriately examined in the context of the study of organizations in Chapter 8. For a detailed discussion of the relations between the leadership and the parliamentary party, see Duverger, Book 1, Chapter 111.

and real power belongs to a particular group revolving round a parliamentary leader. 'The party is concerned only with political questions; doctrine and ideological problems play a very small part. . . .'[1]

By contrast with such 'direct' parties, the British Labour Party is made up of a federation of trade unions, co-operative and friendly societies. Membership is mainly 'indirect' through affiliated organizations, although the proportion of 'direct' individual members increased after the Trade Union Act of 1927 required members to 'contract in' and to declare in writing their willingness to pay the political levy. Since the repeal in 1946 of the 1927 Act, union members are now required to declare that they do not wish to pay the political levy, resulting in a shift towards the indirect pattern.

An important characteristic of political systems is the number of parties. Two-party and multi-party systems provide different mechanisms for expressing and articulating cleavages. In a two-party system, cleavages polarize around one major dimension, and the struggle between factions takes place within each of the major parties. 'If, however, the factions become exasperated and can no longer meet on common ground the basic tendency towards dualism is thwarted and gives way to multi-partism.'[2] In France, the multi-partite division reflects various combinations of a number of dualisms.[3] The Christian Progressives, for example, are pro-clerical and pro-planning but the Socialists are anti-clerical and pro-planning.[4] Duverger shows that the main determinant of the number of parties is the electoral system. 'The simple-majority single-ballot system favours the two-party system.'[5] 'The simple-majority system with second ballot and proportional representation favours multi-partism.'[6]

The political system and culture

Whatever differences there may be between political parties in England, and however bitter the conflict between them may at times

---

[1] *Op. cit.* (1959), p.1.

[2] *Ibid.*, p. 230.

[3] *Ibid.*, pp. 231–4.

[4] The number of parties also has important consequences for the governmental process, influencing the distribution of power between parliament and executive. This is discussed later in the Chapter.

[5] *Op. cit.* (1959), p. 217.

[6] *Ibid.*, p. 239.

be, such conflict is acted out within the framework of agreed rules and procedures. Moreover, it is conflict over a limited range of disagreements, and takes place against a background of substantial consensus over a range of values and beliefs. A high degree of consensus clearly limits the areas of conflict. Moreover, consensus on the norms regulating political activity institutionalizes the modes of conflict. Among the recognized channels of parliamentary procedure are questions, debates, and divisions. Furthermore, the electoral system structures the struggle for power to take the form of periodic contending for votes at general elections.

There is a whole range of political beliefs and values over which there is substantial social consensus; on the value of liberty, the monarchy, of evolutionary rather than revolutionary change, and of English parliamentary and governmental institutions.[1] Differences are more likely to occur over means than about ends. Such consensus is, of course, partly due to political socialization. Respect for the monarchy, for example, is inculcated in the schools, especially through the teaching of history.[2] Moreover, while a few are socialized for leadership roles through attendance at public schools, the majority 'attending secondary modern schools appear to accept the politically passive roles implicitly stressed by the orientation of the schools.'[3]

Most important for any political system is an acceptance of its legitimacy on the part of the governed. It's not wasy to define legitimacy. It is not the same thing as the effectiveness of a government. This is an index of the extent to which its policies have been judged to be successful and is related to the expectations of the electorate. Judgments of legitimacy are affective and evaluative, rather than instrumental.[4] Legitimacy reflects the way in which a society defines the legality of a government and its right or authority to rule. Legitimacy transforms power into authority. This transformation of power into authority is clearly a most important condition for the accep-

---

[1] R. Rose, *Politics in England* (1965), Chapter 2. Forty-six per cent in Britain, 85 per cent in America, but only 3 per cent in Italy, are proud of governmental and political institutions. Quoted on p. 52 from G. Almond and S. Verba, *The Civic Culture* (1963).

[2] R. Rose quotes a Liverpool baker who said that his school 'always had the National Anthem on every occasion and scriptures and prayers. Told to love your own country. Always told our country was the best and still believe it' (*ibid.*, p. 64).

[3] *Ibid.*, p. 67.

[4] S. M. Lipset, in R. K. Merton, L. Broom and L. S. Cottrell, *op. cit.* (1965), pp. 108–9.

tance of rules and orders. Men may accept authority because it rests upon tradition. In stable societies, authority is legitimized by long usage. In times of crisis and change, traditional authority comes to be questioned. Under such circumstances, *charismatic leaders*[1] may emerge, who are obeyed because they are believed to possess special personal qualities.

In large scale contemporary societies, the bases of legitimacy are complex. Power is perceived as legitimate if it is exercised according to rules which have been promulgated by a recognized and accepted procedure. A major function of political philosophies is to provide formulae whereby power may be perceived as legitimate. Rapid changes in society, such as those which accompany industrialization, throw up new groups—both entrepreneurs and factory workers —who seek to influence the decision-making machinery. If a government is to retain legitimacy, and avoid revolution, ways must be found to allow such groups access to power by legitimate means. By extending the franchise to such new groups, states have managed to achieve a substantial degree of political integration among sections with diverse interests. The machinery of election, in fact, plays an important part in ensuring the legitimacy of government. It provides interest groups with a legitimate means for achieving their wants.[2] It is also possible that the monarchy plays an important part in providing stability and lending legitimacy to British governments.[3] The monarch may function as an emotional leader and thus ensure the continued legitimacy of governments even if the political leaders fail instrumentally. Indeed, legitimacy may be a more important determinant of stable government than effectiveness.[4]

But although British governments enjoy a high degree of legitimacy, this has been challenged by some minority groups on issues about which they feel strongly. The Committee of 100, for example, sought to challenge the government's policy on nuclear defence by calculated violations of the law.[5]

---

[1] This term was used by Max Weber. 'The natural leaders in distress have been holders of specific gifts of the body and spirit; and these gifts have been believed to be supernatural. . . .' H. H. Gerth and C. W. Mills, *op. cit.*, p. 245.

[2] See S. M. Lipset, *op. cit.*, Chapter III, 'Social Conflict, Legitimacy and Democracy'.

[3] For a discussion of the monarchy, see E. Shils and M. Young, 'The Meaning of the Coronation', *Soc. Rev.*, Vol. 1, 1953, and the reply by N. Birnbaum, 'Monarch and Sociologists', *ibid.*, Vol. 3, 1955.

[4] S. M. Lipset, *op. cit.* (1965), p. 109.

[5] R. Rose, *op. cit.*, p. 218.

F

POLITICAL PROCESSES

Political philosophers have long discussed both what are and what ought to be 'the functions of the state'. All but the philosophical anarchists would agree on the need for some organ to ensure the integration of the social system through the maintenance of law and order, relying on the ultimate sanction of force. Whatever differences there may be in views about how far the state ought to go beyond this, the fact remains that the modern state in advanced industrial societies has extended its functions far beyond that of integration. More recently, political scientists have returned to the question of the functions of the state, but from an empirical rather than a moral perspective. And it is this functionalist perspective which is resulting in a closer convergence of political science and sociology.

There is a variety of functional models, which view the political system as receiving inputs from the social system and processing these inputs in order to arrive at outputs in the shape of decisions and policies. The results of these in turn, generate feed-back which provide fresh inputs to the system. Easton[1] differentiates between two main types of inputs; demands and supports. Gabriel Almond[2] has suggested that all political systems perform four input and three output functions. The three output functions rule-making, rule-application and rule adjudication have already been mentioned. The political system must also process four main inputs from the social system. Firstly, interest groups must make known their needs and feed them into the political system. This is *interest articulation* and is a function performed by pressure groups. Secondly, political systems must aggregate the various interests and needs of the social system and process these to produce coherent policies which will gain a wide measure of support. *Interest aggregation* is a major function of political parties which act as intermediates between voters and policy makers. They function to process a wide variety of interest inputs into a relatively small number of policies. Thirdly, *political communication* is crucial to the processes of interest articulation, aggregation, and governing. Finally, *political socialization and recruitment* contribute to the perpetuation of prevailing political ideologies, and allocate individuals to their roles in the political system. Of particular interest here is the recruitment of political elites. It is to these functions of the political system that we now turn.

[1] S. M. Lipset and N. Smelser, *op. cit.*
[2] *Op. cit.* (1960), p. 26–52.

Interest articulation and pressure groups

The existence of demands within the social system is not by itself sufficient to ensure that they will be taken into account in the decision-making process. They must first become political issues. Demands may be generated by the experiences of individuals within any of the major sub-systems. Unwanted pregnancies may lead to a demand for changes in the law regulating contraception or abortion, or unhappy marriages to demands for changes in the marriage laws. Unemployment, job insecurity, or poverty may generate demands for changes in the economic system, in the laws regulating relations between employers and employees, or in changes in the distribution of incomes. Some demands may originate from within the political system itself,[1] such as the demand for the extension of the franchise to women, or young voters. In order to become a political issue, such demands must become public and fed into the political system. Pressure groups are one of the major mechanisms for this process.

The term 'pressure group' is however, not entirely satisfactory. The process of consultation between the government and the interests which its actions affect is very extensive and complex. As the functions of government have extended to include the regulation and promotion of a wide range of economic and cultural activities, the need for consultation has extended. This takes place through a wide variety of advisory councils specifically established by the government to offer advice on economic, social and cultural issues, such as the National Joint Advisory Council which includes representatives of the Federation of British Industries, and the TUC. In addition to such well established machinery, other less formal channels of consultation exist whereby ministers and government officials consult the relevant interests involved in seeking information and views relevant to policy or legislation. Moreover, numerous organized interests from the AA to the Lord's Day Observance Society will seek to influence the process of decision-making through the various channels available. It would be preferable therefore, to refer to 'group pressures' rather than to 'pressure groups', but the latter term is too firmly entrenched to be replaced.[2]

Interest groups may be divided into two main types. *Protective* groups defend some interest in society, such as trade unions and pro-

---

[1] Easton suggests the term *withinputs* for such demands. Lipset and Smelser, *op. cit.* (1961), p. 425.

[2] J. D. Stewart, *British Pressure Groups* (1958), pp. 8–10, outlines the complex network of consultation. This book also includes a detailed account of the various strategies for bringing pressure to bear to influence decisions.

fessional associations which protect the interests of their members. *Promotional* groups seek to promote a cause, such as the Campaign for Nuclear Disarmament. Protective groups represent the interests of specific groups in society. By contrast, promotional groups may draw their membership from as wide a cross section of the population as possible, and their representative character is difficult to establish. Moreover, not all interests are 'represented' by organized groups, and others are so large that they do not need organizations to present their case for them.[1]

It is not easy to assess the influence of such group pressures on governmental decisions. It is no longer argued as was once the case, that pressure-groups are by-passing parliamentary functions and threaten democratic processes.[2] No government department would now promote legislation or change policy without appropriate consultation with the interests affected. And this can best be done through those organizations which articulate and represent such interests. The party system will normally ensure that major interests are represented in the parliament, and we can expect the parties to reflect important political issues. On major issues, therefore, group pressures will be faced with party policies. The power of the party rests on much wider basis than that of the pressure group and in arriving at a decision the minister through his party has authority to resist the group.[3] Governments have both the power and the resources to resist group pressures to consider its interests alone. However, over large areas there are no party viewpoints, and on such issues pressure groups may be more influential. A Minister of Agriculture will hear representations from the National Farmers' Union. In the absence of alternative views, there might be a tendency to act as though what was good for the farmers was good for agriculture.[4] But in spite of such dangers, interest groups perform essential functions in articulating interests and providing links between the political and social system. Stewart considers that, in fact, the British system achieves a satsfactory balance between taking account of sectional interests and taking decisions in the wider interests of society.[5]

[1] See J. Blondel, *op. cit.*, pp. 160–7, for a discussion of the representative character of interest groups.

[2] On the role of pressure groups in the political process, see R. T. McKenzie, 'Parties, Pressure Groups and the British Political Process', in R. Rose (ed.), *Studies in British Politics* (1966), pp. 255–66.

[3] J. D. Stewart, *op. cit.*, pp. 240–1.　　　[4] *Ibid.*, p. 242.

[5] *Ibid.*, p. 240. For studies of particular interest groups, see P. Self and H. Storing, *The State and the Farmer* (1962); H. Ekstein, *Pressure Group Politics* (1960); R. Rose (ed.), *op. cit.* (1966), pp. 220–54.

Interest aggregation—political parties and voting
Pressure groups differ from political parties in that, unlike parties, pressure groups do not exist in order to achieve political power. But parties, like pressure groups function to ensure that interests are taken into account in the political process. Moreover, they represent a wide range of interests rather than any narrow sectional interest. No mass party could gain support unless they could convince a substantial section of the electorate that it would govern in their interests. In order to do this, it must aggregate as wide a range of interests as possible into broad policy issues. Parties function to aggregate such interests into alternative government policies.

Such cleavages are not necessarily a threat to the cohesion of society. Indeed, Lipset argues that some measure of cleavage is necessary for a stable democratic system in order to ensure 'that there will be a struggle over ruling positions, challenges to parties in power, and shifts of parties in office'.[1] The study of democracy, therefore, argues Lipset, requires us to focus on the sources of both cleavage and consensus. Without cleavages, there would be no struggle for power. But where cleavages run too deeply and divide too sharply, the possibilities of shifts of party preference and alternative governments would be remote. The party system and the electoral process provides the machinery for both the expression of interests and for their aggregation into alternative policies.

Studies of the relation between class membership and support for political parties in Britain provide evidence for the view that the major political parties do not reflect a hard and clear-cut cleavage of interests on class lines, although class factor obviously play an important part in attracting party support. The Conservative Party, for example, attracts a sizeable proportion of the working-class vote. No Conservative government would, in fact, ever be returned to power without such support, as the working-class vote represents about 70 per cent of the electorate. The Labour vote is more homogeneous, but even this includes about 8 per cent of top business executives. The middle ranges of the social hierarchy, in particular, divide between the two parties. About a quarter of the lower middle-class voting Labour and about one-third of the upper working-class voting Conservative.[2]

On a wide range of issues, there is no marked party cleavage. On

[1] S. M. Lipset, 'Political Sociology', in R. K. Merton, *et al.*, *Sociology Today* (1965). See also S. M. Lipset, *Political Man* (1960).

[2] J. Blondel, *op. cit.*, p. 57. See also John Bonham and F. M. Martin, 'Two Studies in the Middle Class Vote', *B.J.S.*, Vol. III : Sept. 3, 1952.

humanitarian issues such as corporal punishment, and on foreign affairs such as nuclear disarmament and support for the United Nations, differences between Conservative and Labour voters are small. It is only on economic and social issues that cleavages emerge. There are marked differences between supporters on attitudes towards raising the level of surtax and sympathy with workers on strike. But even here, there are many in the Conservative party who adopt 'left' attitudes and in the Labour party who adopt 'right' views. Even on the surtax changes in 1961, 32 per cent of Conservatives were opposed (compared with 67 per cent Labour).[1] What is remarkable is not the difference but the consensus between substantial numbers of both parties. It is this which makes possible the shift of allegiance between parties and which forces parties to compromise and to make concessions in order either to win or to retain a majority.

Such evidence suggests that support for a party is not necessarily support for all the items in its policies. Voting studies indicate that voters are attracted by the general image of the party. This image includes class elements. Part of the image of the Labour Party among its supporters is that it is 'for the working class'. But many Labour supporters disagree with items of its policy, especially on nationalization. However, issues are related to images. For many Conservatives, for example, nationalization figures in their image of the Labour Party.[2] Nevertheless, the fact that voters support a party for its image rather than for any specific item of policy[3] facilitates the task of the party in aggregating a variety of issues into a coherent policy, and ensures continued support in the face of disagreements on specific issues.

Individuals are members of a variety of groups and occupy a variety of statuses. Most are consequently subject to at least some cross-pressures. But where pressures are aggregative, pushing all in the same direction, they are likely to lead to sharp cleavages incapable of compromise. For many, such is not the case, and they do not find themselves unequivocally attached to one party unable to

---

[1] J. Blondel, *op. cit.*, pp. 75–9. See also Mark Abrams, 'Social Trends and Electoral Behaviour', *B.J.S.*, Vol. XIII : Sept. 3, 1962. Surveys in 1949 showed much more marked cleavage.

[2] See J. Blondel, *op. cit.*, pp. 81–4, and R. S. Milne and H. C. MacKenzie, *Marginal Seat* (1958).

[3] A partial explanation of this is the very substantial influence of socialization in determining voting behaviour. Seventy-one per cent of those intending to vote Conservative in 1960 were the sons of Conservative voters (M. Abrams, *op. cit.*, 1962, p. 238).

see any merit in the other. Where one issue, such as race or religion becomes of over-riding importance, then cleavage outweighs consensus and the social conditions favourable to democracy are absent.

Political communication

Political communication is a two-way process. As we have seen, governments receive a variety of influences from organized interest groups. But since the extension of adult suffrage, governments are also concerned with the views of the less organized and articulate public, on whose electoral support they ultimately depend.

The development of various forms of mass communication have given rise to anxiety about their role in the process of political communication and socialization. As we have seen in Chapter 3 on education, the Press is undoubtedly partisan.[1] But the general conclusion of investigations of mass communication in the political sphere confirms the conclusions of our earlier discussion, that the effects of the mass media are less than is frequently supposed. The one intensive study of the influence of television in an election campaign found that its effects were slight.[2] Audience research by the BBC similarly confirms that the impact of political broadcasts is greatly influenced by the predispositions of the viewers, whose evaluation of party broadcasts is closely related to party affiliations. Party identifications are formed by a lengthy process of political socialization rather than by the short-term processes of electoral communications.[3]

Rather less attention has been paid to the question of how far public opinion can influence politics. Modern polling techniques certainly enable governments to keep a finger on the pulse of public opinion. But the concept of 'public opinion' is vague. There is, in fact, a variety of publics and opinions, some informed and some not, and some whose views need to be weighed by governments and others which can be safely ignored. Nevertheless, there is a sense in which there can be said to be a 'climate of opinion', which is some indication of what the public will stand for, rather than a pressure for some particular measure to which governments must respond.[4]

[1] See also R. Rose (ed.), *Studies in British Politics* (1966), pp. 161–90, for a discussion of the Press and politics.

[2] J. Trenaman and D. McQuail, *Television and the Political Image* (1961).

[3] R. Rose (ed.), *op. cit.* (1966), 'The 1964 General Election on Television', pp. 191–8.

[4] R. Rose (ed.), *op. cit.* (1966), p. 154. See also R. Rose, *Politics in England* (1958), Chapter 8.

Political recruitment, elites, ruling class

The social origins of political leaders has been a major preoccupation of sociologists.[1] Much of this interest stems from Marx's notion of the existence of a ruling class, and assumes a conflict theory of power. The 'ruling class' perspective assumes that the social origins of political leaders is a primary factor determining their decisions which flow mainly from their self-interests. It follows that fundamental changes in power can only be made by changing the incumbents of power positions.[2] Such a view is challenged by those who emphasize that the important issue is *access* to power rather than the composition of the political elite.

The notion of a *ruling-class* implies that an economic class rules politically. For Marx,[3] it was the newly emerging class of capitalists, owning and controlling the productive property of society, who not only controlled the machinery of government, but also shaped the ideas of the times. In other words, one class, the bourgeoisie, dominated the total society, including the state, which it used for its own ends.

This is a view which raises the whole question of the relations between property and power, and indeed, the sources of power itself. The state monopolizes the coercive means of power by its control of the police and the army. Power may also be exercised by the manipulation of material rewards; by conferring or withholding rights to enjoy incomes, and property of various kinds. The manipulation of material rewards is, in fact, an extremely powerful means of influencing and controlling the conduct of others. To withhold shelter and above all, adequate food is comparable to physical coercion in achieving compliance.

Those who exercised political power in the nineteenth century were certainly men of property. The political elite was drawn almost entirely from the property-owning class of landowners.[4] But the view that their power derived from property can be challenged. On

---

[1] For a summary of the literature, see T. B. Bottomore, *Elites and Society* (1964).

[2] S. M. Lipset, *op. cit.* (1965), pp. 106–7.

[3] It is by no means clear either from the writing of Marx or from those who have followed him, precisely who are the members of the ruling class. It has been used to include all those having decision-making powers in society, families and individuals whose control of the means of production allows them to dominate society, those linked by property, kinship and inheritance who also govern, or simply the group of capitalist producers. See S. Keller, *Beyond the Ruling Class* (1963), pp. 47–54.

[4] W. Guttsmann, *The British Political Elite* (1963).

the contrary, it can be argued, property depends on power. As we have seen in Chapter 4, property can be defined as a bundle of legally enforceable rights over persons and things.[1] These may include the rights of sale, bequest and exclusive use, or only relatively limited rights may be enjoyed, such as the right to use a post-office telephone or to the labour of an individual between fixed hours. Now only those rights which are ultimately enforceable in the courts can be exercised against opposition. And the decisions of the courts are, in the last analysis, enforceable by the coercive means of the state. Property is, in fact, a bundle of powers. It is force which upholds such powers. Property can be seized by force, by conquest, or by politial revolution. According to this view, it is power, not property, which is the basic issue.[2]

Nevertheless, studies of the social origins of the political elite demonstrates the close connection in the nineteenth century between property and power. (Table 5.1.) Men of property used the machinery of government to strengthen the powers of property and to confer substantial rights and protection on the property owner. Moreover, the man of property was able to extend his power over things to power over people. The factory owner, for example, was able to exercise extensive power over those who depended on him for work as the sole source of income for the necessities of life. Furthermore, the law protected factory owners from countervailing measures by its restrictions on the rights of workers to organize and to strike. Thus the law served to enforce and under-pin the powers of property, and in this way, political power provided the basis for economic power.

But the gradual extension of the franchise has conferred political power on the property-less and increased the autonomy of the

TABLE 5.1*

CLASS STRUCTURE OF CABINETS 1935–55

	1886–1916		1935–55	
	Cons.	Lib.	Cons.	Lab.
Aristocracy	26	23	20	1
Middle class	21	28	40	14
Working class	—	2	2	19

* Compiled from W. L. Guttsmann, op. cit. (1963), p. 79.

[1] 'Things' include intangibles such as patents in inventions, copyright, etc.
[2] This view is supported by R. Dahrendorf, Class and Class Conflict in Industrial Society (1959).

political system. Studies of the social origins of the political elites in Britain shows that since the beginning of the nineteenth century, there has been a gradual increase in the numbers of first, middle-class, and then, working-class members of the cabinet. During the Labour administration of 1929, 67 per cent of the cabinet were of working-class origin. However, during periods of Conservative rule, it remains true that the majority of the cabinet are drawn from the few exclusive public schools and attended Oxford or Cambridge (Table 5.2). In the 1959 House of Commons, 103 Conservative members were directors, manufacturers, landowners and farmers, compared with twelve on the Labour side. The close association between property and Conservative governments in Britain can be interpreted to support the argument that it is power, not property, which is decisive. It is only through the political machinery that the propertied can protect their interests. The loss of political power faces them with the possibility of the restriction of property rights, and the redistribution of wealth and income.

The notion of *elites* has been used by many who criticize or reject Marx's theory of a ruling class. It implies the existence of individuals and groups who occupy dominant positions in a particular sphere

TABLE 5.2*

EDUCATION AND OCCUPATION OF THE POLITICAL ELITE: CABINET MINISTERS 1916–55

	Cons. %	Lab. %
Education		
Elementary	4	51
Grammar	18	18
Eton	32	5
Major Public Schools	33	15
Other	13	11
	100	100
Occupation		
Landowning, Rentier	35	8
Civil Service, professions	43	38
Commerce and Industry (entrepreneurs)	14	6
Manual Workers and TU Officials		46
Others	8	2
	100	100
	(N=100)	(N=65)

* Compiled from W. C. Guttsman, *op. cit.*, pp. 106–7.

by virtue of their qualities of excellence relevant to their functioning. In addition to political elites therefore, there are religious, scientific, intellectual, managerial elites. Indeed, the number of elites will depend on the social system. The growth of division of labour and occupational specialization, and of formal organization will result in the multiplication of elites. They are, that is to say, a function of the increasing structural differentiation of society.

It is such elites, it is argued, particularly those who perform key roles, who are evolving out of earlier core groups, such as aristocracies and ruling classes, as structural alternatives to ruling classes, 'representing a more specialized and advanced form of social leadership'.[1] Their task is to perform the various specialized functions in society, such as production, artistic creation and intellectual advancement. Increasingly, 'the political, economic, scientific, religious, educational, cultural and recreational sectors are organizationally, occupationally, and morally autonomous'. And it is the leaders in these spheres who constitute the increasingly differentiated *strategic elites* of advanced societies. The task of the political elite is rather to act as honest broker in a plural society in which there is mutual interaction between elites. Governments, that is to say, are weak rather than strong. The task of political leaders is to steer a hazardous path between conflicting factions.

Different societies, however, will face different problems. In some societies, the primary problem is integration and the achievement of consensus. Such tasks occupy governments in totalitarian societies and are reflected in the strategies they adopt. Advanced industrial societies however, it is argued, are primarily pre-occupied with goal attainment—specifically with maximizing production and with raising the standard of living as rapidly as possible. Such a task requires the co-ordination of the inputs from a number of specialist elite groups. The economic elite are primarily concerned with the application and allocation of means (adaptive function), but in this they depend heavily on the intellectual elite such as scientists and innovators. In addition to elites primarily concerned with instrumental functions such as adaptation and goal attainment, other elites perform primarily expressive and symbolic functions (latency) —ecclesiastical dignitaries exhorting drivers not to drink and drive or workers to work harder.

Furthermore, we can observe that such functions may be variously distributed among the elements in a social system. In the past, they have been performed by single individuals or groups of individuals,

[1] S. Keller, *op. cit.* (1963).

such as the priest-king who functions both as warrior and moral leader. In feudal societies, a land-owning stratum both organizes the economy, exercises political functions, and maintains internal order and defence. In advanced societies, such roles become differentiated and specialized, resulting in the emergence of specialized elites who each contribute to the maintenance of the social system.[1]

In a society which emphasizes the maximizing of consumption, elites concerned with the instrumental function of goal attainment and adaptation (i.e. the polity and the economy), occupy strategic positions. But no one elite can occupy a predominant position, uninfluenced by pressures from others. Industrialists are preoccupied with production, but politicians are concerned with allocating resources and products for the achievement of societal goals in response to pressures from consumers and workers.[2] It is politicians who make the ultimate decisions on goals, but they do so in response to electoral pressures, and must achieve the compliance of producers in their plans. In other words, we have a pluralist society in which a number of elites and interests exert influence on the decision makers.

What is not clear is precisely how these elites are related to the political system. Keller argues that the task of the strategic elites is to 'co-ordinate and harmonize the diversified activities, combat factionalism, and resolve group conflicts. And they try to protect the community from external danger.' It is difficult to see how the elites which, according to her argument, are increasingly autonomous, are able to perform this integrating function. While it is clear that each may exercise influence, and in this sense no one elite is all-powerful, it is still possible to argue that some elites are more powerful than others. However, their political function appears to be mainly that of pressure groups, articulating interests and influencing the political process. Strategic elites have not usurped the functions of government. This would be to confuse influence with government.

C. W. Mills[3] is more decisive in attributing a dominant position

---

[1] S. Keller, op. cit. (1963).

[2] The fact that such distribution may be left to market forces does not change the essential argument. This is itself a political decision. According to Parsons, the political system is primarily concerned with goal attainment. It is the political system which must make ultimate decisions on the allocation of resources. For this reason, Parsons includes in the polity banking and finance which exercise control over purchasing power. If such decisions are largely influenced by pressures from industrialists, this does not change the basic argument. The economy is primarily concerned with the adaptive function—with producing means in the form of goods and income. See Black, op. cit., pp. 124-6.

[3] C. W. Mills, The Power Elite (1956).

to three elites who together constitute what he calls the *power elite*. He argues that the power elite comprises a close association between the heads of business corporations, the top military and the political elite. The top men in all three areas, he argues, are drawn from the same predominantly upper stratum in society, share the same values and outlooks and pursue the same interests. Membership of these elites is freely interchanged, with generals becoming members of the political administration and politicians being appointed to top posts in the industrial corporations. There is, that is to say, consensus among the members of the power elite rather than a conspiracy to build structural links between property and politics. It is difficult to see how Mills's[1] use of the concept of a power elite differs greatly from the notion of a ruling class. He stresses the unity of the elite and its common origins from the upper classes. But it is not at all clear why power elite constitutes one elite and not three.[2] Mills makes an important distinction between levels of power. While politicians deal with intermediate issues, the power elite take the big decisions, while the masses are powerless.[3] Most, however, who have argued in favour of the idea of elites have rejected the view that the various elites constitute a cohesive group. A recent study[4] for example, concludes that the various elites in British society constitute a cluster of interlocking circles, each largely preoccupied with its own interests, and each group acting as a check on the others.

Governmental processes
The study of political recruitment has unavoidably involved us in some discussion of governmental processes as distinct from political processes. An examination of the social origins of the political elite has frequently assumed that such data enables us to draw conclusions about the exercise of power—about who takes decisions and enforces them. The pluralists have countered the ruling-class model by arguing that a variety of elites participate in the decision-making process. But by so doing, they have blurred the distinction between the political processes of the articulation of interests, the exercise of influence, and the governmental functions of taking and enforcing decisions. The model adopted in this chapter underlines the im-

[1] C. W. Mills, *The Power Elite* (1956).

[2] T. B. Bottomore, *op. cit.*

[3] Some empirical studies which have taken a pluralist position, such as R. Dahl, *Who Governs* (1963), have investigated specific local communities, and are not, therefore, concerned with the level of power discussed by Mills.

[4] A. Sampson, *Anatomy of Britain*. See T. B. Bottomore, *op. cit.*, for a summary of the various elitist theories.

portance of distinguishing between influencing political decisions and taking and enforcing them. The presence of industrialists or landowners in the political elite therefore, tells us something about the channels of access between social groups and the government and indicates the kind of influences and interests to which the government is particularly exposed. But the model also stresses that in making policy, governments have to process a variety of inputs from a large number of interests. Moreover, where periodic elections determine who makes political decisions, the incumbents of such roles must act in ways which meet the interests of a substantial section of the electorate if they are to continue to enjoy its support.

In democratic societies, the governmental functions of rule-making, rule-application, and rule-adjudication are in theory roughly divided among separate agencies. But the separation of functions is not complete. Both the administration and the judiciary have limited rule-making functions. Governmental structures are, to a limited extent, multi-functional. Some societies, such as the United States have sought to place limits on the concentration of governmental powers by its doctrine of the separation of powers and the incorporation of checks and balances whereby the courts can exercise some control over the rule-making function by declaring acts unconstitutional. This existence of distinctive structures and the distribution of functions among distinct structures matches the differentiation of structure and function in the political system, in which interest articulation is primarily performed by interest groups and parties, and interest aggregation is performed by parties and parliament.

Duverger[1] shows that the structure of government is profoundly influenced by the party system. In a single party system, there is marked concentration of powers even where the constitution specifically provides for the separation of powers. In a single party system, executive and legislative are constitutional facades: the party alone exercises power. Duverger[1] argues that even in a two party system, as in Great Britain, a similar situation exists. 'In practice, the existence of majority government transforms the constitutional pattern from top to bottom. The party holds in its own hands the essential prerogatives of the Legislature and the Executive. Government posts are in the hands of its leaders . . . draft Bills are prepared by the party's research groups, tabled in its name by a party representative in the House, voted by the party parliamentary group, and applied by the party Government. Parliament and Government are like two

[1] M. Duverger, *Political Parties* (1959).

machines driven by the same motor, the party. . . . The single-party and the two-party systems differ radically on the limitation of power and the existence of an opposition; they are very close as far as concerns the separation of powers, or rather their concentrations.'[1] Other factors, of course, influence the separation of powers, the concentration being greater in a parliamentary system such as Great Britain than in a presidential system, such as the USA, especially when in the latter, congress and the president represent different parties.

The internal structure of the parties is a further factor. In Great Britain, discipline, centralization, and cohesion are more developed in the Labour Party than in the Conservative party, and hence there is a greater concentration of power under a Labour administration. The size of the majority in office also influences the separation of powers. Where the majority is small, parliament regains its importance.[2]

Multi-party systems, by contrast, tend towards the separation of powers. Governments depend on the stability of alliances and the government is constantly threatened by a parliamentary vote of no confidence.[3]

It can be seen that societies differ considerably in the distribution of governmental processes. An extreme example is where one or a few structural elements dominate in the performance of not only governmental but also political functions. Pakistan, for example, can be described as a 'modernizing oligarchy', in which the executive and the army together dominate in the performance of both political and governmental processes, and in which parliament does not function. Pakistan is deeply divided by internal cleavages deriving from linguistic, cultural, and religious differences. Under such circumstances, it is the executive and the army which aggregate interests and make and enforce rules.[4]

[1] *Ibid.*, p. 394.
[2] *Ibid.*, p. 400.
[3] *Ibid.*, pp. 408–9.
[4] G. A. Almond and J. S. Coleman, *op. cit.* (1960), pp. 572–3. See pp. 52–8 for a more detailed discussion of types of governmental and political systems. For an analysis of the role of the military in emerging states, see M. Janowitz, *The Military in the Political Development of New Nations* (1964). The role of the military in the power structure of society has been largely ignored by sociologists partly perhaps because the military in Western societies has been subordinated to civilian control and has not functioned as a contender for power. However, in the newly emerging states, the military is playing a much more decisive role. Its officers are drawn from an educated stratum, are closely in touch with modern technology, and control an efficient organization and communication system.

POLITICAL SYSTEMS AND SOCIAL CHANGE

Two main views are currently debated among sociologists about political trends in industrially advanced societies. The first, exemplified by Lipset's 'Political Man' argues that the same convergence of factors produced both democracy and capitalism. Protestantism favoured both the development of capitalism, and the emergence of democratic values through its emphasis on individual responsibility. The growth of a burgher class and their alignment with the monarchy extended the acceptance of democracy among the conservative strata. The second theory, the 'mass society' theme, is concerned rather with trends in fully developed industrial societies. It argues that such societies generate conditions which may lead to the emergence of totalitarian states.[1]

In a comparative study of a large number of states, Lipset has attempted to isolate those variables which are associated with 'stable democracy'. He finds that the stable democracies include those societies which are industrially advanced and which are characterized by high standards of living and high levels of literacy. They are also societies in which most own radios and large numbers of newspapers are read (Table 5.3). Although a number of factors interrelated with industrialization seem to hang together in a cluster, the causal links between such factors and political democracy are more speculative. It is reasonable to suppose that the more affluent societies provide a higher level of satisfaction of needs and do not breed the discontents which are generated by poverty and hunger. Moreover, they possess a more elaborate machinery for producing consensus. The schools, radio, and Press all contribute to the socialization process through the transmission of a common culture. And although minority and deviant opinions may be allowed expression through such media, all societies limit the expression of dissent. In the USA for example, communist doctrines and in the USSR capitalist doctrines, are excluded from the normal channels for the dissemination of views and opinions, thus contributing in both societies to a measure of ideological consensus. But it is important to note that some industrially advanced societies such as

Moreover, in many states, the army provides an opportunity for a new elite to form, recruited mainly from the middle strata of society. It would not be surprising, therefore, to find them aligned against the traditional landowning stratum and favouring industrialization and more radical land reforms.

[1] See, for example, W. Kornhauser, *The Politics of Mass Society* (1960), for an analysis and critique of this theme.

Germany had not achieved stable democracies during the first half of this century.

TABLE 5.3*

ECONOMIC DEVELOPMENT AND DEMOCRACY

	European and English-speaking stable democracies	Latin-American stable dictatorships
Per capita income (US)	695	119
Newspaper copies per 1,000 persons	341	43
Radio per 1,000	350	43
Per capita energy consumed	3·6	0·25
Education: post-primary enrolment per 1,000	44	8
Urbanization: per cent in cities 20,000+	43	17

* Based on S. M. Lipset, *op. cit.*, pp. 51–4.

The 'mass society' theme argues that industrialization leads to the alienation of individuals from primary group structures, that is, to the atomization of the social structure. Mass society in this sense is particularly vulnerable to totalitarian movements. Kornhauser challenges the view that modern societies all exhibit like tendencies to develop the characteristics of mass society. Moreover, he maintains that mass society is analytically distinct from a totalitarian society. This distinction can best be exemplified by his analysis of the two main variables which he uses, the 'accessibility of elites' and the 'availability of non-elites.' The first variable refers to the extent to which elites are accessible to influence by non-elites. Mass society is characterized by a high degree of influence over elites. The growth of democracy increases the participation of the masses and leads to the possibility that the masses may dominate elites. The second variable refers to the extent to which the masses are available for mobilization by elites and arises when individuals are divorced from their community and other primary ties including work. Individuals in such a society are atomized. A mass society is one in which elites are accessible and vulnerable to the influence of non-elites, while non-elites are atomized. (Figure 5.1.)

Both totalitarian and mass societies are characterized by atomized masses. But they differ in the vulnerability of elites to influence. The disruption of primary group ties through sudden and extensive

FIGURE 5.1

AVAILABILITY TO ELITES*

		Low	High
		communal	totalitarian
ACCESSIBILITY OF ELITES	Low		
	High	pluralist	mass

* W. Kornhauser, *op. cit.*, p. 40.

changes in the social structure caused by widespread unemployment or military defeat are among the factors favouring the atomization of populations—one of the ingredients of totalitarianism.

It follows from Kornhauser's analysis that an essential condition for a liberal democracy is the existence of a number of autonomous secondary associations which reduces the vulnerability of individuals to elites. In other words, it is to the pluralist type of society to which Kornhauser turns as a protection against any trend towards totalitarianism. 'In summary, a liberal democracy requires widespread participation in the selection of leaders, and a large amount of self-governing activity on the part of non-elites. It also requires competition among leaders and would-be leaders, and considerable autonomy for those who win positions of leadership.'[1] It follows that Kornhauser believes that a plural society offers the most favourable conditions for democracy. In seventeenth-century England, for example, a variety of class and religious groups were developing. And it is in the highly industrialized and urbanized societies that pluralism and democracy are strongest.

One possible threat to pluralism is the growth of large scale corporations which transform the middle-class from property-owning independent entrepreneurs to corporation employees. The threat to autonomy is seen in the inclusiveness of the organization which demands the individual's total allegiance.[2] On the other hand, Kornhauser points to the emergence of new middle-class associations such as the professions and their high rates of participation in voluntary associations.

In short, Kornhauser argues that conditions in industrial society make possible both increased alienation and opportunities for the formation of new associational ties. Clearly, these are matters of continuing debate and will be the object of further studies. Moreover, the very knowledge of the vulnerability of industrial society to

[1] W. Kornhauser, *op. cit.* (1960).
[2] W. H. Whyte, *Organization Man* (1957).

develop mass society characteristics may lead to countervailing measures. For example, anxiety about the possible consequences of mass communications has lead to a substantial volume of research in the USA.[1] One result of these researches, as we saw in Chapter 3, has been in the rediscovery of the primary group and a challenge to the view that mass media operate on atomized individuals. The prevailing view is rather that communication takes place through primary group structures and that the content of mass communication is mediated via opinion leaders in a group context.[2]

SUMMARY AND CONCLUSIONS

The political system occupies a central position in the social structure. Governments take the final decisions on who gets what. The formulation and execution of policies involves interaction with other elements in the social system. And with the growing complexity of society, the task of mobilizing its resources for the achievement of desired goals increases the interaction between governments and the social system. They are no longer concerned simply with the maintenance of law and order, although the state monopoly of legitimate coercive means still provides the characteristic feature of politics.

The extension of state functions has increased the channels of communication between the government and the social system. The political process now includes a multiplicity of agencies, groups, and committees for the articulation of interests. Every extension of government activity generates feedback in the shape of demands on the government from those whose interests are affected and the task of processing such inputs becomes more complex. The shift to government by consent and the extension of the franchise raises further problems of mobilizing support. The search for policies by competing parties which will command the widest possible support in the competition for leadership results in the parties themselves performing part of the function of aggregating a variety of specific demands into broad political policies.

Government by the periodic consent of the governed provides a mechanism for peaceful change. In their search for support, parties are vulnerable to pressure from interests, and even minority interests

---

[1] For a summary of this evidence and a detailed discussion of mass culture and mass society, see Leon Bramson, *The Political Context of Sociology* (1961), Chapters 2, 5 and 6.

[2] One further topic related to political trends is the 'end of ideology' theme. This will be examined in the next Chapter.

may be taken up in this way. But the legitimacy of the system assumes that the struggle for power is real and that oppositions may become governments. Moreover, competition irons out deep cleavages, voters change sides, and both parties are seen as having some of the qualities of the other. But where cleavages are deep and clear-cut, where, for example, a society is split on issues of race or religion and where such splits are taken up into the political system, the system may not be able to accommodate the conflicts.

The use of this model which sees the political system processing a variety of demand and support inputs suggests that preoccupation with political recruitment and the social origins of elites may be less important than much of the literature suggests. The ruling class and elitist controversy places great emphasis on the interest of the incumbents of key roles as the main clue to policy outcomes. Though such interests may well strongly colour policies, the ruling-class and elitist controversy does not appear to take sufficient account of the transformations in the political system which result from the extension of the franchise and the increasing interaction between the political system and the social system which results from the extension of governmental functions. The functions of government are more complex than the ruling class or elitist controversy recognized. Advanced industrial societies with complex technologies and rich resources are preoccupied with problems of goal attainment rather than integration and social control. The maximization of wealth requires the co-operation of a variety of specialized elites who increasingly occupy strategic positions in the social system. Governments, are faced with the task of devising policies for the pursuit of societal goals, and of allocating resources according to priorities. In doing so, they are subject to pressures from organized interest groups, and must achieve the compliance of the strategic elites on whose co-operation they depend. In advanced industrial societies in the West, there is substantial evidence which suggests that the economic and financial elites exercise a predominant influence over government policies, including the distribution of rewards. But they differ from a ruling class in that their positions are more vulnerable, rely less on inheritance, more on achievement, and the policies they favour have to meet pressures from the countervailing influences of organized labour and consumers. The extension of the franchise is a major mechanism by which governments are made responsive to such pressures, though how far the balance of influence remains substantially with the producers and men of property who dominate an apathetic mass society is a matter of controversy.

QUESTIONS AND EXERCISES

1. 'The state is only an element in the political system.' Discuss.
2. How useful is the definition of politics as 'the exercise of power'?
3. 'Pressure groups and parties are boundary structures which link the political system to the social system.' Explain and discuss.
4. 'The notion of a "political system" draws attention to the interrelation between the elements in the system.' Explain and discuss.
5. 'The differences between the structure and functioning of the Labour and Conservative parties have been exaggerated.' Discuss.
6. How would you account for the high degree of legitimacy of governments in Britain?
7. Examine the channels which exist for consultation between interests and the government.
8. Examine the functions of pressure groups in the political process.
9. Discuss the view that the democratic system requires sources of cleavage.
10. Examine the ways in which studies of voting behaviour may illuminate the extent of cleavage and consensus.
11. Discuss the usefulness of the analysis of political recruitment for an understanding of governmental processes.
12. It is no longer very useful to ask the question 'Who governs Britain'? Discuss.
13. Examine critically any one typology of political systems.
14. Examine the relations which have been asserted to exist between mass societies and totalitarianism.
15. How far do you think that industrialization leads to the development of 'mass society'?
16. Examine and compare the relations between political parties and the governmental process in Britain and one other industrial society.
17. 'The separation of powers is a constitutional fiction in many societies.' Explain and discuss.

READING

Gabriel A. Almond and James S. Coleman.—*The Politics of the Developing Areas* (Princeton, 1960), especially 'Introduction' and 'Conclusion'. A functionalist approach to the comparative study of political systems.
S. H. Beer.—*Modern British Politics: A Study of Parties and Pressure Groups* (Faber, 1965).
*J. Blondel.—*Voters, Parties and Leaders* (Pelican Books, 1963). A lucid and concise introduction.
J. Bonham.—*The Middle-Class Vote* (Faber, 1954).
T. B. Bottomore.—*Elites and Society* (Watts, 1964). A concise summary of the literature on elites and the ruling class.
*Robert A. Dahl.—'A Critique of the Ruling Elite Model', and

*David Easton.—'An Approach to the Analysis of Political Systems'. Useful brief summaries of important perspectives, both in S. M. Lipset and N. J. Smelser, *Sociology: the Progress of a Decade* (1961).

M. Duverger.—*Political Parties* (Allen & Unwin, 1959).

W. L. Guttsman.—*The British Political Elite* (MacGibbon, 1963). A detailed source book for data on the social and educational origins of various elites.

S. M. Lipset.—*Political Man* (Doubleday, 1960).

R. T. McKenzie.—*British Political Parties* (Heinemann, 1964), especially Chapters I and XI. The definitive study of the distribution of power within the Conservative and Labour Parties including an analysis of the emergence and structure of the mass party organizations.

*R. Rose.—*Politics in England* (Faber, 1965). A general text using Almond's functional model as a framework for an analysis of English data.

*R. Rose (ed.).—*Studies in British Politics: a Reader in Political Sociology* (Macmillan, 1966).

J. D. Stewart.—*British Pressure Groups* (Oxford, 1958).

Chapter 6

BELIEF SYSTEMS

BELIEF SYSTEMS AND SOCIETY

'What is the purpose of life?' 'Why is there so much suffering and misery in the world? I just can't see why innocent children should suffer senseless pain?' 'Young people have too much money. That's why there's so much delinquency.' 'Happiness is a by-product of hard work.' 'Longer prison sentences would soon put a stop to drunkenness on the roads.' 'A woman's place is in the home.' 'The welfare state saps initiative.' 'To me, the most important single thing is my salvation.'

Beliefs about how to do things, and what things we ought to do are essential for any action. And most of us want some kind of an answer to the problems that life poses. Such beliefs influence the way in which an individual perceives and defines a situation, its meaning for him, and guide his selection of alternative responses. Hard work, for example, will have one meaning for the protestant, and quite another for the Hindu. At the level of society, shared beliefs about what goals are most worth pursuing and how they ought to be pursued serve to integrate the behaviour of large numbers of individuals. In this Chapter, we will explore in more detail the way in which systems of belief are related to the social system. This will involve the attempt to discover the correlates (functions) of belief systems with other elements in the social system.

Belief systems are, of course, a part of culture. The term 'system' stresses the fact that we are now looking at complex wholes, not simply collections of isolated beliefs. Religious beliefs, for example, constitute a system in the sense that they are interrelated. They have a certain internal logical consistency. Indeed, it is this characteristic of belief systems which goes some way to explain their resistance to change. No single element stands on its own in isolation but is buttressed by the logical support it receives from other elements. The same can be said of other systems such as political ideologies, or science. The belief in God as creator and architect of the universe, original sin, predestination, and hell—all hang together. Remove any element in this system and the fabric of interwoven ideas is weakened.

Belief systems are a part of the culture of society in so far as they are shared by others. In this sense, beliefs are social facts which come to the individual from society, and are learned as a part of the socialization process. Thus members of Western industrial societies who have religious beliefs are almost certain to be Christians. But in Asia and the East, they will have learned quite different religious beliefs. Of course, the process is not a simple determinist one, or there would never be innovation. Moreover, we have to account for the fact that within the broad framework of Christianity there has arisen a wide variety of sects and denominations, holding quite different variations on a theme. There are limits to the range of beliefs available in any one society. Science, for example, has emerged only recently as a dominant element in the belief systems of Western society.

Types of belief system

How can we differentiate between religion, magic, science, and political ideologies? One way in which they differ is the extent to which they are capable of empirical verification.[1] The statement 'Longer prison sentences would soon put a stop to drunkenness on the roads' has reference to empirical things 'prison sentences' and 'drunkenness' and the relation between them. The proposition 'God is love' does not have such empirical references and is not capable of verification. A second distinction is between beliefs which refer to what things are and how to achieve ends, and beliefs about values. The belief that divorce is wrong is about values. It prescribes how we and others ought to behave. These two distinctions are related. Our belief that divorce is wrong may rest on empirically verifiable propositions, such as its consequences for the welfare of children. Or it may be essentially non-verifiable, such as when a person appeals to conscience and says 'I just know inside me that it is wrong.' We have, then, four main types of belief (Figure 6.1) according to whether they are empirical or non-empirical and cognitive or evaluative.

In practice belief systems cannot be neatly categorized in this way. Thus a religion may include theological beliefs about the nature of God which cannot be verified, and beliefs about values and morality.

---

[1] Such distinctions raise complex philosophical questions about the nature and meaning of propositions. The classification being put forward here claims only to be useful for sociological analysis.

FIGURE 6.1

TYPES OF BELIEFS

	Cognitive	Evaluative
Empirical	Science	Secular ethics
	Technology	
Non-empirical	Theology	Religious morality
	Magic	

It may also include elements of magical and metaphysical beliefs. It may even include beliefs about naturalistic phenomena such as whether the earth is round and the causes of illness. For most purposes of analysis it is sufficient to arrange belief systems along a continuum according to the extent to which they rest on empirical data. At one end we would have theology and metaphysics, and at the other science and technology.

One type of belief system is of particular importance for sociological analysis, and does not fit easily into such categorization, namely, *ideologies*. The term has, in fact, undergone considerable change in meaning in the course of its history.[1] It has now come to mean more than simply a system of ideas or beliefs. It is essentially a simplification or falsification of beliefs which arises when beliefs are related to actions. Not only this, but ideologies mask particular interests and reflect the needs of groups. They function to provide groups with a legitimation and motivation to action, and it is this imperative which leads to simplification. Any organization, including a church, may thus develop an ideology which may therefore be either religious or secular.

The sociology of knowledge[2]

Many societies have religions which teach doctrines about life after death. How can we explain such similarities? We also find that religious sects are supported by some segments of society and not by others, while political ideologies differ considerably in different sections of society. Marx argued that men's beliefs reflected their material conditions and experiences and these in turn were the result of their roles in society and above all their role in the economic system. But although he took a broadly determinist position, Marx recognized the great complexity of the problem, and that ideologies do not stem in any simple way from a persons objective location in

[1] See D. Bell, *The End of Ideology* (1962 edition), pp. 393–400.

[2] This section has drawn heavily on Merton's essays on the sociology of knowledge in his *Social Theory and Social Structure*.

society. He recognized, for example, that some members of the proletariat accept the ideology of the bourgeoisie—a phenomenon that Engels described as 'false class consciousness'. He also recognised that ideas once born have a certain autonomy and may persist in a society long after the material circumstances from which they have derived have changed.

Sociologists such as Mannheim and Merton have developed rather more sophisticated theories of the variables which have to be taken into account in exploring the relations between belief systems and social systems. A possible theoretical approach can be summarised in Figure 6.2. In exploring the beliefs held by any group of individuals in society we can start from the assumption that they are likely to be related to the needs of the individual. That is to say, beliefs enable individuals to adapt to the situation in which they find themselves, providing some kind of an orientation to life by answering such questions as 'Who am I?' 'What ought I to do?' and giving meaning to experiences. We can secondly explore the extent to which the

FIGURE 6.2

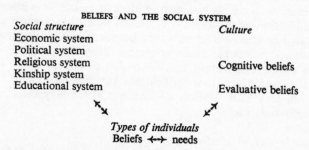

BELIEFS AND THE SOCIAL SYSTEM

Social structure	Culture
Economic system	
Political system	
Religious system	Cognitive beliefs
Kinship system	
Educational system	Evaluative beliefs

Types of individuals
Beliefs ←·→ needs

beliefs of individuals are related to their roles in the social structure. Individuals who experience severe deprivations or frustrations, for example, will seek symbolic means of interpreting such a situation in a meaningful way. It would not be surprising to find them supporting beliefs in a life-hereafter, or in the imminent coming of the millennium in which their sufferings would be rewarded. And finally existing beliefs derived from culture will influence the way in which experiences will be perceived, and interpreted. No one starts from scratch in finding answers to life's problems. He can select from the beliefs which are available from those which come closest to his needs and experiences, and will be motivated to search for new beliefs if none enable him to discover meaning and to adapt to his situation.

This model tentatively suggests that individuals are the intervening variable between culture and the social structure. The individual inherits the shared beliefs of his society through the socialization process. He retains those which are congruent with his experiences and searches for others to meet his needs. These include those needs which are organically determined such as those resulting from illness as well as the socially determined needs which derive from his social roles as husband, worker, and voter.

The model implies a determinist view of beliefs. It would take us too far into philosophical speculation to explore all its implications. But the fact that we construct such a model to help us to analyse a problem does not mean that we are saying that beliefs are determined.[1] In the last analysis this is an empirical question which we are not at the moment in a position to answer. It may be that an element of indeterminacy in beliefs will be found to defy a naturalistic explanation. Meanwhile, we are simply interested in exploring the extent to which variations in beliefs can be explained by relating them to the social system. There is one sense, of course, in which no-one is disturbed by the notion that beliefs are determined. In the field, of science, for example, we believe what the evidence forces us to believe. But the more we move away from empirically verified beliefs, the more the characteristics of the believing subject are likely to influence the content of his beliefs.

Functions of beliefs

We are interested not only in the social factors which shape systems of beliefs but also in their functions in the social system. For the individual, beliefs perform an adaptive function. They enable him to adapt to his role in the social system by providing him with a symbolic interpretation which gives meaning to his experiences, enables him to orient his actions, and to manage the tensions which derive from fears and uncertainties. But they also perform functions in the social system. In organizations, for example, the activities of individuals are integrated by shared beliefs about common goals. Shared beliefs about ways of acting ensure the maintenance of patterns of conduct such as honesty and truth telling, and act as agencies of social control.

One problem which we need to explore is how far alternative

[1] This problem has worried several sociologists who have contributed to the sociology of knowledge. Mannheim, for example, argued that the intellectual in society was the most free from class attachments and therefore most capable of objectivity. (See Merton, *op. cit.*)

belief systems can function, in these ways. How far, for example, can secular systems of belief act as functional alternatives to religion for goal-attainment, adaptation, integration, tension-management and pattern-maintenance?

RELIGION

Religions are systems of beliefs which include a number of elements. But their essential feature is that these beliefs cluster around a core belief in the supra-natural—in phenomena which cannot be explained in naturalistic (empirical) terms. Usually the supra-natural phenomenon is though of in personal terms, whether as spirits and demons, or the almost metaphysical notion of 'personality as the ground and being of existence' held by some contemporary theologians.

It is not surprising that the role of religion in social systems has long occupied the attention of sociologists, and a brief glance at some major theories can help clarify sociological perspectives on this subject.[1] Pareto's contribution represented a particularly important development of the prevailing positivist view which treated the individual actor's orientation to his environment as essentially cognitive and rational. The positivitists had been aware of the fact that men might deviate from action guided by facts and logic through ignorance or faulty reasoning.[2] Pareto drew attention to a second important class of non-logical actions—those which were incapable of being tested by scientific procedures. It is precisely this type of orientation which characterizes religious ideas and beliefs. Religious behaviour is essentially non-logical, and expresses deeply rooted sentiments.[3]

A further important development in the role of rational (empirically verifiable) and non-rational beliefs emerged in the study of religion and magic among the Trobriand Islanders by Malinowski. He showed that activities such as deep-sea fishing and canoe building were guided by a body of sound empirical knowledge and that behaviour was rationally guided by such knowledge. But side-by-side with such knowledge and action, there existed a second set of magical

[1] See T. Parsons, *Essays in Sociological Theory* (1954), Chapter X, for a summary.

[2] Pareto referred to such 'pseudo-scientific' actions as *derivations*.

[3] The precise nature of such sentiments is not clear. Pareto was content to classify the variety of non-logical actions into a number of residual categories or residues.

beliefs and practices. These beliefs related to the occurrence of uncertainty, to outcomes beyond rational control and explanation, such as bad weather, or inexplicable crop failure.

The function of magic is therefore distinct from that of science and technology and should not be treated as a kind of primitive science. Even in advanced industrial societies, 'magical' actions are common. Magic steps in to provide us with a means of adaptation to a situation when empirical means have failed or are inadequate.[1] We can't be absolutely certain that the pilot will take off successfully, or that we can undertake a journey in safety. We can be even less certain that we can survive a battle. So we carry a talisman for luck, or say a prayer—just in case the servicing of the plane and the take-off drill of the pilot let us down. Magic, that is to say, is essentially an expressive action, providing an outlet for frustrations and pent-up emotions in the face of the failure of empirical means. Magic is the use of non-empirical means dirdcted towards the attainment of empirical ends. Religion is the use of non-empirical means for non-empirical ends.[2]

Various theories have been put forward to account for the origins of religious beliefs and the distinction between the sacred and the profane. The naturalist school sees the sacred as essentially the personification of natural forces. Such beliefs provide answers to the problems of adaptation to man's material environment. Crops fail, rivers burst their banks, pestilence strikes the village. The gods are angry and must be placated. Such beliefs give rise to practices which merge into magic. The Greeks had a pantheon of gods which personified natural forces. Sacrifices, or prayers, may influence the gods to smile more benevolently. The churches fill at times of national crisis or calamity, such as war, and prayers are said for rain or victory in battle.

Durkheim, however, pointed to the weakness of such an explanation. The things that are personified or treated as sacred have no common intrinsic qualities. There is hardly anything which in some society or another has not been treated as sacred. The clue, he argued, was to be found in the symbolic nature of sacred objects. Moreover, the thing that they symbolize must command moral respect. Hence

---

[1] In all societies, the fact of death is something in the face of which we are helpless. And in all societies, as Parsons has pointed out, burial involves actions which go beyond the mere utilitarian disposal of the corpse.

[2] A religion may include magical practices, such as prayers for rain, which are linked to the core belief in a deity. But these are peripheral practices, rejected by some.

Durkheim was lead to the view that society is always the real object behind the religious symbols. It far transcends the individual, and it is his experience of society which generates in him emotions of awe and respect.[1] We may not accept Durkheim's explanation, but it does draw attention to the important symbolic functions of religion. Religious symbols serve to underline the significance of solemn occasions such as the opening of parliament and the end of term. The school hymn, the dedication of the national flag, are all examples of the reinforcement of secular meanings with religious symbolic meanings.

Weber still further developed these themes by pointing to the distinction between empirical problems of causation and what he called the 'problem of meaning'. Religious systems can provide a variety of 'meanings'—various ways of making sense of everyday life. Moreover, such meanings and explanations have an important relation with the actions men adopt in response to similar situations, and especially in the goals they seek. Specifically, Weber demonstrated the significant differences between Catholics and Protestants in their economic behaviour, and argued for the substantial influence of Protestantism in generating worldly ascetism (hard work, thrift, and abstinence), and its role in the rise of capitalism.[2]

THE FUNCTIONS OF RELIGION

Such theories suggest that religious beliefs perform necessary social functions. They assist the individual man in adapting to his environment and in dealing with uncertainty. Religious and magical beliefs and practices provide tension-management and pattern maintenance mechanisms. While science may be superior as an instrumental means, it may be doubted whether it can perform adequately expressive functions. But one instrumental function has been claimed for religion—as a means of integration. We must now turn to investigate the social functions of religion in contemporary society.

Social functions of religion

It is not easy to measure the significance of religion in the life of contemporary society. Statistics for church attendance or church membership are only crude indications of belief, although it is

---

[1] *The Elementary Forms of the Religious Life* (189).

[2] *The Protestant Ethic and the Spirit of Capitalism* (1930). For a criticism of Weber, see R. H. Tawney, *Religion and the Rise of Capitalism* (1926).

reasonable to suppose that they bear some relation to intensity of belief. On this criterion, religion is declining in England. The broad trend shows a steady rise in church attendances reaching a peak in the 1880s, followed by a steady decline. A religious census of 1851 returned 39 per cent who had attended a place of worship on a particular Sunday. Studies of church attendance in York show a decline from 25 per cent in 1900 to 14 per cent in 1948.[1] The following table of Easter communicants shows a similar decline, with a slight rise in recent years above the record low of 1947, but still well below the pre-war figures. Infant baptisms and church marriages have also declined. Other indices of religious behaviour show that traditional religious beliefs are no longer held by significant sections of the population. Seventy-two per cent believe in God, 47 per cent in an after-life, while 46 per cent claim to pray daily.

In interpreting these trends however, we must avoid generalizations from only one industrial society. Comparable figures for the USA show a much higher proportion of weekly church attendance (43 per cent), belief in God (95.5 per cent) and in an after-life (72 per cent). Fewer, however, pray daily (42.5 per cent) and could name the four Gospels (35 per cent compared with 61 per cent).[2]

TABLE 6.1

PAROCHIAL EASTER DAY COMMUNICANTS OF THE CHURCH OF ENGLAND*
(per thousand over 15)

Year	Communicants
1885	84
1911	98
1921	87
1931	81
1939	73
1947	54
1958	63

* Central Board of Finance, *Facts and Figures about the Church of England* (1962).

It is not easy to assess the significance of such evidence. Recent American researches suggest that religious influences are mediated not only through formal membership of a religious association but also by being involved in a religious sub-community composed of members of the same faith, which 'is a vehicle by means of which large numbers of persons are effectively indoctrinated with the norms of the group',[3] even where associational ties are weak. In

[1] M. Argyle, *Religious Behaviour* (1958).
[2] *Ibid.*
[3] G. Lenski, *The Religious Factor* (1961), p. 327. This distinction originates from W. Herberg, *Protestant, Catholic, Jew.*

fact, the influence of religious community may sometimes run counter to the association, fostering and encouraging 'a provincial and authoritarian view of the world.'[1] Lenski's researches confirm Herberg's view that urbanism does not, in fact, break up communal life. On the contrary, the impersonality of urban living strengthens the need for communal relationships, and for a sense of identity. Contrary to the accepted theory of urbanism, the specialization and compartmentalization characteristic of urban society is transforming religious life from specialized associations to groups which are more communal in character.[2] For example, although there has been a marked decline in associational membership among Jews, the majority stated that nearly all their friends were Jews, and all were married to a life-long Jewish spouse. By contrast, the Catholics has strong associational ties but weaker communal ties, while the white Protestants were weaker by both criteria. Nevertheless, a significant proportion of both reported that nearly all their close friends were of the same faith. Moreover, Lenski's findings confirm Herberg's prediction that the disintegration of the old ethnic sub-communities is leading to a religious survival as Americans turn to religion as a source of identity.

Clearly, such conclusions cannot be lifted and applied to the English social system. But Herberg's theory may account for what appears to be a major difference between England and America— the evidence of a religious revival in the USA compared with a continued decline in Britian. More important, the data on declining church membership in the UK may give a misleading picture of the significance of religion in modern England, since it ignores the possibility that some form of religious sub-communities may exist here as well.

One important social function claimed for religion is its ability to integrate members of a group through shared beliefs and values. But religious beliefs may also be divisive; separating believers from non-believers. Many religions, including Catholics and Jews in contemporary society are endogamous. Some of the bitterest wars in history have been between rival religious groups. Sacred objects and rituals also serve as symbols of common beliefs and interests and thus serve to enhance the consciousness of belonging. Shared rituals serve to unify members of the group through shared activities. Profane objects such as flags and other symbols are consecrated and thus become themselves sacred symbols.

[1] *Ibid.*, p. 328.
[2] G. Lenski, *op. cit.* (1961), p. 11.

English studies suggest that religion fails to perform an integrative function. On major social issues, Christian churches are divided. Not only are there differences between denominations on questions such as birth control, divorce, and the use of atomic weapons, but also on some issues within denominations. But on major political and economic issues, the views of members of churches appear to reflect their social roles rather than a specifically religious viewpoint. Indeed, on such questions, as Wickham shows, the churches have, by and large, failed to concern themselves, nor have they expressed any clear policies. A similar verdict is reached from a study of the decline in religion in South Wales.[1] This research shows that the main topics discussed at conferences and in church publications in the 1940s were Sunday observance, temperance, gambling and the preservation of Welsh culture. Moreover, it is argued, this neglect of concern with political and social issues reflected the different and opposed attitudes and interests of the leadership of the Welsh chapels, drawn as they were from both middle and working class. Any decisive line on the burning issues of unemployment and housing would inevitably have alienated some members of the congregation. The authors conclude that religion has, therefore, failed to perform a integrative function in Welsh society. It has failed to provide a set of shared values which could guide conduct in such spheres as work and politics.

A second possible social function of religion is the enforcement of morality. Supernatural sanctions, such as the threat of hell, it can be argued serve to underpin the moral beliefs of a society and to maintain the accepted patterns of conduct. Thus the Christian churches have stressed monogomous marriage, and opposed birth control and divorce.[2] The fact that the rules are derived from core theological beliefs puts them into the category of sacred objects. To challenge or to alter them is defined as heresy, and such rules therefore become particularly resistant to change. The doctrine of the divine right of kings functioned in a somewhat similar way to legitimize and sanction the authority of the monarch.

How far religion underpins the morality of the individual and regulates his conduct it is difficult to say. Fertility rates among Catholics are only slightly higher than those for the corresponding non-Catholic section of the population. Crime rates are not signifi-

[1] T. Brennan, E. W. Cooney and H. Pollins, *Social Change in South West Wales* (1954).

[2] On divorce, see O. R. MacGregor, *op. cit.* (1957).

cantly lower for church members. Religious people have a lower level of sexual activity.[1] The evidence is inconclusive, but does not support the view that the conduct of the religious in England differs significantly from the non-religious in the same segments of society.

Lenski however, concludes that 'religion in a variety of ways is constantly influencing the daily lives of the masses of men and women in the modern American metropolis. More than that: through its impact on individuals, religion makes an impact on all the other institutional systems of the community these individuals staff. Hence the influence of religion operates at the social level as well as at the personal level.'[2] Religion was found to influence attitudes towards work, saving, the welfare state, freedom of speech, racial integration, close family ties, having a large family, intellectual autonomy, and social mobility. Again, no support was found for the theory that urbanization would increase the homogeneity between religious groups. Religion was found to be comparable to social class in both potency and range as an index of behaviour and attitudes.[3]

Religion and the individual

The religious beliefs of the individual are largely inherited with other elements of culture through the socialization process. This accounts for the fact that most individuals will believe only some of the total range of religious perspectives of mankind. They are most likely to accept the shared beliefs of the particular society in which they live, and of that segment of society in which they have been socialized.

But the association between the beliefs of parents and children is not a determinist one.[4] We may expect the individual to retain those beliefs which are congruent with his experiences and which meet his needs. We may expect, therefore, significant differences between the religious beliefs of different segments in society which reflect their social roles and experiences and the needs which these generate. Thus we find in contemporary society that religious beliefs are more widespread among widows, and among combat troops exposed to the danger of death.[5] They are also more widespread among old

[1] M. Argyle, op. cit. (1958)
[2] Op. cit. (1961), p. 320. This influence was significant when controls were introduced for class.
[3] Ibid., p. 326.
[4] There is a correlation of 0·65 between the religious beliefs of parents and children. M. Argyle, op. cit. (1958).
[5] Ibid.

people, but this may be because their beliefs perpetuate the stronger religious convictions of earlier generations.

One of the most vivid illustrations of this thesis is the occurrence through history of revolutionary millennial sects which promised the imminent overthrow of the existing social order and the reign of the dispossessed who would be elevated as saints to positions of pɔwer and influence. Such movements took place within the framework of Jewish and Christian doctrine which includes a substantial body of prophetic belief about the final state of the world (eschatology). Christianity teaches, for example, that in the last days, God will return to judge the world. Professor Cohn[1] shows that there were numerous examples of such emotional mass movements in Europe between the eleventh and sixteenth centuries which gained their main support from those exposed to poverty and catastrophe. Such outbreaks occurred during times when society was disrupted by famine, plague, and war. They were concentrated too, in the growing urban communities in which the traditional supportive network of social relations had been disrupted.[2]

Studies of sects in society have similarly demonstrated the association between the social roles and characteristics of supporters and major elements in their teachings. Jehovah's Witnesses, for example, teach that the end of the world is at hand when the wicked will be destroyed and the rule of God established. Studies in the United States show that its membership attracts the underprivileged strata. A detailed study by Bryan Wilson of the Elim, Christadelphian and Christian Science sects in England clearly supports the association between religion and socio-economic conditions.[3]

Both the Elim and Christadelphian movements have drawn in the 'poor, socially neglected and culturally deprived'. God will not only give the saints a heavenly reward, but will also benefit them on earth by their ecstatic experiences and the gift of tongues. In this way, Elim compensates both the economically disinherited, and those disillusioned and embittered by their experience. ' . . . The Elimites are workers, often factory hands, who obtain from religion a transvaluation of life: it reassures them of their ultimate worthiness and provides exciting escape from the dull routine of daily life.'

By contrast, the Christian Scientists adopt an optimistic attitude to the prevailing social order and attract the more wealthy. 'It is the religious expression of the well-to-do and comfortable . . .; it confirms

[1] *The Pursuit of the Millenium* (1957).
[2] N. Cohn, *op. cit.*, pp. 21–32.
[3] B. R. Wilson, *Sects and Society* (1961).

them in the righteousness of their possessions, or of their striving.'[1]
It is in no way opposed to the values of the established order, nor is
it primarily preoccupied with life after death. It is concerned rather
with the application of religion to everyday life, including the world of
business. It provides its adherents with esoteric knowledge which will
enable him to adapt more effectively to the world as he finds it, and
to maximize his enjoyment of health, wealth, and happiness, by
teaching that evil and unhappiness are illusions. Faith can conquer
the fear out of which such illusions arise; evils are explained away
by the constant affirmation that they do not exist. Its emphasis that
illness is an illusion attracts many who have a morbid preoccupation
with bodily health. It flourishes particularly in watering places and
health resorts.'An analysis of Christian Science testimonies shows that
80 per cent were from women. In 93 per cent of the letters the
maintenance of health was the primary subject discussed. Wilson
concludes that it can 'certainly heal the wounded spirit and restore
otherwise hopeless people to cheerfullness and hope'.[2]

This functional relationship between the doctrines of sects and the
needs of their members faces churches and denominations with a
particular problem. In the United States for example, the predominantly middle-class protestant churches have found difficulty in
spreading their liberal doctrines among the lower strata, who wanted
ministers who would preach hell-fire and salvation.[3] A church which
derives its members from one segment of society is likely to support
social policies which alienate those whose social role makes such
policies unacceptable. Bishop Wickham[4] shows, for example, that
the churches have failed to win support among the industrial working
classes of England. Although the Methodists succeeded in winning
some support from the well-paid artisans, the bulk of the manual
workers remained outside the church. The major factor contributing
to this alienation was the social and political policies which the
denominations supported and the attitudes of the predominantly
middle-class congregations. The churches in the nineteenth century
were preoccupied with their own affairs—with disestablishment,
ritualism, Sunday observance, and the drink question. 'The political
composition of the churches . . . precluded any sympathy towards the
new working-class political organizations that were being born.'[5]

[1] *Ibid.*, p. 317.
[2] *Ibid.*, p. 212.
[3] S. M. Lipset, *Political Man* (1960).
[4] E. R. Wickham, *Church and People in an Industrial City* (1957).
[5] *Ibid.*, p. 198.

Bishop Wickham quotes Arthur Henderson's comments on the churches before the First World War. 'Some of our churches are little better than religious hot-houses for the preservation of the interests of middle-class society . . . The attitude of the churches towards social questions has been a powerful factor in creating the present situation . . . they have (given) . . . relief by way of opening soup kitchens or doling out coal or blankets, instead of using their magnificent opportunities to go to the root of the evil . . .'[1]

The limited evidence which we have does not permit any firm conclusions on religious trends. It is clear that for many, religion continues to perform important functions. The support for chiliastic sects among those experiencing major problems of adjustment, and the higher rate of belief among the widowed and the aged is evidence of such a role. Moreover, it is unlikely that those who still take the trouble to leave fireside and television set to attend church services do so simply out of habit or response to social pressures. But there is little doubt that religion has changed in its significance for many individuals. The eclipse of the chapel by the trade union in South Wales demonstrates the shift to secular agencies as the means of adapting to the economic system. Yet those for whom such organized responses are frustrated, such as the American negroes, continue to support chiliastic movements which combine revolutionary aims with religious beliefs.

The decline in the adaptive and tension management functions of religion may also be traced to other social changes. Death is now a less frequent event in the life of the individual who is now much less likely to experience untimely bereavement from the death of wife or child. Pain and suffering are largely controlled, and poverty greatly diminished. Science has proved to be a more reliable providence in the control of famine and disease.

This does not mean, of course, that major disruptions and catastrophies no longer occur. And the fact of death remains as the ultimate and inescapable fact. But such events occur in a cultural context in which alternative belief systems exist. Professor Cohn for example, argues that secular ideologies such as communism and fascism now function for many to take the place of the medieval millennial cults—a view which will be examined in more detail later.

Those who reject a religious view of life must find an alternative mode of adjustment to the inevitability of death, to apparently senseless suffering, and to fortuitous calamity. The Greek philosopher Epicurus, for example, argued that we should not fear death because

[1] Quoted, *op. cit.*, p. 280.

we ourselves can never in fact meet death: 'when we are, death is absent from us; when death is come, we are no more'.[1] Some find exhilaration and challenge from the view that life has no extrinsic meaning. 'There is only one solution to his (man's) problem: to face the truth, to acknowledge his fundamental aloneness and solitude in a universe indifferent to his fate, to recognize that there is no power transcending him which can solve his problem for him. . . . If he faces the truth without panic, he will recognize that there is no meaning to life except the meaning man gives his life.'[2] A less sophisticated solution is an acceptance of fate—that we must take what is coming to us—a view which characterizes working-class subculture.[3]

How far such non-religious philosophies may eventually replace religion is a matter of speculation. Those who hold such views are at the moment a small and unrepresentative section of society. A recent study of the British Humanist Association found that its members are mainly drawn from those with above average education. Moreover, they are predominantly from the upper socio-economic categories.[4]

RELIGION AND THE SOCIAL SYSTEM

In the more complex societies religious beliefs become the basis for groupings and organizations. Churches evolve with a priesthood, and hierarchical organizational structure. In other words, religious organizations always exist as a part of a social structure. And this brings them into interrelation with other elements in the social structure. In order to survive they have to achieve some kind of congruence with the political system and the economic system. In England, for example, there is a close association between church and state. Parliamentary sanction is required for some kinds of ecclesiastical laws, there is state patronage of benefices, religious rites are incorporated into the coronation of the monarch, while the state protects the church's property. The church is brought into particularly close association with the economic system through its ownership of land and its investments. The need for survival has resulted in Christian churches accommodating to both democracies and to

[1] Quoted H. Sidgwick, *Outlines of the History of Ethics* (1919).
[2] E. Fromm, *Man for Himself* (1947), quoted by H. C. Bredemeier, R. M. Stephensen, *Analysis of Social Systems* (1962), pp. 300–1.
[3] R. Hoggart, *The Uses of Literacy* (1957).
[4] C. Campbell, 'Membership Composition of the British Humanist Association', *Soc. Rev.* (1965), pp. 327–36.

totalitarian and even to communist regimes.[1]

Any major strain between religion and the social system could be expected to result in some accommodating adjustment, either on the part of the social system or religion. Hoult[2] concludes after an extensive comparative study that such socio-cultural compatibility is the rule. A study of Christian documents on social issues illustrates such compatibility very forcefully. As we have seen in Chapter 4, the encyclical 'Revum Novarum' (Leo XIII) of 1891 is a powerful plea for private property, a condemnation of socialism, and a defence of laissez-faire. A chief function of the state ' . . . is the duty of safeguarding private property by legal enactment and protection. Most of all it is essential, where the passion of greed is strong, to keep the people within the line of duty; for if all may justly strive to better their condition, neither justice nor the common good allows any individual to seize upon that which belongs to another, or, under the futile and shallow pretext of equality, to lay violent hands on other people's possessions.'[3] In this document powerful religious support is lent to a particular social system, while urging at the same time that is should be operated in a just and humane way. It epitomizes in fact, liberal capitalist opinion at the end of the nineteenth century.

The fact of congruence does not enable us to draw any particular conclusion about which is the dependent variable—religion or society. The evidence suggests that religion may function in both ways. But the dominant trend in advanced industrial societies seems to be that religion reflects social change. An example is the changing religious attitude to birth control Most previous societies have urged the duty of child-rearing and condemned practices which aim at the limitation of fertility. Such a policy is essential for survival where mortality is high. But the decline in mortality since the eighteenth century has resulted in a new situation, the population explosion, which make high fertility rates a threat to the future of mankind. Yet the condemnation of fertility control has been incorporated into Christian teaching. In 1908, for example, the Lambeth Conference of the Church of England resolved: 'The Conference regards with alarm the growing practice of the artificial restriction of the family, and earnestly calls upon all Christian people to discountenance the use of artificial means of restriction as demoralizing to character and hostile to national welfare.' But the same conference in 1958

[1] T. F. Hoult, *The Sociology of Religion* (1958).
[2] T. F. Hoult, *op. cit.*
[3] Catholic Truth Society, *The Pope and the People* (1943), p. 154.

rejects the view that procreation is the ruling purpose of marriage, and allows family limitation by artificial methods. 'The questions, How many children? At what intervals? are matters on which no general counsel can be given. The choice must be made by parents together, in prayerful consideration of their resources, the society in which they live, and the problems they face.'[1] There are many other such examples of changes in religious views on questions such as the status of women, social equality, and slavery. Such re-thinking of religious viewpoints on a number of moral and social questions is now taking place in all churches, and it. is reasonable to predict that further changes will occur in religious teachings over the next decade.

Religious beliefs are a part of culture. Its beliefs, both cognitive and evaluative must exist side by side with secular beliefs in the intellectual life of society. The social structure provides a part of the existential basis for the culture of society. Men seek to interpret their experiences in a meaningful way, but there are obviously a variety of possible interpretations, and consequently a variety of cultural beliefs which are compatible with any particular social system. Thus in both capitalist and communist societies there are elements in culture which explain the meaning of work and legitimize and motivate work. It is possible for religious beliefs to exist side by side with secular beliefs about the social system and to provide alternative meanings and explanations.

Religious beliefs however, must be compatible not only with the social system, but also with other elements in culture. Science, for example, offers an alternative explanation of natural phenomena. For a considerable time, such alternative explanations existed side-by-side, although frequently contradictory. The Copernican revolution eventually challenged successfully the prevailing religious view that the earth is the centre of the universe; and in the nineteenth century, the confrontation between religion and biology resulted in the triumph of the Darwinian view on evolution. As the areas of indeterminancy and ignorance have receded with the growth of science, religious explanations have given way to secular explanations. But religion remains as an alternative view in those areas where science cannot provide an answer. On questions such as 'what is the purpose of life?' many still find that religion provides a satisfactory explanation.[2]

One important thread in intellectual history has been man's self-

[1] *Report of Lambeth Conference*, 1958.
[2] Science, of course, would not claim to be able to answer such questions.

conscious examination of the actual processes of knowing. In recent years there has been an increasingly rigorous examination of the nature of belief and the language which we use to discuss such philosophical questions. As a result, there has been a more critical appraisal of many traditional religious beliefs. Theologians, for example, have re-examined Christian theology in the light of developments in linguistic philosophy which has challenged the meaning of many propositions previously acceptable.[1] The resulting revolution in theology has lead to the rejection of mythological elements in Christianity to the 'death of God' as traditionally believed. Whether such a de-mythologized religion is capable of performing the same tension-management and adaptive functions remains to be seen.

SCIENCE AND THE SOCIAL SYSTEM[2]

Science is usually conceived as a relatively recent development in human history. But there is a sense in which this is not so. It is true that the beliefs of man in the past have been dominated by non-empirical beliefs in magic and the supernatural. Yet, as Malinowski has shown in his studies of the Trobriand Islanders, magical beliefs exist side by side with a great deal of practical know-how on navigation, boat-building and cultivation. But such practical and empirical knowledge is not quite what we mean by science. Science consists of theories which relate concepts in a systematic way and which rest on objective empirical inquiry. Moreover, in the scientifically advanced societies science becomes a distinct activity, with its own organizations, culture, and personnel, while the products of science have wrought a profound change on the whole fabric of social life. One has only to think of the staggering consequences of nuclear fission and mortality controlling drugs.

Scientific beliefs, like religious beliefs and political ideologies, do not exist in a social vacuum, but are functions of social systems. At the level of the individual, there must be persons who not only feel free to pursue their inquiries but who are also strongly motivated to do so. At the structural level, there must be adequate organizational support for the individual and a recognized social role for him to play. At the level of culture, there must be congruence be-

---

[1] The writings of Dr Robinson, Bishop of Woolwich, are an example of such re-thinking, e.g. *Honest to God* (1963).

[2] For a review of the earlier literature on the sociology of science, see *Current Sociology*, Vol. V, 1956.

tween the cognitive and evaluative beliefs of science and non-science.

Science and culture

The recognition of science as a part of culture is a relatively recent development. Indeed, it is only since the Second World War that the notion that an educated person could be largely ignorant of science has been challenged. 'Traditionally, natural science was subordinated to theology and philosophy.'[1] Its status as an intellectual activity was considered to be inferior to that of the arts. Its establishment in Europe was the result in part of the growing recognition of its practical utility by the rising class of merchants and artisans. But it also had to overcome not only the apathy, but even the hostility of the prevailing religious culture.

The connexion between Protestantism and the rise of science has been fully documented by Merton and Ben-David. Unlike the Catholic church, Protestantism in Europe did not everywhere possess a constituted religious authority.[2] Moreover, its doctrines left the interpretation of the Bible to the individual. Consequently, 'a Protestant who felt that God's will and the discoveries of science were in harmony could go ahead with a good conscience . . . Protestantism thus provided the legitimation for the formulation of a new utopian view where science, experiment, and experience . . . were to form the core of a new culture.'[3] Protestantism came to encourage empircal inquiry 'to discover the true Nature of the Works of God', in the belief that such discoveries would manifest 'the Glory of the Great Author of Nature'.[4] Merton found that 42 per cent of the sixty-eight original members of the Royal Academy for whom data are available were Puritans—although they constituted only a minority in the population. Protestantism, then, not only stimulated speculation, but encouraged its application to the empirical world.

Although its connection with practical affairs earned support from some strata in society, this connexion has also played a part in ensuring its relatively inferior status as a part of culture. The pre-

---

[1] J. Ben-David, 'The scientific role: the conditions of its establishment in Europe', *Minerva*, Vol. IV, No. 1, 1965.

[2] The exceptions were the small self-contained Protestant communities such as those in Geneva and Scotland, where science fared worse than in the great Catholic centres. See J. Ben-David, *op. cit.*, 1965, p. 42.

[3] *Ibid.*, p. 41.

[4] From the last will and testament of Robert Boyle; quoted in R. K. Merton, *Essays in Social Theory and Social Structure* (1957), Chapter xviii. See also B. Barber and W. Hirsch, *The Sociology of Science* (1952), Chapters. 2, 3.

vailing aristocratic values in England have premiumed non-utilitarian knowledge and have been reflected in the relatively lower prestige of science compared with the arts in the universities.[1]

Science and the economy

One important stimulus to science has derived from its adaptive function. Merton[2] has shown that much of the great increase in scientific activity in sixteenth and seventeenth-century England was directed towards the solution of practical problems. Newton, for example, made use of astronomical observations which were the product of Flamsteed's work at Greenwich Observatory, constructed at the command of Charles II, for the benefit of the Royal Navy. Napier's invention of logarithms in 1614 made a valuable contribution in calculations of longitude and latitude. Such problems led to a variety of astronomical investigations and stimulated the development of accurate chronometers. Nearly 60 per cent of researches reported to the Royal Society for the periods 1661-2 and 1686-7 could be related directly or indirectly to practical problems. After 1760, there was a rapid increase in the number of patents from 92 for 1750-9 to 477 for 1780-9. Seventy-five per cent of the patents of this period related to mining. Merton is not, of course, saying that economic and military needs alone can explain the growth of science, only that they provided a stimulus and gave it direction.

The considerable expansion in science in recent decades can similarly be traced to the growing recognition of its importance for economic growth[3] and for military security. A substantial measure of support for science now comes from state sponsored research, much of which is for military purposes.

Science and the political system

The articulation between science and the political system hinges around two main points. In the first place, the political system ultimately determines the allocation of societal resources. As we have seen, the growing numbers, wealth, and influence of the merchant and artisan class was an important factor in the emergence of a social structure favourable to the growth of science in sixteenth- and seventeenth-century Europe. More recently, the growing awareness of the economic significance of science stimulated state sponsor-

---

[1] N. Hans, *New Trends in Education in the 18th Century* (1951); S. F. Cotgrove *Technical Education and Social Change* (1958).

[2] R. K. Merton, *op. cit.*, Chapter 19.

[3] S. F. Cotgrove, *op. cit.*, 1958, Chapter 7.

ship for scientific research, exemplified by the setting up of the Department for Scientific and Industrial Research in 1916. Secondly, the increasing military significance of science in the fields of nuclear fission and space research have not only channelled substantial economic resources into state support for science but have also resulted in a growth of political control over science, and in a challenge to its cherished claim to freedom of inquiry and publication. This situation poses particular problems for scientists engaged in research which is involved in state security, and has led to considerable heartsearchings among scientists about their social role. Such scientists are no longer autonomous and free from public pressures.[1]

Science and scientists

It is not easy to explain why some individuals turned to scientific activities in the sixteenth and seventeenth centuries. The association of scientists with dissenting religion is capable of a variety of explanations. While such religions may have provided more encouragement to independent thinking, they may also have attracted innovating personalities who were seeking more radical explanations of things both spiritual and temporal. Moreover, the new discoveries and innovations in industry and trade had created a class of persons with an interest in change. But once established and institutionalized, science achieves a measure of autonomy and generates its own momentum. Science becomes a career with recognizeable rewards. Posts become available in universities, schools, and industry, while scientists form learned societies and professional associations to promote their interests.[2] This view receives strong support from researches into scientific productivity in the nineteenth century. Ben-David[3] has calculated the number of discoveries in the medical sciences in the nineteenth century, and shows that whereas the contribution from Britain and France increased only slightly, that from Germany increased markedly. In 1880–9, for example, Germany had six times as many discoveries as England. The clue to the difference was the decentralization of the German universities which

[1] See R. Jungk, *Brighter than a Thousand Suns* (1958), for a vivid account of the dilemma of atomic scientists and their growing involvement with politics. See also, B. Barber and W. Hirsch, *op. cit.* (1962), Chapters 36 and 37, and N. Kaplan (ed.), *Science and Society* (1965), pp. 373–89.

[2] D. S. L. Cardwell, 'The Organization of Science in England', *op. cit.* (1957).

[3] Joseph Ben-David, 'Scientific Productivity and Academic Organization in Nineteenth Century Medicine', *A.S.R.*, Dec. 1960. Reprinted in B. Barber and W. Hirsch, *op. cit.* (1962), Chapter 20.

generated competition between them. Increasing subdivision and specialization lead to competition between universities to attract able scientists. 'Successful scientists were rewarded with university chairs and facilities. Their success encouraged others to take up science and, incidentally, transformed the pursuit of science into a regular professional career; it created pressure for further expansion of facilities and training, and exposed the inadequacies of out-of-date traditions.'[1]

The relatively slow growth of science in England before 1940 can be explained in similar terms. Career prospects were restricted. Not only were there few opportunities in the universities, but industry too employed few scientists, and then only in relatively subordinate positions. By contrast with Germany and France, qualifications in science and technology were unlikely to lead to a seat on the board. Moreover, in the scientific civil service, career prospects were inferior to those in the administrative grades. It is only since the increasing employment of scientists in industry mainly after the Second World War that there has been a marked expansion in those seeking scientific qualifications.[2]

Science as a belief system is more than simply a body of knowledge. Success in the world of science is judged by contributions to knowledge. The value of knowledge comes to be shared by the community of scientists[3] and in this way, its value becomes institutionalized. Various other values of science are generated in this way. The pursuit of knowledge as the primary goal for the scientist implies the subordination of other goals such as material gain or self interest to the quest for scientific truth. It requires, too, free communication of results, cutting across national and class barriers, and is hence universalist. Since the appeal of science is to empirically observed facts, personal bias must be avoided, and the personal characteristics of the investigator are irrelevant. It requires too, suspended judgment and an attitude of scepticism.[4] Such values, as we have seen in Chapter 8, may face the scientist with major conflicts as scientific careers are increasingly to be found outside the universities and research institutes, in industry and military research.

[1] *Ibid.*, p. 842.
[2] It is important to note that there has also been a large increase in the numbers of arts students so that the ratio of science to arts has not greatly changed. For a discussion of the relations between industry, science and technology, see S. F. Cotgrove, *Technical Education and Social Change* (1958), Chapter 7.
[3] For a discussion of the implications of the growth of the scientific community, see W. O. Hagstrom, *The Scientific Community* (1966).
[4] See R. K. Merton, *op. cit.* (1957), for a discussion of the values of science and their institutional imperatives.

IDEOLOGIES AND THE SOCIAL SYSTEM

Ideologies, as we have seen, are essentially related to action. Or as Bell has put it, 'ideology is the conversion of ideas into social levers.'[1] In order to win the widest possible support, they are couched in simple terms, reducing the complexities of social reality to ideological definitions. Moreover, they reflect the needs of specific groups for a guide to action and a legitimation of their claims. Mannheim has drawn a useful distinction between those ideas which defend existing interests, namely *ideologies*, and those which seek to change the social order, which he calls *utopias*.

There is some evidence for the view that secular ideologies can function as alternatives to religion. Support for the more extreme political ideologies appears to come from the same strata which also provide recruits for chiliastic movements. Trotsky recruited the first members of the South Russian Workers' Union from members of religious sects.[2] As Cohn points out,[3] revolutionary political ideologies have certain resemblances to their religious counterparts. In both, a final solution is envisaged which by a single revolutionary event (the proletarian revolution) will usher in the millennium. Hitler, for example, spoke of the Third Reich lasting for a thousand years. Cohn argues that when the existing structure of society is undermined, members of that society become less able to face calamity. When some major catastrophe strikes the lower and more exposed strata, the way is open for chiliastic social movements, couched in either religious or secular terms. Thus defeat in war, and unemployment, paved the way for the support of fascism by those whose social world had been most disrupted and who were then exposed to the catastrophic inflation of the late 1920s. It was from the lower middle class of small proprietors in particular, that Hitler gained much of his support.[4]

Political ideologies then, can be functional alternatives to religions. They offer alternative modes of adaptation to cope with situations of strain and conflict. Studies in Holland and Sweden show that communism is strongest in regions which were once centres of fundamentalist religion.[5] Moreover, some ideologies such as nationalism, by providing a shared goal, would appear highly successful in inte-

[1] D. Bell, *op. cit.* (1961), p. 400.
[2] S. M. Lipset, *op. cit.* (1960), p. 108.
[3] *Op. cit.*
[4] S. M. Lipset, *op. cit.* (1960), pp. 140–8.
[5] *Ibid.*, p. 108.

grating diverse religious and tribal units. Once independence is achieved, the integrating function of nationalism becomes less effective and the underlying conflicts reassert themselves.

Bell has argued for the 'end of ideology', claiming that today, the old ideologies are exhausted, and nothing has emerged to take their place. Events such as concentration camps and the suppression of the Hungarian workers have resulted in a disenchantment with utopias, and blueprints for social engineering, while the rise of the Welfare State has removed the existential basis for protest movements. Moreover, there is considerable convergence of ideas, and the old extreme positions on the role of the state are no longer held. Only in the newly emerging states of Africa and Asia are ideologies still alive, but they arise out of different social contexts and are ideologies of industrialization, modernization and nationalism, distinctively different from the ideologies of equality and freedom of the nineteenth century. There is a rejection of the older chiliastic vision of a 'new society'. The very absence of modern causes is reflected, he argues, in the anger of recent left wing writing,[1] which is remarkable for its failure to define the 'cause' which they seek.[2] Such a view perhaps under-emphasizes the continued existence in contemporary society of poverty and restricted opportunities. Race, for example, remains an explosive question, around which ideological movements might again crystallize, as they have in the past.

SUMMARY AND CONCLUSIONS

The role of beliefs in the social system is complex. The ways in which we define our experiences and the ways in which we react to circumstances are greatly influenced by our beliefs. Although these may largely reflect the prevailing beliefs of society, they must also meet the needs of individuals to adapt to their environments, and to cope with tensions and frustrations.

A wide variety of differing beliefs is capable of performing such functions. For some magic, for others religion, or a political ideology may provide a mode of orientation, adaptation and adjustment. Just which, will depend to some extent on those elements of the prevailing culture to which the individual has been exposed through socialization, and to some extent on the specific problems which his roles in society, or his physical and biological experiences have generated. In this way, the economic system and the political system

[1] E.g. *Convictions*.
[2] D. Bell, *op. cit.* (1961), pp. 402-7.

constitute important elements in the existential basis of beliefs. But they do not determine beliefs in any mechanistic way. Man's response will be shaped by the prevailing culture whether predominantly religious or secular.

But if man's beliefs respond to his changing environment, they also profoundly shape his environment. Science has enabled us to adapt to and to control our material circumstances and in this sense, it could be argued that ideas are the dynamic force in social change. To do so however, would be to overlook the complex inter-action between man and his material and cultural environment. Any such one-sided emphasis can only be avoided by conceptualizing the relationship as a system of inter-related elements in which culture, the social structure, and individuals are inconstant interaction.

The possibility that secular belief systems can perform the function of religious beliefs has been demonstrated. The trend away from religion, and certainly the transformation of religion in response to the challenge of science and philosophy to something much closer to contemporary secular beliefs appears to be established. Such trends prompt the question whether religion may eventually be replaced by non-religious beliefs? The major task facing such alternatives is the problem of tension management for those for whom life poses special problems. Where empirical means for the achievement of empirical ends have failed, the attraction of the non-empirical may well prove irresistable.

QUESTIONS AND EXERCISES

1. 'Religion is the use of non-empirical means for the attainment of non-empirical ends.' Explain and discuss the usefulness of this definition for sociological analysis.
2. How would you differentiate between magic and religion?
3. To what extent are non-religious beliefs functional alternatives to religious beliefs?
4. Examine the view that millenial cults are the response to extreme social conditions.
5. 'Religion is the opiate of the masses.' Is it?
6. Examine the alienation of the working classes from religion in nineteenth-century England.
7. Examine the problems involved in attempts to estimate trends in religious belief.
8. What is the social role of religion in contemporary England?
9. How would you account for the changing attitudes of the churches towards birth control?

10. What reasons have been put forward to account for the rise of science in the sixteenth and seventeenth centuries?
11. How would you account for the slow rate of growth of science in Britain compared with some European countries?
12. 'The end of ideology.' Discuss.
13. 'Politics is increasingly threatening the autonomy of science.' Discuss.

READING

M. Argyle.—*Religious Behaviour* (Routledge, 1958).
*D. Barber and W. Hirsch (eds.).—*The Sociology of Science* (Free Press, 1962), Chapters 2, 3, 4, 8, 18, 20, 36, 37.
D. Bell.—*The End of Ideology* (Collier Macmillan, 1962), especially Part III, 'The Exhaustion of Utopia'.
T. Brennan, E. W. Cooney and H. Pollins.—*Social Change in South West Wales* (Watts, 1954), Chapter 4. Explores the religious life of the Swansea area, and its declining influence for adaptation and integration.
D. S. L. Cardwell.—*The Organization of Science in England* (Heinemann, 1957).
N. Cohn.—*The Pursuit of the Millennium* (Secker & Warburg, 1957), Chapter 1 and Conclusion. A study of the sociological context of the chiliastic cults of the eleventh to sixteenth centuries, plus a brief comment on the view that political ideologies are their contemporary counterpart.
G. Lenski.—*The Religious Factor* (Doubleday, 1963). Explores the religious revival in America, and establishes by empirical research the role of religious sub-communities and the influence of religion on a number of variables.
*S. M. Lipset.—*Political Man* (Heinemann, 1960). Chapters IV and V analyse the factors making for support for extreme political ideologies. See especially pp. 106–8 for a summary of data on support for chiliastic religion.
R. K. Merton.—*Social Theory and Social Structure* (Free Press, 1957).
*K. Nottingham.—*Religion and Society* (Random House, 1954). An introductory text outlining the sociological perspectives on religion.
E. R. Wickham.—*Church and People in an Industrial Society* (Lutterworth Press, 1951). Argues that the industrial working class has always been alienated from the churches. The failure of the churches to meet the political and social challenge of industrialization plus the growing challenge of science is now losing them their traditional middle class support.
B. R. Wilson.—*Sects and Society* (Heinemann, 1961). An analysis of the teachings, social composition and functions of three sects (see especially Introduction and Conclusion).
*J. M. Yinger.—*Religion, Society and the Individual* (Macmillan, 1957). Includes a particularly useful section of thirty-nine 'readings'. See especially Introduction and Chapters 2, 3, 4, 5, 8, 9, and readings 8, 17, 20, 28, 29, 31.

Chapter 7

SOCIAL DIFFERENTIATION AND STRATIFICATION

Rich and poor, powerful and weak, honoured and despised—such dichotomies are widely characteristic of human societies. Prophets have denounced the exploitation of the poor, idealists have sought to establish utopian communities in which all are equal, and political reformers have set their feet on the road to a classless society. And yet differences in wealth, in power and in prestige stubbornly persist. Are such differences necessary for the functioning of any social system? Or are we, in fact, moving towards a more equalitarian society?

TYPES OF STRATIFICATION

We are confronted at the outset by a considerable semantic confusion. The word 'class' for example, is frequently used in everyday speech and writing with a variety of meanings. The lack of consensus among social scientists still further complicates the matter. We must distinguish, for example, between the facts of objective differences in income, prestige and power and the existence of *classes*, which are more than mere statistical aggregates of individuals, differentiated according to some such criterion. Class refers to the existence of solidary groupings which arise on the basis of such differences. Furthermore, we must distinguish between *class* and *stratification*. The latter term refers to the existence in a society of a hierarchy of layers marked off by differences in status. Thus, the nobility in feudal Europe constituted a *stratum*. Strata emerge therefore where there are clear-cut and consistent differences in the distribution of status which makes it possible to allocate individuals to a particular layer in the hierarchy.

There is, in fact, a variety of types of stratification, of which social classes are only one. These types can be distinguished according to the rigidity of the grades and the possibility of mobility between them, the nature of the sanctions by which the divisions are enforced, and the degree of functional specialization.[1] The estate system of feudal society was characterized by very restricted mobility, the divisions were enforced by legal sanctions, and each estate performed characteristic functions. The noble strata performed the political and military functions while the peasantry and serfs carried out menial tasks. Somewhat similar functional distinctions between prayers, fighters, and workers exist in the caste system of India, but here there is no possibility of movement between the rigid caste grades. Birth determines caste, and the distinctions are upheld by strong social and religious taboos which enforce rules of commensality and endogamy.

By contrast, in a social class system of stratification, there are no legal distinctions between classes—all are subject to the same laws and all have equal citizen rights.[2] The barriers to mobility are largely those of opportunity. How far differences in income, property, status and power underly the existence of distinctive classes, is a matter to which we shall now turn.

THE DISTRIBUTION OF DIFFERENCES

Differentiation and the economic system
Sociological researches have now provided us with a very substantial amount of empirical data on the differential distribution of property and income, power and prestige. But such material is largely descriptive. There has been less success in relating the facts of social differentiation to any satisfactory body of theory which provides a coherent explanatory framework. Much of the research on social differences has not, of course, been directed to any such attempt to understand the workings of social systems. In Britain, for example, much of our data has been collected as a basis for administrative policies to solve the problems of poverty. Booth's survey of poverty in London provided authoritative data on the size of the problem by demonstrating that one-third of the population of London in the

[1] M. Ginsberg, *Sociology* (1934).
[2] For a discussion of the extension of citizenship, see T. H. Marshall, *Citizenship and Social Class*, 1950.

1890s was living in poverty.[1] He also showed that over half this poverty was the result of irregular employment and low wages, while a further substantial fraction (about a quarter) was due to circumstances largely outside the control of the individual such as illness, infirmity, and large families. In the light of such data, it could no longer be argued that poverty was mainly a question of thriftlessness, or drink, and the case for state action in the form of unemployment insurance, labour exchanges, health insurance, and family allowances was greatly strengthened.[2]

Subsequent researches such as Bowley's survey of five towns showed a substantial reduction in the incidence of poverty in 1923-34 to only one third of that in 1913, due to two main causes—the decrease in the size of families plus higher wages.[3] In the inter-war years, unemployment became a primary cause of poverty, especially in the depression around 1930. But substantial differences in both income and property remain. Moreover, a relatively small number (1 per cent) of incomes of over £2,000 after tax take 5 per cent of the national income. Although taxation has reduced the differences in net incomes, there are still 28,000 incomes of over £4,000 net.[4] Moreover, it is probable that official statistics underestimate the size of real incomes enjoyed by the well-to-do, as they fail to take account of incomes in kind and other emoluments.[5]

Differences in the distribution of property are even more marked. The top 10 per cent of incomes own 43 per cent of the total liquid assets.[6] Less than 6 per cent of income units own stocks and shares, while these are heavily concentrated (52 per cent) in the top income groups (£2,000 plus). Twenty-two per cent own houses, but 10 per cent still have mortgages to pay off.

Such differences are clearly related to the position occupied by individuals and groups in the economic order. For Marx, for example, the key is to be found in the relation to property. Those who own productive resources such as factories, capital and land are contrasted with those who have only their labour to sell. The incomes derived from these sources (profits, interest, rent, and wages) differ greatly in size and security. A relatively small group of individuals take a disproportionately large share of the national product in the

[1] C. Booth, et al., Life and Labour of the People in London, 17 vols., 1902.

[2] M. Abrams, Social Surveys and Social Action, 1951.

[3] A. L. Bowley, Has Poverty Diminished? (1925).

[4] National Income and Expenditure.

[5] R. Titmuss, Income Distribution and Social Change (1962).

[6] H. F. Lydall, British Incomes and Savings (1955). See also A. M. Carr-Saunders, et al., op. cit. (1958), Chapters 11 and 13.

form of rent, interest and profits, (Table 7.1) although the marked decline in the share taken by property after the Second World War is notable.

Marx's approach, however, does not help us to explain the substantial differences in income among the propertyless. For Weber, the key to class differences is to be found in market situation, which

TABLE 7.1*

DISTRIBUTION OF THE NATIONAL INCOME

	1938 %	1952 %	1960 %
Wages	38	42	41
Salaries	18	21	24
Other	3	7	7
Self-employment	13	12	10
Rent, interest, profits	22	11	11
National insurance benefits	5	7	8

* National Income and Expenditure (1961).

he defined as '. . . the typical chance for a supply of goods, external living conditions, and personal life experiences, in so far as this chance is determined by the amount and kind of power . . . to dispose of goods or skills for the sake of income in a given economic order'.[1] Such an approach directs our attention to the factors which influence the 'amount and kind of power' in the market, such as skill and security. We have already seen in Chapter 4 that occupations adopt a variety of strategies to strengthen their market situations. There is little doubt that such techniques can have a considerable influence on the relative income of an occupation, particularly where (as in the printing trades) the union is able to exercise close control on recruitment through apprenticeship. But it is a matter of controversy whether the shift in the share of the national income going to wage-earners since 1938 is due to union action or to scarcity of labour.[2] In other words, income differentials can be seen partly as a function of the efforts of an occupational group to increase its share of the cake and partly as a function of the use of differentials by employers to stimulate the supply of both the quantity and quality of labour power. And since the division of labour results in differential skills, it can be argued that differential rewards are necessary to call them forth in the required amounts—a question to which we shall return later.

[1] H. H. Gerth and C. W. Mills, op. cit., p. 181.
[2] Full-employment and the increasing employment of married women have also contributed substantially to rising prosperity of manual workers.

Differentiation and the political system

The analysis so far implies that economic differentiation is entirely a function of the economic system. But, as previous chapters have shown, the economy is not autonomous, being particularly closely related to the political system. It could also be argued that the political system plays a major role in determining the distribution of rewards. It is political laws which confer powers in the market and over property. And political action can abolish the whole class of factory owners and businessmen. Moreover, political action has influenced the distribution of the national product through taxation. The bargaining power of labour has been strengthened by the right to strike, unemployment insurance, and full-employment policies. How far social benefits have redistributed incomes is more problematic. Vaizey has calculated that although the middle-class contribute a higher proportion to the costs of education, they also consume more, and on balance enjoy a net gain.[1] Martin[2] has demonstrated the differential consumption of health services; prescriptions for middle-class patients involving significantly greater cost than those for working-class patients.

But the relations between social differentiation and the political system are more fundamental than simply the effect of politics on economic rewards. The differential distribution of power and authority is as much a characteristic feature of societies as economic differences. Indeed, since organization is an essential feature of large scale societies, it can be argued that differences in power are a functional necessity. We have already seen in Chapter 5 that there is substantial concentration of political power, and that there is a close association between the economically and politically dominant strata. But whether social differentiation is best understood as a function of the political system or of the economic system and the relative importance to be attached to each, is still a matter for controversy.

Differentiation and Culture: The Status System

Utopia's frequently envisage an ideal society in which all men are judged to be equal. But with few exceptions, 'the differential evaluation of men as individuals and as members of social categories is a universal, formal property of social systems'.[3] The fact that there are

---

[1] J. Vaizey, *The Costs of Education* (1958).
[2] J. P. Martin, *Social Aspects of Prescribing* (1957).
[3] R. Williams, *American Society* (1961), p. 88.

differences in skin-colour, income, position, age, sex, intelligence, does not by itself result in *social stratification*. This depends on the meaning which society gives to the objective differences. It is the cultural definitions and meanings of wealth, skin colour, sex or age which gives them social significance. The differences can persist, but the cultural definitions change. Money or birth can become more or less important as bases for social stratification.

It is this fact which Max Weber stresses when he insists that status differentiation is analytically distinct from economically determined differences in class situation.[1] Status is the social evaluation of the individual—the degree of honour which society confers on him. Income and property do not by themselves ensure the conferment of high status although in the long run, they are closely related to it. Titles are examples of status in our society. Wealth by itself does not carry the automatic right to a title, nor does its absence debarr a title. Empirical studies of the prestige of occupations confirm that the criteria by which an occupation is allocated to a position in the prestige hierarchy are complex. The ranking of occupations in terms of prestige does not correspond exactly to their ranking in terms of income, although there is normally a significant correlation between the two rankings. Other factors may enter into the ranking process. Status may be *ascribed* or conferred on the basis of the possession of some quality. Birth, for example, or inborn personal qualities such as skin colour, may be the criterion for status ascription. Or status may be *achieved* by personal effort, such as the passing of examinations and the conferment of degrees or titles. Parsons[2] has identified six main criteria: (1) birth, (2) possessions, (3) personal qualities, (4) personal achievement, (5) authority, (6) power.

The relation between an individual's ranking on a number of criteria, such as occupation, income education, and ethnic group can be close, or there may be a lack of congruence between such rankings. If there is a good 'fit' between a persons position in each of the major rankings, then this indicates a high degree of *status consistency* (or status crystallization).[3] A person may, for example, be highly qualified educationally, but be a member of an ethnic group or occupation with a relatively low status. Where there is a high degree of status consistency, we may refer to the individual's status profile

[1] H. H. Gerth and C. W. Mills, *op. cit.* (1947), pp. 186–7.

[2] T. Parsons, 'An Analytical Approach to the Theory of Social Stratification', *A.J.S.*, May 1940, pp. 848–9.

[3] See L. Broom, 'Social Differentiation and Stratification', in R. K. Merton, L. Broom and L. S. Cottrell, Jr, *Sociology Today: Problems and Prospects* (1959).

as flat, compared with the irregular profile of status inconsistency.

There is a considerable volume of empirical research which demonstrates general agreement on the social grading of occupations, and shows that there is substantial congruence between the rank order of different industrial countries. Hall and Jones asked respondents to rank thirty occupations in relation to each other according to their social standing in the community. Differences in the age, sex, or occupation of the respondents were found to have little effect on the ranking. The investigators had previously allocated each of these occupations to seven categories, differing in degrees of specialization, skill and responsibility. The researches confirmed that the general public were agreed in ranking occupations in the same order of prestige as that adopted by the researchers in allocating occupations to the seven categories.[1] Comparable studies in America and elsewhere show that differences are small.

Perhaps the most significant inquiry is that of Young and Willmott[2] among a working-class sample in East London. They found that about one-quarter of their respondents ('deviants') differed significantly in their ranking. Skilled manual jobs were elevated while non-manual occupations such as insurance agent, clerk, and shop assistant were lowered. The 'deviants' differed greatly from the 'normal' in their criteria for judgment, all but one giving 'social contribution' as the basis for elevating or depressing the prestige of an occupation.

Status rankings function to legitimize differences in the distribution of wealth and power. Those who have power are honoured, and their status underpins their exercise of power. The enjoyment of deference and privileges, such as exemption from unpleasant tasks, special immunities (from taxes, military service, prosecution by the common courts) is tolerated while it is accepted that rank confers a title to such privileges. An example of this is the view often expressed by non-manual workers that they 'ought' to be better paid than manual workers, even though their work may be less skilled.[3] This is simply another way of saying that in a stable social system, we can expect congruence between the values of society and other aspects of the social structure. Those who occupy dominant roles largely control the manipulation of rewards, including the conferment of such

[1] J. R. Hall and C. A. Moser, 'The Social Grading of Occupations', in D. Glass (ed.), *Social Mobility in Britain* (1953), Chapter II.

[2] M. Young and P. Willmott, 'Social Grading by Manual Workers', *B.J.S.*, Dec. 1956.

[3] See also discussion of status in Chapter 4.

symbols of status as honorific titles. And if property and income are highly valued, material rewards will also function as symbols of social honour, while those who are honoured will be defined as entitled to wealth and privilege. The ranking of individuals in society is *institutionalized* in the sense that it reflects the norms of society. Of course, such norms may come to be challenged, as when the legitimacy of the claims of an aristocracy is called in question.

CLASS SOLIDARITY

So far, this discussion has deliberately avoided using words like 'middle-class' and 'working-class' wherever possible. Such words in the vocabularly of social differentiation are ambiguous in meaning and present considerable difficulty. They imply the existence of a group of individuals which is more than simply a statistical aggregate like 'tall men'. Indeed, some textbooks of sociology include a discussion of social classes as part of the analysis of the organization of society.

Now we need to tread cautiously in moving from a description of the distribution of differences in income, property or prestige to the assumption that actual groupings have evolved on the basis of such differences. Marx, for example, was aware of the fact that the common experiences of those occupying similar roles in the production process did not necessarily result in the formation of a class. It is only when such individuals become aware of their common fate and come together for collective action that they are transformed from a 'class in itself' to a 'class for itself'. The facts of class, as Tawney[1] has reminded us, are not the same thing as the consciousness of class.

We need further to distinguish between a *class* and a *stratum*. Social strata are aggregates of individuals with similar social status. Strata are statistical constructs. But where a stratum is relatively homogeneous, composed of individuals with flat status profiles, there is more likelihood that its members will become aware of the stratum as a distinct entity, and its relation to others in the hierarchy of strata. Such shared perceptions and awareness of shared interests can become the basis for the transformation of a stratum into a class.[2]

We can then distinguish four main elements in the process of increasing social solidarity on the basis of the differential distribu-

[1] R. H. Tawney, *Equality* (1952).
[2] L. Broom, *op. cit.*

tion of rewards.[1] Firstly there is the consciousness of identity, of belonging to a group with common characteristics and a common fate. Secondly, there is the emergence of shared beliefs, attitudes and values (culture). Thirdly, there is the increasing interaction between members of such emerging groups. And finally, there is concerted action for the pursuit of common interests through the formation of class associations such as political parties.

Class identity and class consciousness:

In a study by F. M. Martin,[2] subjects in Greenwich and Hertford were asked 'How many social classes would you say, there are in this country?' 'Can you name them?' 'Which of these classes do you belong to?' Ninety-six per cent of the sample saw society as being divided into three main classes, upper, middle, and working, 36.6 per cent replying that they were 'working-class' and 42.5 per cent 'middle-class'. A further 9 per cent replied 'lower-class' or 'poor'. Most, that is to say, think of society as being divided into two main classes and are able to allocate themselves to one of these categories. The relation between occupation and class identity can be seen from Table 7.2. Two-thirds of non-manual workers thought of themselves as middle-class, compared with one-quarter of manual workers.

TABLE 7.2

	Occupation	Class identity	%
A.	Professional, managerial	Middle class	93
B.	Other non-manual	Middle class	65
C.	,, ,,	Working class	32
D.	Manual	Middle class	26
E.	,,	Working class	70

To know that a person thinks of himself as middle-class tells us little unless we also know the meaning which he gives to the term. The 'deviant' groups C and E in Table 7.2 are of particular interest in this context, that is to say, non-manual workers who identify with the working-class and manual workers calling themselves 'middle-class'. Martin found that these two groups in fact gave rather different answers to the questions, 'What sort of people belong to the same class as yourself?' Most respondents defined the working-class in occupational terms as manual workers, factory workers, or artisans. But group D who defined themselves as middle-class, also had a

[1] R. Williams, *op. cit.*, p. 92.
[2] In D. V. Glass (ed.), *op. cit.* (1954), Chapter 3.

different frame of reference by which they assessed membership of the working class. They were much more likely to define working class in terms of low income and standard of living and in moral and evaluatuve terms such as laziness and lack of ambition. Similarly, group C defined 'working-class' as 'everyone who works for a living' and extended the working-class to embrace minor non-manual occupations. It is not suprising, too, to find that respondents differed in their allocation of occupations to class categories. Group C, the salaried working-class, tended to extend the description 'working-class' to workers in occupations similar to their own.

Such data confirm that although the notion that society is divided into classes is widely accepted, that there is considerable confusion as to what constitutes the basis for inclusion, in either main category. It is difficult however to know what significance to attach to these findings. Existing researches do not tell us the degree of importance which respondents attach to their class identity. For some, being 'working class' may be a most significant element in their identity which influences their behaviour in a number of ways, especially voting behaviour. For others, it may be a largely meaningless label. We will therefore turn to such evidence in a later section. One other tentative conclusion can be drawn. Those who are not rewarded by the existing social system by income and prestige, can adopt a number of strategies. One, we have already seen, is to reject the prevailing social norms which fail to attach sufficient value to their particular role. Another is to redefine the norms themselves in such a way that the prestigeful categories are extended to include them. This is apparently the strategy of many manual workers who are rejecting the label 'working-class'.

Class sub-cultures

On theoretical grounds, it is to be expected that different experiences will be associated with differences in beliefs and values.[1] In Chapter 4 we have seen that occupational experiences can have a significant influence on beliefs and behaviour. There is a wealth of data which demonstrates large differences in beliefs between aggregates of persons classified according to income, degree of skill, whether owners of businesses or workers, and other variables. But such aggregates do not constitute 'classes'. What is much more difficult to demonstrate is the existence of distinctive class sub-cultures, held by those who are conscious of a class identity. Differences in cultural orientations associated with differences in the distribution of rewards,

[1] See Chapter 6.

prestige, and power will first be outlined before attempting an answer to the more difficult question as to how far such differences coalesce into distinctive class sub-cultures.

TABLE 7.3*

INCOME AND THE CONSERVATIVE VOTE

	%
Well-to-do	86·5
Middle	68·5
Lower	40·5
Very poor	27·5

* Tables 7.3, 4, and 5 are adapted from J. Bonham, 'The Middle Class Elector', *B.J.S.*, Sept. 1952.

TABLE 7.4

INDUSTRIAL STATUS AND THE CONSERVATIVE VOTE

	%
Business proprietors	
Middle income	78
Lower income	71
Employees	
Middle income	62
Lower income	38

TABLE 7.5

MANUAL/NON-MANUAL WORK AND THE CONSERVATIVE VOTE
(employees, lower income)

	%
Non-manual	52
Manual	31

Studies of voting behaviour offer indirect evidence on the relation between beliefs and social differences. Business proprietors, for example, have a high conservative vote compared with employees, where the decline in the conservative vote is particularly marked in the low income group. (Table 7.4). Manual workers are also less likely to vote conservative than non-manual workers in the same income group.[1] (Table 7.5.)

The support of lower paid manual workers for the Labour Party

[1] This is far from a complete explanation of voting behaviour. A number of other factors, such as social origins, are also significant variables. Manual worker parentage reduces the Conservative vote from 69 per cent to 31 per cent.

is not by itself evidence of distinctive class attitudes. There is, however, direct evidence that many see political parties as pursuing class interest, and that their support is influenced by their own class identity. A study by Mark Abrams[1] showed that those who do not support the Labour Party see themselves as middle-class and identify the Labour Party with poor people and factory workers Other researches demonstrate that those who identify with the working class are more likely than others to vote Labour (Table 7.6).

TABLE 7.6

CLASS IDENTITY AND THE LABOUR VOTE*
(Greenwich, 1951)

	Identity	Per cent voting Labour
Non-manual —	middle class	22
	— working class	44
Manual	— middle class	51
	— working class	72

* Adapted from F. M. Martin, 'Social Status and Electoral Choice in Two Constituencies', *B.J.S.*, Sept. 1952.

One further aspect of differentiation which has been shown to be related to political radicalism is status consistency. Lenski has found that low status consistency is associated with political liberalism in the United States, particularly where relatively low ethnic status is accompanied by relatively high income, occupational or educational status.[2]

Inconsistency between subjective and socially ascribed status could also be expected to be associated with political radicalism. If status rankings are, in fact, evidence of consensus on the legitimacy of the differential distribution of power, and income, then we could expect 'deviants' to question the legitimacy of the existing order and to adopt radical political attitudes. Young and Willmott[3] recognize this, and their inquiry provides some supporting evidence. Moreover, as they point out, such attitudes are consistent with the traditional ideology of the Labour movement which challenges the justice of the established distribution of rewards.

[1] M. Abrams and R. Rose, *Must Labour Lose?* (1960).

[2] G. E. Lenski, 'Status Crystallization: A Non-Vertical Dimension of Social Status', *A.S.R.*, Vol. 19, 1954. Status inconsistency has also been found to be associated with psychological and physical symptoms of stress. E. F. Jackson, 'Status Consistency and Symptoms of Stress', *A.S.R.*, Vol. 27, 1962.

[3] *Op. cit.*, 1956.

But the differences in attitudes and beliefs in English society go beyond beliefs on economic and political issues. There is a wealth of documentary evidence on the cultural differences between broad strata such as manual and non-manual workers. Klein[1] draws a distinction between the traditional and the mobile among both manual and non-manual workers, which helps to throw light on the extent to which such differences are related to class identity and consciousness. The sub-cultural orientations of manual workers will be taken as an example.

Traditional manual-workers live in relatively stable communities, characterized by a close-knit social network.[2] These are conditions which favour concensus on norms and the perpetuation of tradition. Neighbourliness, a sense of community and mutual self-help are highly valued. There are permissive and indulgent attitudes towards children and adolescents—'you're only young once'. There is a deep emotional attachment to home, and a reluctance to move far away. Pleasures are taken as they come (short-term hedonism)—there is little long-term saving, and the periodic 'splash' on the occasion of a wedding, Christmas, holidays or similar event absorbs a large part of the budget. But at the same time, there is an emphasis among the 'respectable' stratum on cleanliness, thrift, and self-respect. The 'splash' is an institutionalized and regulated extravagance which co-exists with an anxiety to avoid being submerged by poverty and circumstances. Above all, the traditional working man seeks to make 'them' appreciate his respectability. The world is seen in terms of 'them' and 'us'—'They' are the bosses, people at the top, tell you what to do 'treat y' like muck'.[3]

Many aspects of this traditional culture are undergoing change. Although some of these changes are associated with the growth of new housing estates, the movement of populations from traditional areas, while it is disruptive, does not lead to changed patterns of living unless other social changes take place at the same time (such as the effect of war, affluence, and the mass media).[4]

With the decline in the close-knit social network, there is more emphasis on individual self-reliance. There is a new attitude towards saving, with a shift of expenditure towards household furnishings and consumer durables, with much time spent on redecorating—the growth of home-centredness. Borrowing and popping in and out are no

[1] J. Klein, *Samples from English Culture* (1965), Vol. 1.
[2] See Chapter 2 for a more detailed discussion of this concept.
[3] Summarized from J. Klein, *op. cit.* (1965), Chapter 4.
[4] *Ibid.*, p. 222.

longer approved. But a more complete analysis of changes would raise the question whether the working-class are becoming middle-class, which must be postponed until a later section. So, too, must the question whether the distinctive subcultures of manual-workers is in any sense a class subculture.

Interaction and association

Reference has already been made to the distinctive interaction patterns which characterize the traditional manual-workers' community. The close-knit community leads to informal relations but notions of privacy exclude strangers who are not close friends or kin. Under such circumstances, there may be less need for membership of formal associations and consequently there is considerably less joining of clubs and voluntary associations. The associations joined such as darts clubs, require relatively little organization and will largely exclude non-manual workers. In other words, for many, the pub is also the club, providing a locus for whatever association is needed outside the informal relations of the social network. There is, in other words, a full associational life, but it takes place largely outside formal organizations.

There appear to be a number of factors underlying this reluctance of working men to join formally organized associations. Among these is a fear of commitment which inhibits entering into any obligation which looks like a contract, together with a dislike of being pushed around. Problems of communication between different strata are also contributory factors. Bernstein[1] has drawn attention to the restricted language forms characteristic of close-knit kinship system which hinder the verbal expression and therefore social inter-action outside the network, Working-men's teams and clubs are differentiated from the more formal associations by what Klein[2] calls 'effortless sociability'. Notification is casual, and no one worries if he is absent. Middle-class associations require more formal commitment, and activities are planned further ahead. But there is no doubt that 'there are strong influences towards segregation in accordance with occupational status'.[3]

Other evidence of the restricted interaction between strata comes from data on marriage. There is a particularly high degree of association between the social origins of brides and grooms at the top and bottom of the social ladder, although there has been a slight decline

[1] B. Bernstein, in A. H. Halsey, *et al., op cit.* (1961).
[2] *Op. cit.* (1965), p. 212.
[3] *Ibid.*

over the last fifty years.[1] There is also a tendency for grooms to marry brides with a similar educational background, which is particularly strong among those with secondary or further education.

SOCIAL MOBILITY

One factor influencing the extent to which strata coalesce into solidary groupings is the degree to which they are self-recruiting. Restricted mobility facilitates the protection of privileges by a stratum and the development and persistence of a unitary culture. It is widely believed, particularly in America, that modern industrial societies in fact make possible a substantial degree of mobility and are in this sense 'open' societies, in which there is a reasonably close relation between a person's ability and his position in society. Status is achieved on the basis of merit rather than ascribed by birth. Before examining the relevant evidence, it is first necessary to look more closely at what we mean by social mobility, how it is measured, and the factors which offset it.

In investigating mobility, we want to know how the position which individuals achieve in society differs from that of their family of origin. The method widely used by sociologists is to compare the status of fathers and sons, using occupation as the index of status. The same status scale is used by classifying both fathers and sons and it is assumed therefore, that there have been no marked changes in occupational status. Such an approach measures mobility by using only one dimension of stratification—*status*—and ignores others such as *power* and *class*. It also faces the practical difficulty that at the time of the inquiry, sons may not have reached the height of their careers. However, movement within a generation is very much less than between generations.[2] Seventy-nine per cent of those who begin as manual workers remain in this category.[3]

Even when we know how the statuses of fathers and sons compare, there is still a considerable problem of interpretation. Industrialization has resulted in a very considerable change in the occupational structure. There has been a relative decline in the primary extractive industries such as agriculture, and an increase, especially in the later

[1] D. V. Glass (ed.), *op. cit.* (1954).
[2] D. V. Glass, *op. cit.* (1954).
[3] G. Thomas, *The Social Survey: Labour Mobility in Britain* 1945–1949. With the increase in the importance of education as the determinant of occupation, there are signs of a *decrease* in career mobility. See Acton Society Trust, *Management Succession* (1956).

stages, of tertiary service industries, including clerical work, and professional and technical occupations.[1] In other words, there has been an increase in the proportion of higher status non-manual occupations. This alone will account for some improvement in the statuses of sons compared with fathers. In 1881, for example, 21.5 per cent of occupied males in England were non-manual workers, compared with 27 per cent in 1951.

A second factor influencing comparisons of intergenerational status is a demographic one—the relative fertility rates of different strata.[2] Since non-manual workers have smaller families, some non-manual jobs will have to be recruited from the sons of manual workers, even if the proportion of such jobs remains constant.

The comparisons of statuses between generations raises a further difficulty. In a society in which 80 per cent of the population are peasants and agricultural labourers, we could expect 80 per cent of their sons to remain peasants and labourers, assuming a perfectly random distribution of occupations among sons, with no bias whatever. In other words, we have to take account of the size of various occupational groups in our attempts to measure the degree of mobility.[3] The more closely the numbers recruited to any status category are proportionate to their numbers in the population, the nearer we are to 'perfect' mobility.[4]

The extent of mobility
Perhaps the simplest picture of the extent of mobility in Britain can be gained from Table 7.7. From this it would appear that around 40 per cent of sons are upwardly mobile, and that there has been little change over the last five decades. The decline for those born in 1920–9 must take account of the fact that at the time of the survey (1949), these men were between 20 and 29 and had not therefore reached the top of their careers.

Precise international comparisons are not possible since surveys in other countries are not strictly comparable. But the proportion of non-manual sons of manual fathers varies from 29 per cent in Germany to 33 per cent in the United States and 45 per cent in Switzerland.[5] It is interesting to note that the perception which

[1] See Chapter 4.
[2] See Chapter 2.
[3] See D. V. Glass, *op. cit.* (1954), Chapter 8, for a discussion of statistical methods of calculating an index of mobility.
[4] This phrase does not imply that such a degree of mobility is desirable.
[5] S. M. Lipset and R. Bendix, *Social Mobility in Industrial Society* (1959), p. 24.

individuals have of the opportunity structure does not necessarily correspond to the facts, notably, the view that mobility is high in the United States and low in Europe.

Two points need to be made to qualify this picture. Firstly, the amount of movement is limited—typically one or two status categories. Secondly, such data fails to bring out the high dgree of self-recruitment in the higher strata. This can be made clearer by referring to the index of association between the statuses of fathers

TABLE 7.7*

PERCENTAGE OF SUBJECTS WITH HIGHER OR LOWER STATUS THAN THEIR FATHERS

Date of birth of subjects	Higher %	Lower %
Before 1890	31·8	34·8
1890–99	43·1	23·0
1900–09	44·1	21·5
1910–19	42·7	10·9
1920–29	33·7	29·3

* Taken from D. V. Glass, *op. cit.* (1954), Table 8, p. 188.

TABLE 7.8*

ASSOCIATION BETWEEN STATUSES OF FATHERS AND SONS

Status category	Index of association
1	13·158
2	5·865
3	1·997
4	1·618
5	1·157
6	1·841
7	2·259

* *Ibid.*

and sons (Table 7.8). This index takes account of the relative size of status groups and the fact that if there were 'perfect' mobility strata would be recruited proportionately to their size in the population. An index of '1' indicates perfect mobility in this sense.

The high degree of self-recruitment of status categories 1 and 2 can be seen in Table 7.8. By contrast, category 5 (skilled manual and routine non-manual) includes only slightly more sons whose fathers were in the same group than could be expected from the fact that this group comprises nearly 50 per cent of the population. For category 1, nearly 50 per cent of the fathers were in the same category, but as this is a small group, the index of association (ratio of self-recruitment) is high. To put it more simply, nearly half those in status category 1 are the sons of a small group comprising only 3.7 per cent of the population.

In summary, although rather more than one-third of sons have a higher status than their fathers, the shift is seldom more than one category, and takes place mainly in the middle ranges of the status hierarchy. Moreover, mobility to the highest stratum is relatively small.

Elite mobility
Studies of the recruitment of particular elites provide more detailed and precise information on elite self-recruitment. About 60 per cent of the businessmen in Britain[1] and the United States are the sons of businessmen. Studies of the higher civil service show that 48 per cent attended public schools while 30 per cent came from families of property owners and professionals which comprise only 3 per cent of the population.[2] Studies of high court judges, bishops, and cabinet ministers show a similar preponderance of those drawn from the upper echelons of society. Such evidence supports the view that industrial societies are characterized by a high degree of mobility only if mobility is conceived in a somewhat restricted sense. It also suggests the mobility to positions of power is even more restricted and in this sense, there is still relatively little mobility in contemporary societies. Elite strata have, that is to say, a number of strategies, such as the public schools, which enable them to preserve their positions for their sons. But although the movement between one generation and the next may be less than supposed, the cumulative effect of changes over a number of generations could be expected to be considerably greater.

The process of social mobility
Most research on mobility has concentrated on the amount of movement between generations. Less is know about the mobility process, and the actual mechanisms by which individuals move up or down the social ladder and the consequences of such movement.

The chances of movement between generations depends not only on variables such as differential fertility and occupational change. It depends too, on the avenues which exist for upward or downward mobility and the existence of barriers hindering mobility. One major

[1] G. H. Copeman, *Leaders of British Industry* (1955); Acton Society Trust, *Management Succession* (1956).
[2] R. K. Kelsall, *Higher Civil Servants in Britain* (1955).

reason for expecting an increase in mobility in industrial societies is the growth in the numbers of occupations requiring educational qualifications, and in the expanding role of bureaucratic organizations such as central government and large scale industrial and commercial undertakings using formal criteria for recruitment and promotion. There has been a corresponding decline in the number of inheritable positions. But although these changes have opened up fresh avenues of mobility, it must also be remembered that other avenues have become more restricted. The increasing capitalization of production has made successful entrepreneurship more difficult. Moreover, it is becoming increasingly hard for the small shopkeeper to survive, whereas in the latter part of the nineteenth century, rapid population growth, urbanization, and rising levels of living had resulted in retail trade providing a significant avenue for mobility.

There is considerable evidence on the role of education in mobility and on the relation between ability and occupational achievement. Studies in Britain show that the type of schooling significantly affects the association between the statuses of fathers and sons. The grammar school is the decisive stage. But as we have seen,[1] both access to education and educational achievement are heavily influenced by parental background. Consequently, the influence of education modifies but does not destroy the association between the status of father and son. Thus in the British mobility survey 40 per cent of the sons of status category 5 (43 per cent of the sample) who attended independent schools achieved categories 1 and 2, compared with only 2.3 per cent of those attending elementary schools.[2] By contrast, 66 per cent of the sons of categories 1 and 2 (8 per cent of the sample) attending independent schools achieved categories 1 and 2, but so did 26 per cent of those who had not attended grammar school.[3] In other words, not only are the chances of attending a grammar school less for able children in working class homes, but the chance that a grammar school education will lead to the higher rungs of the occupational ladder are also considerably reduced for the sons of manual workers. That is to say, education is a factor in social mobility, but it is by no means the only one. Not only is educational opportunity restricted for those from working-class homes, but so are the occupational opportunities of those who have reached similar levels in the educational system.

[1] Chapter 3.
[2] This term refers to the non-grammar schools pre-1945 in which education normally ceased at fourteen.
[3] D. V. Glass, *op. cit.* (1954), Chapter 10.

But mobility is a function not only of the opportunity structure and the ability of the individual. It is related also the extent to which the individual is motivated to climb the social ladder. And this in turn will be determined in part by the culture of society, specifically the prevailing mobility norms which may value or discourage upward striving, and the extent to which society is defined as providing opportunities for mobility. But there is also evidence to suggest that quite complex personality differences exist which help to explain why individuals with similar levels of ability experience differing degrees of mobility.[1] Studies suggest that the upwardly mobile have received earlier training for independence, have had more opportunities for interaction with adults, have the capacity to deal with others instrumentally, rather than emotionally, have learned to defer present gratifications, and have higher rates of mental disturbances. Researches also indicate that such differences are related to sociological variables such as parent-child relationships. It suggests, for example that upwardly-mobile children are likely to come from homes where parents have adopted higher status groups as reference groups and have subjected their children to anticipatory socialization into middle-class norms, and in which parental approval is conditional upon the mastery of tasks.[2]

Further evidence on the mobility process comes from studies of the factors influencing the choice of, and entry into, occupations. Children from working-class homes have a restricted knowledge of the range of occupations open to them. They are unlikely to have relatives who are accountants, solicitors, or businessmen. They are far more likely to be influenced in their occupational choice by *significant others*, such as father, elder brother or uncle, and for this reason, many will follow in the footsteps of an admired relative.[3] It is first occupation which is the crucial choice. Once a manual job has been taken, there is little chance of mobility. In short, the boy whose father is semi- or unskilled is handicapped in a variety of ways. Early socialization is unlikely to have developed the personality characteristics of the upwardly mobile, such as deferred gratification and strong achievement motivation; he is likely to be an under-achiever at school and to acquire a distaste for his studies; his range of occupational

[1] For a survey of the literature, see D. F. Swift, 'Social Class and Achievement Motivation', *Educational Research*, Feb. 1966.

[2] See S. M. Lipset and R. Bendix, *op. cit.* (1959), for a summary of such researches.

[3] R. F. L. Logan and E. M. Goldberg, 'Rising Eighteen in a London Suburb', *B.J.S.*, Vol. 4, pp. 323–45; M. Carter, *Home, School and Work* (1962), and *Into Work* (1966).

choice will be restricted by inadequate educational qualifications, and by lack of knowledge of the requirements and strategies for occupational mobility. His subsequent choice is likely to be strongly influenced by admired individuals within his own immediate social sphere, and once chosen at 15 or 16, his future career is more or less determined.

Social mobility and the social system

Social mobility is not only a function of the occupational structure, differential fertility, and cultural variables. It also has consequences for the social system. A society which rewards success raises problems for those who fail. Upward mobility it must be remembered, also implies related degrees of downward mobility. Underlying much research and writing on mobility, there is the assumption that it is a 'good thing' and that a high rate of mobility is both socially and morally desirable. Such judgments can only be sustained on the basis of factual knowledge as to the actual consequences of high and low rates of mobility.

One of the most interesting findings is that the consequences of mobility vary considerably according to the society. In America, for example, the upwardly mobile are more conservative than the group from which they came, whereas in Germany, Norway and Sweden they are more radical. A possible explanation is that in Europe, shifts from one class to another require greater adjustments in the style of life than in America. In Sweden, upwardly mobile workers who adopt middle-class styles of life, exemplified by acquiring a car, are much more likely to vote non-socialist.[1]

Such differences however, do not appear among the downwardly mobile. In all countries, these give less support to working-class organizations and politics than those who inherit working-class status. One possible result of downward mobility therefore, is to weaken working-class solidarity.[2]

Some indication of the possible strains generated by mobility comes from evidence on the incidence of suicide and mental disorder, which is higher among the mobile than the non-mobile. A possible explanation is that mobility removes the individual from the primary-group support which results from the disruption of family and friendship cliques.[3] But the possibility that a degree of mental disorder is a cause rather than a consequence of mobility must not be overlooked.

[1] S. M. Lipset and R. Bendix, *op. cit.* (1959), pp. 66–7.
[2] *Ibid.*, pp. 69–70.
[3] *Ibid.*, p. 65.

Cultures such as America which stress the value of success raise particular problems of adjustment for failure. As we have seen in the last chapter, one possible mode of adjustment for those who fail to achieve success by legitimate means is to seek illegitimate and deviant avenues. Another possible adjustment is support for transvaluational religions or radical politics.[1] A third possible adjustment is to become child-centred and to seek vicarious satisfaction in high aspirations for ones children. All such evidence suggests that high rates of mobility are to some extent disruptive. But they do not by themselves result in social instability as there are examples of stable societies such as Britain and America in which mobility is relatively high. By contrast, the acquisition of wealth by the eighteenth-century French bourgeoisie generated status discrepancies and revolutionary zeal among those who felt that they were being denied status and power commensurate with their wealth—a further reminder that it is not enough to study mobility along one dimension only.

UPPER, MIDDLE AND WORKING CLASSES

Although the evidence is far from complete, there seems little doubt that classes exist in a more solidary form than mere statistical aggregates of individuals of similar income, occupation, or prestige. There is a consciousness of kind, of belonging to perceived and defineable groups, marked off by differences in beliefs and values and styles of life. Visiting, eating together (commensality), intermarriage, membership of clubs,—all of these interactions are structured by an awareness of status differences. It is status groups, differentiated by occupation and styles of life which are the basis of such distinctions. Above all, it is the divide between banausic manual work and higher status white-collar jobs which is particularly significant. And it is an emphasis on consumption rather than role in the production process which is crucial. Such 'estates' are particularly clear-cut at the top, where membership of 'society' is a matter of acceptance. Here, a small elite of wealth and power are united by multiple bonds of association, intermarriage, and membership of exclusive clubs.[2] It is such considerations which have led some sociologists to argue that it is status rather than class which is the characteristic feature of contemporary industrial societies.[3]

[1] The evidence for this was examined in Chapter 6.
[2] A. Sampson, *Anatomy of Britain* (1962).
[3] In my view, this argument attaches insufficient importance to the very real differences in income, property and, above all, power which exist.

It is in this sense then, that we can speak of upper, middle and lower classes. They are not clear-cut groups, nor are they organized. But there is a consciousness of identity with others among those from broadly similar income and occupational groups which leads to support for political parties which are believed to pursue class interests, and which is the basis for segregation in associational membership and which structures social interactions.

STRATIFICATION AND SOCIAL CHANGE

Two main debates provide clues on the possible long term trends in stratification in industrial societies. In America, a paper by Davis and Moore in 1945[1] started one of the most long-lived discussions in contemporary sociology. Moore explained the universality of stratification in functional terms, arguing that differentiation is a functional necessity in any society. It functions to motivate individuals to fill the various positions required by the division of labour and to carry out the necessary duties. It follows, therefore, that there are limits to any trend towards equality. On the other hand, it has been argued that industrialization is resulting in substantial convergence between the stratification systems of advanced societies in which all are moving towards a minimizing of differences and towards a greater consistency between income, education, and prestige. In Britain, considerable debate has centred around the view that affluence and mobility are eroding the traditional working-class with its support for working-class associations such as the Labour Party, and trade unions.[2]

The embourgeoisement of the working-class

Many in both the United States and in Europe have claimed to detect a trend towards the blurring of class lines, and the disappearance of cleavage between manual and non-manual. The argument rests on the assertion that income differentials have declined and that the achievement of middle-class incomes by many manual workers is accompanied by the adoption of middle-class styles of life.

A careful study of the empirical evidence however, does not support this view. American data shows that the apparent overlap between clerical and skilled manual median incomes ignores the influence

[1] Kingsley Davis and Wilbert E. Moore, 'Some Principles of Stratification', *A.S.R.*, Vol. 10, 1945.
[2] This debate has largely centred round the electoral position of the Labour Party. See Mark Abrams and Richard Rose, *Must Labour Lose?* (Penguin, 1960).

of sex and age. Clerical work employs large numbers of women, while for many men, it is a stepping stone to managerial positions which are reached in middle age. When these two factors are controlled, clerical incomes are considerably above those of craftsmen and foremen except for the over-45s, which includes mainly those males who have been unsuccessful in achieving promotion. If foremen are excluded from the manual group, the differences increase.[1] Studies in Germany suggest that there has, in fact, been a widening of the gap between middle and working-class judged by the percentage owning consumer durables in 1953 and 1959.

But the achievement of comparable incomes does not in any case justify the assumption that these will be spent on similar 'life-styles'. German evidence shows marked differences between manual and non-manual workers in the ownership of durable consumer goods, even when income is controlled.[2] Middle-class homes have more luxury goods and expensive household aids. Working-class homes are superior to the equivalent middle-class income group mainly in possession of more expensive television sets and record-players; that is, in items of home entertainment. There also are marked differences in attitudes toward liquidity and savings. In a more impressionistic study, Zweig[3] found similar attitudes and patterns of expenditure among British workers.

But even if it could be demonstrated that some manual workers aspire to middle-class styles of life, this is not evidence of assimilation. It must also be shown that such manual workers take the middle-class as a reference group and desire to be accepted as members of the middle-class. Goldthorpe and Lockwood doubt whether in fact, the evidence supports the view that any such substantial embourgeoisement of the working-class in this sense has occurred.[4] Despite the fact that many now own cars, television sets, and refrigerators, this has not led to their acceptance by their white-collar neighbours on equal terms. Willmott and Young report marked

[1] Richard Hamilton, 'The Income Differences between Skilled and White Collar Workers', B.J.S., Vol. XIV, Dec. 1963. Much of the improvement in the relative position of manual workers derives from full-employment and the increasing employment of their wives. J. H. Goldthorpe, 'Stratification in Industrial Society', Soc. Rev. Monograph No. 8, 1964.

[2] Richard F. Hamilton, 'Affluence and the Worker: The West German Case', A.J.S., Vol. 71, Sept. 1965.

[3] F. Zweig, The British Worker (1952).

[4] For a discussion of this thesis, see J. Goldthorpe and D. Lockwood, op. cit., July 1963, and W. G. Runciman, ' "Embourgeoisement", Self-Rated Class and Party Preference', Soc. Rev., July 1964.

status segregation in the middle-class suburbs to which the more affluent workers are moving.[1] Goldthorpe and Lockwood suggest that the subordinate status of the manual worker in the work situation spills over into community and associational context. They question whether similarities of income and life-style can iron out barriers to social intercourse which derive from different positions in the authority structure of industry.[2] They doubt too, whether the attitudinal changes are as dramatic and far-reaching as some writers have supposed. True, there has been a decline in the cohesion of the working-class community as families move to new housing estates, and the emergence of home and family centredness.[3] There is more preoccupation with money, a decline in short-term hedonism and the emergence of a longer view. But the working-class has never been homogeneous and has always included a 'labour aristocracy' of highly paid craftsmen who have in many ways been similar to the middle-class in outlook and values.

Goldthorpe and Lockwood suggest three stages in the embourgeoisement of the worker. Firstly, there is a decline in involvement in the traditional working-class community and in acceptance of its norms. At this stage the worker does not aspire to acceptance of membership of the middle-class. He has become 'privatized', withdrawn into a private world of home-centredness. It is this which Goldthorpe and Lockwood believe to be the condition of the affluent worker. The next phase, the socially aspiring worker identifies with the middle-class, accepts their norms, and wishes to be accepted by them. Only when such workers are fully accepted by the middle-class can embourgeoisement be said to have taken place. And from the evidence, this does not appear to be the case. Nor is there much evidence to suggest that such a trend is likely to occur. The limited chances for promotion, and the subordinate position of the manual worker remain distinctive characteristics of the working-class situation. Under such circumstances it is difficult to see how manual workers will shift their social perspectives from the traditional working-class 'power' model, which sees society dichotemized into 'them' and 'us', to the middle-class 'status' model of society as a hierarchy of open strata up which the individual can climb by his own efforts.

[1] P. Willmott and M. Young, *Family and Class in a London Suburb* (1960), Zweig (1961), quotes one respondent: 'I am working-class only in the works, but outside I am like everyone else.'
[2] J. H. Goldthorpe and D. Lockwood, *op. cit.* (1963).
[3] These trends were discussed in Chapter 2.

The fact that an increasing number of manual workers are calling themselves middle-class is not, by itself, evidence of embourgeoisement; as this would require that they were also accepted by the middle-class. Runciman argues that the evidence on class identification supports the 'privatization' hypothesis. The fact that many manual workers who call themselves middle-class reject working-class identity, on evaluative or income grounds supports privatization. However, it can also be argued that the many who call themselves middle-class define the middle-class in terms of approval, suggests that they may be aspiring to membership. They are not merely status-dissenters but are positively adopting the middle-class as their reference group; they are socially aspiring. Evidence for this view is the fact that manual workers in Woodford, who call themselves middle-class show a shift towards middle-class values and behaviour in other ways. Fifty-two per cent (compared with 36 per cent) go to church, and 42 per cent (compared with 27 per cent) go to social clubs. This is more than simply an enjoyment of middle-class material standards. All that can be said at this stage is that the evidence is neither unambiguously for or against the embourgeoisement hypothesis.

The functional theory of differentiation

The Davis-Moore position stated in its simplest terms stresses the functional necessity of social differentiation and therefore, the limits to any trend towards equality. Social inequality is the device '. . . by which societies ensure that the most important positions are filled by the most qualified persons. Hence every society, no matter how simple or complex, must differentiate persons in terms of both prestige and esteem, and must therefore possess a certain amount of institutionalized inequality.'[1]

The early stages of the debate were marked by semantic confusion which has since been clarified. As Buckley[2] has pointed out, Davis and Moore failed to differentiate between social differentiation and stratification. The existence of social differences does not necessarily give rise to strata. What Davis and Moore have argued is that social differences are a functional necessity. But as Tumin insists, differences in income need not be taken up into the stratification system and become the basis for invidious distinctions in social ranking. And it is in this sense that the principal protagonists have

---

[1] Davis and Moore, *op. cit.* (1945).

[2] W. Buckley, 'Social Stratification and the Functional Theory of Social Differentiation', *A.S.R.*, Vol. 23, 1958.

defined the notion of stratification as 'the presence in any society of a system by which various social units are ranked as inferior and superior to each other on a scale of social worth...'[1] Strata emerge then when clear-cut and consistent statuses attributable to individuals could be generalized into categories for individuals of 'similar' status, and the categories ranked as 'strata'.[2]

It would be possible therefore to have a stratified society reflecting social differences in rewards, which was not a 'class' society. In such a society, a person's social position would be determined entirely by his abilities and efforts. That is, it would constitute a 'meritocracy'.[3] But the possibility of achieving a classless society in this sense has not been examined by the functionalists. It would be necessary to explore the possibility of ensuring equality of access to positions, a subject which the functionalists have only touched on. Their main concern, it now becomes clear, has been to argue the necessity for unequal rewards for positions of unequal importance.[4]

The core problem, as Tumin[5] has pointed out, is how to judge functional importance in order to avoid the purely circular argument that the most important positions are the most highly rewarded because they are the most important. Moreover, the precise amount of differentiation is indeterminate. Furthermore, the functionalists appear to be arguing that most of the differences can be explained as functional. Thus the magnitude of the differences will reflect the scarcity of talent and the sacrifices involved in training. This involves a logical confusion. To argue that differences in function lead to the necessity for differences in reward does not justify the conclusion that all differences in reward are due to differences in function. It is on this point that the functionalist case appears to most naive. There are only the most occasional hints that other mechanisms may be at work contributing to differentiation.[6] Most notable is an absence of any discussion of the strategies which are used to increase differ-

[1] M. Tumin, 'On Inequality', *A.S.R.*, Vol. 28, 1963. The controversy had failed to distinguish as Weber had done, between market and status situations.

[2] W. E. Moore, 'But Some Are More Equal than Others', *A.S.R.*, Vol. 28, 1963. This notion of strata takes no account of the literature on status consistency from Lenski (1954) onwards.

[3] M. Young, *The Rise of the Meritocracy* (1961).

[4] W. E. Moore (1963). This article shows a considerable shift from the original which sought to explain the universality of stratification in functional terms. It recognizes, for example, the possibility of status inconsistency.

[5] M. W. Tumin, 'Some Principles of Stratification: A Critical Analysis', *A.S.R.*, Vol. 18, 1953.

[6] Davis and Moore (1945) recognize that where a priestly guild controls membership, this may prevent competition. Moreover, they recognize that property

ences in rewards, such as the strategies adopted by trade unions and professions for limiting entry to an occupation and thus strengthening their market positions. The income differences which result can hardly be described as functional requisites.

The functional argument assumes that there are no barriers to the mobilization of talent. But, as mobility studies show, such barriers do exist. There is little reference to the 'contrivances of various elites who find the social situation to their liking and wish to preserve it'.[1] Indeed, stratification systems which have coalesced into classes are in many ways dysfunctional. The discovery of talents is limited by unequal access to motivation, recruitment and training. Class systems therefore set limits to the expansion in the supply of talent.[2]

To sum up, the functionalist debate has to a considerable extent developed out of a semantic confusion between social differences, social strata, and classes. It has failed to establish that differences of any specific magnitude are essential or to identify clearly what are the positions of most importance. Nor has it shown that all differences can be explained as reflections of a society's efforts to mobilize talent. It has neglected to explore the sources of inequality which derive from the organized efforts of groups to increase their shares, and from the intervention of the political system in the distribution of rewards. While it now recognizes the dysfunctional aspects of differentiation, it continues to stress its functional necessity.

SUMMARY AND CONCLUSION

The differential distribution of property and economic rewards, of power, and of status, characterizes all complex societies. Such differences arise partly out of the division of labour and the resulting distribution of roles within the political and economic systems. The fact that some must govern, and some must direct production makes such differences in power inevitable. But the extent to which power carries with it economic rewards and status is less rigidly determined. Insofar as property and power are in the same hands, we could expect those with power to enjoy advantages in the possession of property and wealth, and those with wealth to seek to safeguard it through the political machinery of society. To some extent, it can be argued, there is evidence of correlated changes in both wealth and power, but the evidence is not conclusive. The growing power of

ownership introduces a compulsive element into contractual relations. Yet the profound implications which this has for the theory are not discussed.

[1] M. Tumin (1963).
[2] *Ibid.*

organized labour has been accompanied by some shift in the distribution of the national income from property to labour, but some would argue that this reflects full employment rather than trade-union bargaining.

Although poverty has been largely abolished, this has been the result of economic growth as well as an extension of equality. But substantial differences in the distribution of incomes, and above all in the distribution of wealth remain. Some have argued that such differences are a functional necessity in industrial societies. The prolonged training and high degrees of skill which industrialization requires can only be achieved, it is argued, if appropriate rewards are offered. Such a view assumes that there is, in fact, a close association between monetary rewards and effort—a view which is hardly supported by the available evidence. While some differences can be argued to be functional in this sense, others are more plausibly explained as the result of the influence of economic and political power. Moreover, the economic rewards of the individual cannot be divorced from his evaluation by society. High status both legitimizes high rewards and provides a lever for bargaining.

Some have gone further than this and have argued that industrialization is resulting in substantial convergence between the stratification systems of advanced societies in which all are moving towards a minimizing of differences to a greater consistency between income, education and prestige. Such an argument assumes that the economic system is the main determinant of stratification and ignores the influence of the political system and of culture. As Goldthorpe[1] has pointed out, there are considerable differences in the stratification systems of societies at similar levels of development. In totalitarian societies such as the USSR, the political system dominates the economic system and deliberately manipulates the distribution of incomes and prestige to ensure loyalty to the regime and compliance with its policies. Stratification systems are influenced too, by ideologies, which generate purposive social action. Thus in the USA, the gap between rich and poor appears to be diverging, especially with the growth of unemployment among the unskilled, whereas in Sweden deliberate social policies have helped to maintain a high general level of employment and welfare.

The differential distribution of rewards cannot be assumed to generate unitary groupings automatically. But the evidence shows that classes do exist in the sense that individuals are conscious of their

[1] J. H. Goldthorpe, 'Social Stratification in Industrial Society' (*Soc. Rev. Mon. No. 8*, 1964).

identity with those sharing a common fate, and that such groupings are marked off from each other by differences in culture and styles of life. Some would argue that affluence has not led to the embourgoisement of the working-class, but rather to the 'privatized' worker, though there is evidence that some better paid workers are 'aspiring' rather than 'privatized'. However, a major characteristic of the working-class condition persists—his subordination in the authority structure of industry. But even here automation may well bring significant changes, subordinating the individual to the impersonal control of technical processes rather than the personal inferiority to management. Moreover, political measures, such as those adopted in Yugoslavia where workers' councils are the ultimate authority, can substantially change the distribution of power.

The existence of persisting groupings is still further evidenced by the data on mobility. Although considerable movement up and down the occupational ladder does exist, this is mainly in the middle ranges, and seldom involves moving more than one or two rungs. While this may blur the boundaries between skilled—manual and non-manual, the top stratum of society remains highly self-recruiting. And in spite of the equalizing tendencies of the spread of education, its distinctive position is further reinforced by the public schools, to which its sons are sent and from which its recruits are largely drawn.

Studies of the process of mobility throw some light on the mechanisms which ensure a substantial degree of class self-recruitment. For many, the cards are so stacked, that upward mobility is the exception. Such studies show too, that the mechanisms at work are complex and subtle, and unlikely to be solved by simple administrative solutions such as improvements in the Youth Employment Service or better student grants, however necessary such changes may be. There is little evidence to support the view that industrial societies have become 'meritocracies' in which rewards reflect the merits of the individual. Family background is still highly correlated with achieved status. In other words, although there has been a shift from status ascription to status achievement, the opportunities for achievement remain unequally distributed.

In this chapter, we have sought to distinguish quite clearly between the differential distribution of rewards and privileges, and the existence of groupings such as the 'middle-class', which depend on a consciousness of belonging and a measure of interaction arising out of common consciousness and awareness of shared interests. Such an approach reminds us once again of the point made in earlier chapters that much of the research on class has been based on an inadequate conceptualization of the variables involved. Crude categories such as 'the working-class' fail to identify the sociologically significant components of class situations, such as the work-situation. Manual workers in the same income-group, may experience totally different work-situations, and such differences, as has been shown, can be highly significant for leisure patterns, conjugal roles, and political attitudes. This is not to say that such crude categorizations are never useful, or that they have not been useful in the past. But further advances in knowledge are more likely to derive from the identification of significant variables hidden within such categories, and the further development of analytical rather than discriptive concepts.

QUESTIONS AND EXERCISES

1. 'The concept of class has outlived its usefulness as a tool of sociological research.' Explain and discuss.
2. 'The status system functions to legitimize the differential distribution of rewards.' Discuss.
3. 'The facts of class are not the same thing as the consciousness of class.' Explain, and examine the evidence for the existence of 'class-consciousness'.
4. 'We are all middle-class now.' Are we?
5. What evidence is there for the existence of distinctive class sub-cultures?
6. 'The embourgeoisement of the working-class.' Explain and discuss.
7. ' "Status", not "class", is the dominant feature of industrial societies.' Explain and discuss.
8. How far can Britain today be described as a meritocracy?
9. 'Studies of social mobility have paid insufficient attention to the processes of mobility.' Discuss.
10. Examine changes in the amount and character of mobility in this century.
11. 'The influence of the extension of educational opportunity on social mobility is less than is popularly supposed.' Discuss the evidence for this view.
12. What are the possible consequences of an increase in social mobility in societies undergoing rapid industrialization?
13. Examine critically the functional theory of stratification.
14. 'Industrial societies are characterized by a convergence of social classes.' Explain and discuss.

READING

Acton Society Trust.—*Management Succession* (Acton, 1956).

*R. Anderson and R. Blackburn.—*Towards Socialism* (Fontana, 1965), pp. 77–113. A summary of the debate on the withering away of class.

R. Bendix and S. M. Lipset.—*Class, Status and Power* (Routledge, 1953).

T. B. Bottomore.—*Classes in Modern Society* (Ampersand, 1955). Discusses Marx's theory and includes a brief comparison of Britain, USA and USSR.

L. A. Coser and B. M. Rosenburg.—*Sociological Theory* (Collier Macmillan, 1964).

C. A. R. Crosland.—*The Future of Socialism* (Cape, 1964), Part 4.

D. V. Glass (ed.).—*Social Mobility in Britain* (Routledge, 1954), Chapters 1, 2, 3, 8, 10.

J. H. Goldthorpe.—'Social Stratification in Industrial Society' (*Sociological Review Monograph No. 8*, 1964), pp. 97–139.

W. Guttsman.—*The British Political Elite* (MacGibbon, 1964).

R. K. Kelsall.—*Higher Civil Servants in Britain* (Routledge, 1955).

J. Klein.—*Samples from English Culture* (Routledge, 1965).

S. M. Lipset and R. Bendix.—*Social Mobility in Industrial Society* (Heinemann, 1959). A summary and analysis of the available data on mobility in industrial societies.

S. M. Lipset and R. K. Bendix.—*The Sociology of a Decade* (Prentice Hall, 1961), pp. 469–94.

T. H. Marshall.—*Sociology at the Crossroads* (Heinemann, 1963).

*K. B. Mayer.—*Class and Society* (Doubleday, 1955). An introductory text, with data for the USA.

R. K. Merton, L. Broom and L. S. Cottrell.—*Sociology Today: Problems and Prospects* (Harper, 1965), Chapter 19.

S. M. Miller.—'Comparative Social Mobility', *Current Sociology*, Vol. IX, No. 1 (Blackwell, 1960).

Chapter 8

ORGANIZATIONS

During the course of a typical day, we go to school or college, office or factory. We use public transport, go to the pictures, watch a TV programme. Less frequently, we may go to church, hospital or prison. We may belong to a trade union or frequent a bingo club. Each and all of these activities involves an organization. We work, study, and play in them. They are present when we are born and they undertake the disposal of our mortal remains. They touch our lives at countless points; their influence is pervasive. Indeed, one of the most distinctive ways in which an advanced industrial society differs from a pre-industrial society is in the complexity of its network of numerous associations and organizations. This trend from *community* to *association*[1] has been emphasized by some sociologists, such as Tönnies as a major social trend differentiating between social structures.

GROUPS, ORGANIZATIONS AND BUREAUCRACY

Specialization and division of labour is the key to organizations. Men form associations in order to pursue goals more effectively. If you are keen to play tennis you join a club. Trade unions enable workers to achieve goals through collective action. Associations then, are a form of social division of labour. Of course, an organization may exist to pursue more than one goal. Some trade unions, for example, provide friendly society benefits, and churches arrange social activities, But they differ from a community which is inclusive rather than exclusive in the goals it pursues. By contrast with an association, a community functions to meet a more or less inclusive range of needs.

We are members of many groups which are not organizations, such as friendship cliques. Such groupings are more than random

[1] Associations are examples of organizations. The term is used here to refer to the voluntary organizations formed for the pursuit of common goals.

associations of individuals. The behaviour of members is structured in the sense that there are regularities in the shared ways of acting, thinking and feeling. These pattern the interactions of members. A group of friends may meet to discuss a common interest. Students, for example, may meet to discuss their subject. The shared value in the importance of, say, sociology structures their activities (place, time, and frequency of meeting) and their interactions (content cf discussion; deference paid to the more knowledgable members). But such a group is not an organization. Organizations are groups, but in addition to possessing a structure and culture they are characterized by having a decision-making and enforcing machinery, deliberately set up and constituted for the pursuit of their common goals. A group of students may form themselves into an organization by electing a committee, drawing up terms of reference (a *charter*, or statement of formal aims), and a machinery for admitting members. They may do this because they find the informal meetings unsatisfactory. Discussion is unplanned and uncontrolled, and there are differences of opinion about priorities in discussion. Once a committee is set up, machinery is established for taking decisions and executing them.

An organization then, has a formally defined structure. A set of rules regulates the activities of members, and who makes decisions. It also has goals towards the achievement of which the activities of members are directed. But clearly, both the structure of the organization (committee, board of directors, hierarchy of ministry officials) and the methods by which it controls its members (coercion, incentives, moral pressures) are likely to vary widely. The attempt to arrive at some general understanding of the ways in which the great varieties of organizations are structured and function is one of the most interesting recent developments in sociology. But to help in understanding the more complex organizations, we will first examine the classical model of an organization as described by Max Weber.

Bureaucracy

It must be remembered that Weber was attempting to construct a model of the typical characteristics of bureaucracies. In his own terminology he was constructing an *ideal type*,[1] that is to say, the 'idea' of bureaucracy. In constructing his model he derived his concepts from an examination of the administrative machinery of

[1] Weber did not mean the term to be prescriptive. He was not describing the 'best' type of bureaucracy, although he did, in fact, believe bureaucracy as he described it to be the most efficient form of administration.

modern governments and large scale business organizations. Bureaucracy as he understood it is, in fact, only to be found in its fully developed forms in the modern state, in which rational techniques of administration have reached their highest forms of development.[1]

The two main characteristics of bureaucracy, according to Weber, are division of labour and a hierarchical structure of officials. The organization chart of a large company, army unit, or civil service section, is a typical example. Each official in the hierarchy is allocated specific tasks. Moreover, he is responsible to, and is controlled by the, official next above him in the hierarchy and in turn controls those next below him. The hierarchy of officials thus ensures the co-ordination of the various functions and provides formal channels of communication from the board down to the operatives through directors, managers, supervisors, foremen, and chargehands.

FIGURE 8.1

A TYPICAL ORGANIZATION CHART

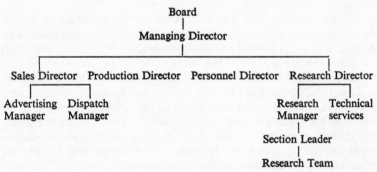

Weber believed that such a structure was not only the most rational but also the most efficient form of administration. The tasks of the organization are distributed in a rational way; each official has defined duties, and his activities and interactions with others are governed by the formal rules of the bureaucracy. The official does not act arbitrarily, nor are his actions influenced by personal considerations. A student applying for a grant, for example, completes a form which is then sent to the appropriate official in his local authority for a decision. If he comes within the categories to which grants are

[1] H. H. Gerth and C. W. Mills, *From Max Weber: Essays in Sociology* (1947).

allowed he receives one, even if he has offended the official by a rude telephone call. If his case is not allowed by the rules, then no grant is given, even if the official is his uncle. The rules ensure uniformity, rational decision-making, efficiency, co-ordinate the actions of officials and promote continuity (since any qualified individual can take over the tasks of an official after appropriate training).

A major criticism of Weber's theory is that he has confused concepts about the structural characteristics of bureaucracy with hypotheses about its functioning. He considered a fully developed bureacratic organization to be technically superior to other forms of organization. Specifically, he considered it superior in its 'Precision, speed, unambiguity, knowledge of files, continuity, discretion, unity, strict subordination, reduction of friction, and of material and personal costs . . . '[1] Subsequent researches have brought to light the dysfunctional and unintended consequences which characterize bureacratic structures. They have demonstrated for example, that an administrative structure which functions effectively in the army or civil service, does not necessarily work in a university or in a business undergoing rapid change. Furthermore, bureaucracies are often inefficient and fail to achieve their intended goals. Both Merton and Gouldner[2] have pointed to the dysfunctions of bureaucracy. These include a tendency towards over-rigid adherence to the rules, timidity, secrecy, red-tape, jealousy of other departments, and inflexibility under changed conditions.

Argyris[3] has also criticized Weber's hypotheses. He found that extreme specialization leads to psychological difficulties at the lower levels which prevent individuals from becoming more expert in their field. Moreover, bureaucratic detachment among top management has led to mistrust, lack of confidence, and lack of understanding between individuals and groups. But it is useful to start with the Weberian model because it is relatively simple and logical. Moreover, it is the model which is widely accepted among administrators as the one to which their behaviour should conform in spite of the fact that it does not accurately describe administrative behaviour.

One of the most influential theories in the classical tradition was the work of Frederick Taylor which has come to be known as Scientific Management. Taylor was mainly interested in industrial management. His model of the structure of administration was

[1] *Ibid.* (1947), p. 214.
[2] R. K. Merton (ed.), *et al.*, *Reader in Bureaucracy* (1952); A. W. Gouldner, *Patterns of Industrial Bureaucracy* (1955).
[3] C. Argyris, *Integrating the Individual and the Organization* (1964).

basically the classical model put forward by Weber. But his interest
in the behaviour of workers rather than managers led him to formulate a different theory of compliance. Researches had shown that
fatigue was an important factor influencing the output of the
worker. By changing the physical conditions of work (e.g. shortening
the length of the working day) fatigue could be reduced and output
increased. Taylor linked this with the view that the individual is
mainly driven by the search for profit. In order to maximize output
therefore, what is needed is to link work done as closely as possible
with payment made, and to minimize fatigue by making sure that the
operations are carried out in the most efficient way possible. The
results of Taylor's recommendations then were piece-work and time
and motion studies.

The basically Weberian approach has been developed and elaborated by more recent researches. March and Simon, for example,
continue to view administrative organizations as formal decision-
making structures. But unlike Weber who prescribed the 'right'
structure, the more recent approach has been to investigate
empirically ways in which the goals of an organization are achieved.
Weber, for example, ignored the possibility of conflict within the
organization and assumed that the rules of the organization would
ensure the smooth co-ordination of the various levels. The more
recent approach has been to investigate the various ways in which
organizations, in fact, resolve conflict. Another recent trend arises
out of the classical emphasis on rational decision-making. This has
lead to the development of decision-making theory which aims to
analyse logically the steps which a decision-maker should follow.
Although largely theoretical and prescriptive, such recent efforts
have attempted to analyse actual decision-making and the conditions
under which rational decisions are likely to be made,[1] and to discover
the factors which restrict rationality.

Human relations
Reactions against classical organization theory arose on two main
counts. Firstly, they were based on a false image of man. Taylorism,
for example, rested on an inadequate theory of motivation and
accepted the classical economist's view of economic man, responsive

---

[1] H. A. Simon, *Administrative Behaviour* (1950); J. G. March and H. A. Simon,
Organizations (1958). For a summary and discussion, see P. M. Blau and W. R.
Scott, *Formal Organizations* (1963). There is also a large literature on the 'principles of management' and 'administrative science' which has grown out of the
classical Weberian approach and which is basically prescriptive.

primarily to monetary incentives. Secondly, there were serious discrepancies between the model of rational organization and the realities of organizations.[1]

The breakthrough came as the result of the now famous series of researches in 1927–32 at the Hawthorne Works of the Western Electric Company—probably one of the most written about and most influential of all social investigations. The researches were in the 'scientific management' tradition and were aiming to measure the effect of illumination on production. Contrary to expectations, the productivity of workers in the experimental room continued to increase not only when illumination was improved, but also when it was decreased to a very low level. Other experiments with rest pauses confirmed that there was no simple connexion between fatigue and output. Further inquiries at the same plant proved that workers had deliberately restricted their output to a level far below that which they were capable of reaching, even though this meant that they failed to earn a production bonus. The simple assumptions of scientific management had been decisively challenged. The reduction of fatigue and the linking of payment to output did not necessarily maximize output. And workers did not work as hard as they could to maximize their income.[2]

The Hawthorne inquiries brought to light two main discoveries. Firstly, that the classical view of organizations ignored the existence of informal groupings which play an important part in influencing the achievement of organizational goals. Secondly, that workers respond to non-economic rewards and sanctions. Workers, it was found, formed informal groups which were not part of the official organization of the plant. This organization within an organization had evolved its own culture comprising beliefs about what would happen if they worked harder (their pay would be reduced) and a set of norms about what constituted a fair day's work. Both 'rate busters' who exceed the norm and 'chisellers' who failed to reach it, were subject to punishment ranging from 'symbolic' sanctions in the shape of losing the respect and affection of the group, to physical sanctions in the form of mild punch-ups during horseplay.[3]

Classical theory then had failed to recognize the importance of

[1] For a critique of theories and bibliography, see Renate Mayntz, 'The Study of Organizations', *Current Sociology*, Vol. XIII, No. 3, 1964. See also W. G. Scott, 'Organization Theory: An Overview and Appraisal', in J. A. Litterer, *Organizations: Structure and Behaviour* (1963), pp. 13–26.

[2] H. A. Landsberger, *Hawthorne Revisited* (1958).

[3] This is another example of the strategies available to workers to control aspects of their work and market situations, discussed in Chapter 4.

informal organization and of informal leaders. The *human relations* school had demonstrated the great influence which informal leaders of work groups exercised—far more effective than the formal leadership of foremen and inspectors in setting the level of output. The human relations school therefore came to stress the importance of the foreman and supervisor as the last link in the chain between management and men, and of leadership styles. 'Democratic' styles which sought to gain the participation of followers were demonstrated to be more effective in achieving goals, while 'democratic leadership is more likely to overcome resistance to change. Moreover, in order to maximize the participation of the lower ranks in striving for organizational goals, good communication is essential. If the reasons for courses of action are explained and communicated, and if the active involvement of the lower ranks is sought by democratic styles of leadership, then the result, it is argued, will be the co-ordination of efforts towards the achievement of organizational goals. Conflicts and non-co-operation, it was believed, are the result of the neglect of these maxims.

In this description of the work of the human relations school it has been difficult to separate an account of the findings of empirical inquiries, the interpretation placed upon them, and the prescriptions for action derived from such interpretations. Management wanted answers to administrative problems. It is difficult for those who have to take decisions to maintain the attitude of scepticism and suspended judgment of the scientist. The human relations school, therefore, found itself involved in advising management on solutions to administrative problems, and its findings were incorporated in the teaching at schools of management which grew up first in America, and after the Second World War in this country. The perspective of such studies was essentially slanted towards management—concerned with devising administrative techniques which would assist management in achieving the compliance of workers with organizational goals. It is not surprising that it has earned the epithet 'Cow sociology', or how to produce happy and contented workers. But this should not blind us to the fact that it has resulted in significant advances in our knowledge of organizational behaviour.

ORGANIZATIONS AS SYSTEMS

Further understanding of the structure and functioning of complex organizations has come as a result of the extension of researches to the study of a variety of organizations. Whereas earlier studies had concentrated mainly on industrial bureaucracies, recent inquiries have looked at prisons, mental hospitals, research laboratories and colleges. As a result, the various 'schools' are moving closer together, and a more inclusive body of theory and research is emerging. It is now becoming clear that there is not one administrative structure which is always superior, nor one best way of achieving compliance. Rathere there is a complex inter-relation between types of organizations, and forms of leadership and control. What works in a business or army won't work in a college. The administration of prisons, hospitals, and social work agencies cannot be the same. Nor can we manage scientists and college lecturers in the same way that we would manage clerks or production workers.

This extension of research has raised a number of problems for the development of a theory of organizations. Such researches have been mainly case studies of conventional categories of organizations, not of examples of a theoretically derived typology. There have, however, been a number of more recent attempts to evolve typologies of organizations and to relate empirical researches more explicitly to theoretical issues. Goffman's notion of *total institutions*,[1] for example, characterized by a high degree of *scope* and *pervasiveness* can be applied to prisons, mental hospitals, boarding schools, and even some types of firms. But there remain questions about trade unions, research laboratories, schools etc, which are specific and not therefore capable of being explored within the framework of generalized theory.[2]

Recent developments in organization theory have been along two main lines. Firstly, it has been recognized that there are a number of possible models for organizations, unlike the classical view of one model of rational bureaucracy. Secondly, organizations have been conceptualized as systems, and this has lead to a search for significant organizational variables. Among the main variables examined have been socialization and selection, organizational goals, rewards and sanctions, communication, adaptation to the external system, and boundary maintenance. But there has not so far been much success in demonstrating the interdependence between such variables. If organizations are systems, we can expect key variables to exercise constraint on others. Among the more interesting attempts in this field has been the classification of organizations according to rewards and sanctions (modes of compliance) by Etzioni.[3]

[1] This will be examined more fully later in the Chapter.

[2] P. M. Blau and W. R. Scott, *Formal Organizations, A Comparative Approach* (1962); R. Mayntz, *op. cit.*, p. 111.

[3] A. Etzioni, *A Comparative Analysis of Complex Organizations* (1961).

Models of organizations

There is still some controversy as to whether one basic model can be used for the study of all organizations, or whether different models are appropriate for different circumstances. Gouldner[1] exemplifies the first of these positions. He argues that two opposing theories have dominated the literature, neither of which is adequate, but which can provide the basis for a single synthesized model. The *rational model* is exemplified in the work of Weber and the classical school which has already been discussed. Here the organization with its division of labour and hierarchy of offices is the rationally devised means for the efficient attainment of given organizational goals. 'Fundamentally, the rational model implies a "mechanical" model, in that it views the organization as a structure of manipulable parts. . . . '[2] By contrast, the *natural-system model* regards the organization as a natural whole or system, which strives to survive and to maintain its equilibrium, even though this may lead to the distortion of the organization's goals (goal displacement). This model focuses attention on the unplanned and informal aspects which contribute to survival.[3] But it tends to neglect planned and rational administration.

As a result of empirical studies, Burns and Stalker[4] have arrived at a somewhat similar distinction between what they call *mechanistic* and *organic* structures. The former corresponds to the classical model in which communication and authority flow vertically, mainly from top to bottom. In the organic model, authority and communication flow laterally as well as vertically. There is a complex network of control and communication. But unlike Gouldner, Burns and Stalker see these two types as descriptions of empirical reality, each of which is appropriate for different circumstances. The mechanistic structure is more suitable for the execution of policies in relatively stable organizations where the goals are fixed and where there is little innovation of either means or ends. The organic model is more relevant for organizations undergoing change. Responsibility and knowledge are more widely distributed, there is more horizontal interaction, and compliance is achieved through the

[1] A. W. Gouldner, 'Organizational Analysis', in R. K. Merton, L. Broom and L. S. Cottrell, *op. cit.* (1965).

[2] *Ibid.*, p. 405.

[3] The informal groups described by the Hawthorne studies, for example, pursued policies aimed to ensure their survival rather than the company's goal of maximizing production. This model has been influenced by cybernetics and has incorporated concepts such as feedback, and homeostasis.

[4] T. Burns and G. Stalker, *The Management of Innovation* (1960).

commitment and involvement of individuals rather than through commands.

Likert's[1] model is rather more elaborate since it involves two dimensions, the amount of control exercised over individuals and the motives used to control and co-ordinate. This yields two main types (authoritative and participative) and two sub-types. The *exploitative authoritative* uses both physical and economic sanctions and exploits the need for security. It uses mainly threats and punishment, decisions are made at the top and there is little communication. There is little interaction and an attitude of hostility towards the goals of the organization. The *benevolent authoritative* appeals mainly to economic motives, and uses rewards as well as punishment. The *consultative participative* offers satisfaction of a wider range of needs, there is two-way communication, and decision-making is more widely distributed. In the *group participative* model, compliance is achieved through a high level of group participation in decision-making, with high levels of communication and the absence of suspicion in interactions.[2]

Organizational variables[3]
It can be seen that these typologies select a number of different variables as bases for differentiation. Moreover, they hypothesize that the differences between the variables are not random, but fall into a number of patterns. Thus the distribution of authority is related to communication, interaction, sanctions, and goals. This line of reasoning suggests an alternative approach. It can be argued that the above models try to tell us too much. They not only seek to discover significant variables but also to state the relations between them. A more modest approach would be to seek to discover significant organizational variables which would provide a systematic approach for organizational research and attempts to discover empirically the main modes of relations between variables. Such data would then provide the basis for constructing generalized models of various types of organization. These variables will include both structural variables such as authority structures and sanctions, and functional variables (processes) such as selection, control, communication, goal-attainment and boundary maintenance.

[1] R. Lickert, *New Patterns of Management* (1961), Chapter 14.

[2] These types are similar to Gouldner's 'punishment-centred' and 'representative' bureaucracies in *Patterns of Industrial Bureaucracy* (1955). In the latter authority is based on expertise, there is collaboration in the initiation of rules, and persuasion and education are used to obtain compliance.

[3] See W. G. Scott, 'Organization Theory: An Overview and Appraisal', *op. cit.*, 1964, pp. 19–24.

A recent attempt to construct 'profiles' of organizations along these lines is the work of Lupton and his associates.[1] Their first step has been to attempt to isolate and conceptualize a number of structural dimensions. They hypothesise six primary dimensions of organizational structure; (1) specialization (the number of specialisms and the degree of role specialization), (2) standardization (for example, of decision-making and communication procedures) (3) formalization (how far communications and procedures are written down and filed) (4) centralization (the location of decision-making at particular points in the authority structure), (5) configuration (exemplified primarily by the organization chart, and including height, width, spans of control) (6) flexibility (changes in the organizational structure). The great advantage of this approach, they claim, is that it provides a conceptual scheme for the empirical investigation of organizations, and facilitates the generation of hypotheses.

The analysis of the structure of organizations cannot be separated from a study of their functioning. It is to studies of organizational functions and processes that we now turn.

Selection and Socialization

Most organizations are faced with the problem of selecting individuals who possess the characteristics appropriate to the performance of organizational tasks. The selection process includes both self-selection by individuals and selection by organizations. Selection functions to help maximize the congruence between the expectations of the individual about role requirements, the demands of the organization[2] for role performance, and the possession of the requisite personal skills and qualities. A high degree of congruence minimizes the need for organizational controls. A research laboratory, for example, will seek to recruit scientists who are not only qualified scientifically but who are also willing to pursue the research interests of the company, and will not object to the restraints on publication which industrial research involves. Scientists will similarly seek jobs which are congruent with their interests and expectations.[3] Similarly grammar schools seek to select pupils with

---

[1] D. S. Pugh, *et al.*, 'A Conceptual Scheme for Organizational Analysis', *Admin. Sc. Qu.* (3), 1963, pp. 289–315.

[2] It is, of course, recognized that the term 'demands of organizations' involves reification. In the last analysis, there are only *individuals*, and organizational demands are made by definable individuals. We return to the role of the individual in a later section.

[3] S. Box and S. Cotgrove, 'Scientific Identity, Occupational Selection and Role Strain', *B.J.S.*, March 1966.

both the interest and capacity for academic achievement. By contrast, secondary modern schools are unselective and therefore face more difficult problems in achieving the compliance of pupils with the aims of the school. Clearly, organizations such as prisons whose inmates have not chosen to enter, face even more difficult problems.

Congruence between individuals and organizations can be increased by subsequent socialization. Some firms will try to socialize scientists by a fairly lengthy process of gradually channelling research interests into the direction of most use to the firm, allowing the new recruit a fair amount of freedom. Scientists who have been employed in industry for a long period of time appear to become adjusted to conditions of industrial employment, and to attach less importance to publication. Under some circumstances, socialization may become dysfunctional for the organization. Merton[1] discusses the tendency in bureaucracies for officials to become over-conformists, to adhere rigidly to the rules and regulations for their own sake. A major structural pressure to behave in this way stems from the fact that the official's life is planned for him in terms of a graded career. The rewards for conformity are promotion, security and eventually a pension. These pressures to conform induce timidity, and conservatism. Moreover, strict conformity to the rules protects the individual against criticism, and may be a device sought by the timid. The result is that importance comes to be displaced from ends to means; from organizational goals to rules. How far this process is the result of the socialization of the official and how far it is due to a tendency for bureaucracies to attract less adventurous types of personality, it is difficult to say.

The influence of an organization in socializing the individual can be seen most clearly in the case of the more extreme types of organizations. *Total institutions*, to use Goffman's[2] term, are marked by a high degree of what Etzioni calls *scope* and *pervasiveness*. The scope of the organization refers to the number of activities carried out jointly by the participants, while pervasiveness refers to the extent to which the organization seeks to control the life of the individual. Churches, for example, seek to regulate the conduct of members not only in the performance of specifically religious activities, but in a wide range of activities carried on outside.

[1] R. K. Merton, 'Bureaucratic Structure and Personality', in *Social Theory and Social Structure* (1957). L. Reissman has suggested a more elaborate classification of types of bureaucrat: functional, specialist, service and job ('A Study of Role Conceptions in Bureaucracy', *Social Forces*, 27: March 1949).

[2] E. Goffman, *Asylums* (1961).

Total institution can bring about profound modifications in the personality of the individual. At the outset, the neophyte is subjected to what Goffman calls a 'mortification' process in which elements of his personality are stripped off. The cadet at the American military academy, for example, is completely socially and geographically isolated. Uniforms are issued which remove distinctive styles of dress, and discussions of family background are taboo.The cadet is stripped of all clues which would enable him to retain his original identity. His personality may be further attacked by degrading initiation ceremonies and an inferior status conferred by the use of terms such as 'swab'.[1] In prisons similarly, all supports for individual identity are abruptly chopped off. Family, occupational and educational status are completely excluded and the prisoner is stigmatized by the anonymous status of a number.

While this breaking down of identity is in progress, the inmate is exposed to the incentives and rewards of the privilege system. It is around these that some re-building of the self takes place. Because there is no escape from the institution, and because it is total in its scope, such rewards and punishments take on a disproportionate significance. A few cigarettes, or the threat of losing a minor privilege constitute severe pressures to conform.

A variety of responses are adopted to these attacks on identity and pressures to conform. Some inmates withdraw attention from everything except immediate events. A second adjustment is the complete acceptance of the inmate world in an attempt to extract the maximum satisfactions which are available. In mental hospitals such individuals have become completely institutionalized and do not wish to leave.[2] A more extreme form of adjustment is conversion in which the inmate accepts the perspectives of the staff and tries to act the role of the perfect inmate. In concentration camps, inmates sometimes go so far as to talk and behave as camp guards, fully identifying themselves with their role.

The breakdown and restructuring of personality that can occur in total institutions (including mental hospitals) seldom appears to have a permanent effect. Return to the original environment provides all the familiar supports for the old identity and the experience may have only relatively short term consequences.

Achieving compliance

One major problem which faces any organization is how to ensure

[1] M. Janowitz, *The Professional Soldier* (1960).
[2] E. Goffman, *op. cit.* (1961).

the compliance of its members. Officials must carry out their tasks conscientiously, while workers in factory and offices must similarly do their jobs at bench and desk. Weber was concerned with the compliance of officials. According to Weber, there are a number of factors which ensure that the official keeps the rules. His job is a career, which provides him with a secure income, regular promotion, and a pension. That is to say, the organization can reward devoted service. But more important, Weber stressed the fact that the rules of the bureaucracy are seen as legally constituted and formal, and therefore legitimate. The acceptance of the rules as legitimate is ensured partly by the careful selection of its officials by the bureaucracy and partly by the fact that they have undergone an appropriate and lengthy education and training. The officials comply with the rules because they accept them as legitimate.

Now we have seen that not only was Weber's model of bureaucracy inadequate as an account of the structure of organizations. It also failed to discuss the means by which they achieve the compliance of individuals other than officials with organizational demands. Both the Scientific Management and Human Relations theories have suggested that the mechanisms are in fact complex. The incentives which lead the official in a public bureaucracy to conform are hardly likely to be effective with the assembly-line worker or the prison inmate. Moreover, Gouldner[1] has distinguished punishment-centred and representative bureaucracies according to the means of control, while Likert[2] has examined the variety of sanctions used to achieve compliance in different types of organizations.

Etzioni[3] has suggested that there are, in fact, three main types of power available (physical, material and symbolic), and each typically produces a different form of compliance. In prisons, for example, coercion is the main means of power; in factories, material rewards are offered such as wages and bonuses; while colleges and churches use moral power.

The use of different means of control has consequences for the responses elicited. Moral power uses symbols to manipulate behaviour, particularly verbal expressions like: 'You've done well.' Individuals are rewarded by prestige, approval or affection. The use of moral power, is more likely to result in normative compliance, that is to say, compliance because, as with Weber's officials, it is

---

[1] *Op. cit.* (1954).
[2] *Op. cit.* (1961).
[3] See A. Etzioni, *op. cit.* (1964), for a simplified analysis of types of power and compliance.

believed to be right. By contrast, coercion is unlikely to generate any commitment; it is, that is to say, more alienative. The individual feels powerless but is forced to comply with orders to which he attaches no value and which he does not define as right. The use of utilitarian power such as wage incentives, results in *calculative involvement* in which actions are performed on the basis of calculated self-interest.[1] In practice, of course, control is seldom exercised by one means alone, and compliance may involve elements of all three types. All that Etzioni is saying is that the dominant element in the methods of control is likely to result in the predominance of one type of compliance.

Prisons are examples of organization where the problems of achieving the compliance of inmates are extreme. Inmates do not identify themselves with the goals of the organization or accept them as either desirable or legitimate. The sources of power available for control therefore are extremely limited. Utilitarian power can be used to a small extent by granting privileges and remission of sentence for good conduct. But coercion is of necessity the main source of power, and since its use is strictly regulated, it proves to be an inadequate means of control.

The lack of support among the inmates for the goals of the organization and the desire to protect themselves as far as possible from the rigours and isolation of prison life favours the development of a strong informal organization with its own leaders, communication network, and culture. There is a more extreme form of the informal organization and culture which sometimes develops in industry, where as we have seen, the workers wish to pursue goals contrary to the offical aims of the organization. The aim of the inmate code is to provide support for other inmates, to avoid trouble, and to maintain a sharp distinction between inmates and officials.

However, the limited strategies of control available to the prison officers frequently results in a breaking down in such sharp distinctions. In practice they may enlist the support of some of the inmates and exercise control through the unofficial inmate organization. Inmate leaders who are usually long-term prisoners, share with the officials the desire to lead a quiet life and avoid trouble; insist that all inmates are equal and that 'outside' criteria such as wealth will not be used to determine special privileges in prison. Such leaders will help to enforce official rules in return for small privileges.

[1] Etzioni stresses that the responses to types of power will depend in part on the characteristics of the participants. The contemporary worker will react differently to physical violence from his nineteenth century counterpart.

In this context it can be appreciated that therapeutic activities such as psychiatric work are of limited success in traditional prisons. Their coercive nature generates a protective inmate culture which to some extent, isolates the prisoners from any kind of personal relationship with the staff. Therapeutic and custodial goals require different systems of control, and the attempt to increase the therapeutic functions of prisons is presenting difficult problems. Similar difficulties also face borstals, approved schools and mental hospitals.

Control; participation and communication

A debating society is run for the benefit of its members. An army serves to protect society. It is reasonable to suppose that such different organizations will adopt different solutions to the problems of control, and will devise different structures. In order to explore such differences, we may take as a starting point Blau and Scott's[1] classification of organizations based on prime beneficiary. They suggest four main types; (1) mutual benefit associations (e.g. trade unions), (2) business concerns (where the owner is the prime beneficiary), (3) service organizations (where the client is prime beneficiary, e.g. hospitals and schools), and (4) commonwealth organizations (where the prime beneficiary is the public at large, such as the army, and prisons).

Trade unions are an example of organizations in which the prime beneficiary is the membership, and in which the participation of members and their control over its policies could be expected to be high. The evidence however, shows that active participation in union affairs by the rank and file is generally low. Voting typically involves 15–25 per cent of the membership and in some unions can be as low as 2 per cent. In others, however, such as printing, a much higher proportion vote—nearer 70 per cent. In part this is because attendance at some meetings is compulsory, and the meetings occur at the place of work. But the nature of the work, and especially the amount of interaction it generates both on and off the job seems to be an important variable. Thus miners, who develop a strong *occupational community* have a higher rate of participation.

Another aspect of the failure of internal democracy is the tendency for the leadership once established to become stable and irremoveable, whether elected or not. This tendency towards the concentration of power in the hands of a few has been observed to occur in a wide range of organizations, including political parties. In fact, Michels considered this to be an inevitable tendency in all such

[1] *Op. cit.* (1963).

organizations and referred to it as the *iron law of oligarchy*.[1] Weber made somewhat similar observations about officials in government bureaucracies.

According to both Michels and Weber, a major reason for this tendency to oligarchy is the fact that the officials develop vested interest in maintaining their positions. For trade unionists, for example, the loss of paid office may mean return to the bench.[2] When this happens, there may be a tendency for the union to become a business concern, run partly for the benefit of the officials.

English students of trade union structure however, have argued that the unions have chosen to sacrifice democracy to the need for efficiency. Allen argues that as the unions have grown in size, and their tasks increased in complexity, officials have been forced to take decisions with a minimum of recourse to the cumbersome machinery of democracy. Moreover, the complexity of the issues has made democratic participation more difficult. A result has been the drying up of branch democracy.[3]

This discussion of course, assumes that a high level of active participation by the rank and file is necessary if the union is to meet the needs of its members. Allen[4] challenges this assumption and questions whether organizations such as trade unions need to provide exercises in self-government. The membership supports the actions of its leaders by belonging and paying its dues. Once the leaders lose the support of the rank and file, they will vote with their feet, and the officials will be faced with declining membership. This mechanism, Allen argues, is sufficient to ensure the responsiveness of the leaders to the members, where membership is voluntary.

Roberts[5] however, places a different interpretation on the evidence. He agrees that unions have tended towards bureaucracy, and have developed routine office administration and impersonal control. But, he argues, that there are powerful forces at work keeping the officials under the control of the rank and file. He cites as evidence the relatively low ratio of officials to members, and the low salaries paid to top officials who are also overworked—evidence he believes of the sacrifice of efficiency to democracy.

[1] R. Michels, *Political Parties* (1959). For a summary, see Broom and Selznick, *op. cit.*, pp. 247–50.

[2] The 'professionalization' of leadership by recruiting graduates or others who had not worked their way up might reduce this tendency.

[3] V. L. Allen, *Power in Trade Unions* (1954).

[4] *Op. cit.* (1954).

[5] B. C. Roberts, *Trade Union Government and Administration in Great Britain* (1956).

The administration and control of functions such as research or teaching, presents quite different problems. The study of the organization of hospitals, colleges, and research departments brings to light an ambiguity in Weber's analysis of bureaucratic authority. What kind of an expert is the official? Is Weber referring to his expert knowledge of the files of the bureaucracy? Or to the special knowledge derived from the officials's formal education? If we look at a college, for example, or at a hospital, the difference between these two kinds of expertise becomes clearly apparent. The expert knowledge of the professor of physics is quite different from that of the registrar. In industry, knowledge and qualifications are more likely to be concentrated at the middle levels in the research and development departments than on the board of directors.

A further related distinction is also important—that between administrative and professional authority. The authority of the official is based upon his position in the bureaucratic hierarchy. The authority of the professional, however, is based on knowledge.[1] His actions are based on his professional judgment and he alone, or in consultation with his professional colleagues (peers) is in a position to decide. The professor of physics, not the college administrator, decides what to teach. The surgeon, not the hospital administrator, decides whether to operate. In the sphere of professional conduct, therefore, the professional expects and demands freedom to exercise his own judgment; he expects professional autonomy.

Organizations have adopted a variety of solutions to the resulting problem. One method is to attach experts in an advisory capacity to the organization. They may have little or no executive authority. This is the solution frequently adopted by industry which distinguishes between *staff* (advisory) function and *line* (executive) functions. But the difficulty is that the staff section may find itself out on a limb, isolated and playing little part in the life of the organization. The research and development department, for example, may frequently find itself in such a position. Or it may find that its primary function of development is being hindered by constant requests from production for 'trouble-shooting' help or product testing. In such circumstances, a struggle for power may develop in which research and development seeks to dominate production. Another possible solution to such conflicts is that suggested by Burns and Stalker,[2] which has been mentioned earlier; the adoption of an *organic* as

[1] A. W. Gouldner, 'Organizational Analysis', in Merton, Broom and Cottrell, *op. cit.* (1965).
[2] T. Burns and G. Stalker, *op. cit.* (1960).

distinct from a *mechanistic* structure of control. They argue that instead of the hierarchical model in which communication and authority flow vertically, mainly from top to bottom, that there should be a much more complex network of communication, horizontally as well as vertically.

One result of the growing insights which were inspired by the human relations approach was an increasing emphasis on machinery to improve communications between management and men in industry. To this end, works councils and works committees have been set up by many firms, while an elaborate consultative machinery was insisted upon in the nationalized industries. But there has been some ambiguity in the aims of such efforts. The dominant aim has been to reduce misunderstandings and conflicts between management and men, to put the workers in the picture, and to ensure that they have a fuller appreciation of the goals of the firm. Some, however, have gone further and sought to increase the participation of workers in the decision-making process.

Such efforts have come up against difficulties. We have seen in the previous chapter that workers experience varying degrees of alienation resulting from their roles in the socio-technical system of production. Consequently, many workers are simply calculatively and not normatively involved. Put another way, they are not work-centred. It is not surprising therefore, to find that efforts to increase worker-participation have often met with apathy rather than hostility. There is little support for attending meetings during, or still less, after hours. This explanation is confirmed by the findings of an inquiry by Banks[1] that participation increases with the level of skill of the worker.

Difficulties have also been experienced in gaining the support of some levels in management. One obvious objection has come from those who see the works committee as a threat to their authority. This applies particularly to middle-management and supervisors, who feel that the works council by-passes them when top management meet the workers face-to-face. A similar objection has come from the shop-stewards who see the works committee as a possible threat to the union.

Communication and decision-making control variables are closely related. Decisions are based on information received from parts of the system and control is exercised by communications originating

[1] J. A. Banks, *Industrial Participation* (1963). See also W. H. Scott, *Industrial Leadership and Joint Consultation* (1952). For a development of methods of increasing participation, see Wilfred Brown, *Explorations in Management* (1960).

from decision-making centres.[1] The study of cybernetics has had considerable influence on this aspect of organization theory. Cybernetics is mainly concerned with problems of automation, and with devising feedback and control mechanisms in engineering which function to maintain the system in equilibrium (homeostasis). Such notions of automatic and self-regulating control mechanisms are clearly attractive to administrators. The development of accounting and electonic data processing, for example, means that many decisions which were once taken on the basis of individual judgment, now emerge as the result of impersonal electronic data processing. Costing, quality control and critical path analysis are all ways in which rational decision and control mechanisms have been built into the organization.[2]

Closely related to this is the impact of technological innovations on management. A study of one hundred firms in South-East Essex[3] showed considerable differences in their organization which were related to differences in techniques of production. Unit (batch) production firms were characterized by the centralization of authority, while delegation of authority was more general in mass production firms. In the process industry, there was a higher degree of specialization of functions such as production and marketing, combined with co-operative decision-making within each function. Moreover, the most successful firms approximated to the medians of the group, indicating that each had devised a pattern of organization appropriate to its particular technology.[4]

INDIVIDUALS AND ORGANIZATIONS

In the last analysis, it is individuals who carry out the tasks in organizations. And as we have seen in Chapter 4, there may well be a lack of congruence between the characteristics which an individual brings with him to the performance of organizational roles and the characteristics which the role requires. Moreover, as we go down the organizational hierarchy, there is a decline in autonomy and skill. Tasks become increasingly fragmented and control over performance

[1] K. W. Deutsch, 'On Communication Models in the Social Sciences', *Public Opinion Quarterly*, 16 (1952).

[2] S. Beer, *Cybernetics and Management* (1959).

[3] Joan Woodward, *Management and Technology* (1958).

[4] See also F. J. Jasinski, 'Adapting Organization to New Technology', in J. A. Litterer, *op. cit.*, 1964. See also Scott, *op. cit.*; F. C. Mann and L. R. Hoffman, *Automation and the Worker* (1960); A. Tourraine, *et al.*, *Workers' Attitudes to Technical Change* (1965).

declines. We have seen that workers adopt a variety of responses, both individual (strategies of independence) and collective (occupational strategies including informal organization and trade-union activities). And although socialization and selection function to minimize the discontinuities between the needs of individuals and organizations, there remains a gap between needs and satisfactions.[1]

Now the relevance of such data to organizational analysis is obvious. Division of labour, fragmentation of skills, subordination and lack of autonomy all result from the fact that production (and teaching and research) is carried out by large-scale organizations. And the adaptive responses of individuals (absenteeism, restrictive practices, trade union demarcations, withdrawal from work, and alienation) are unintended consequences of organization. In this section we are concerned with the organizational response to such problems.

Argyris argues that typical organizational responses exacerbate the problem.[2] At all levels, the consequence of the lack of congruence between the needs of individuals and organizations are dysfunctional for the achievement of organizational goals. Unintended consequences become institutionalized. Efforts to introduce a measure of control over the pace of work become institutionalized as informal group norms. Such institutionalization distorts the flow of communication by inhibiting information about the true state of affairs. Management reacts to apathy and restriction by stronger leadership, tighter controls, and stiffer penalties. Even 'human relations' programmes may be perceived as attempts at manipulation. Such actions stimulate even stronger defensive reactions. 'This forms a closed loop of activity which is repetitive and compulsive; rather than solving the underlying causes, it actually helps to deepen them.'[3]

The solution suggested by Argyris to the problem of integrating the individual and the organization is to modify the organization in ways which release psychological energy for productive effort by devising conditions which make it possible for individuals to experience 'self-actualization', that is, 'psychological success and opportunities

[1] C. Argyris quotes evidence to show that such needs as the opportunity for interesting work, to make decisions, exercise responsibility, and make the most of capacities are not simply middle-class values. Moreover, the increased satisfactions resulting from job enlargement are evidence of the frustrations experienced by manual workers. *Op. cit.* (1964), pp. 82–6.

[2] See also A. Gouldner's discussion of punishment-centred bureaucracies, *op. cit.* (1955).

[3] C. Argyris, *op. cit.* (1964), pp. 110–12.

for self-responsibility'. This will include work which uses the skills and abilities of the individual and is intrinsically satisfying. Above all, this involves a modification of the pyramidal structure of command which centralizes control at the top. Ways must be found to extend and increase autonomy and control down through the organization. This does not mean going to the other extreme and abolishing a hierarchical command structure entirely. Nor will the exact position be the same for all organizations, or for the different situations within the same organization. The degree of 'mix' is largely a matter to be determined by further empirical research.

As Argyris recognizes, his solution is similar to those suggested by Shepard, Burns and Stalker, and by Likert. He is proposing something very similar to Burns and Stalker's 'organic' type and to Likert's 'participative group'. The main difference claimed by Argyris is that his model, unlike the others, is derived from theoretical propositions about the characteristics of organizations. Moreover, Argyris suggests a continuum between two polar 'ideal types', the precise 'mix' differing according to circumstances.

Argyris recognizes that such modifications in organizations demand corresponding modifications in individuals. Working-class culture has institutionalized values and perspectives such as apathy, indifference and fatalism. The perpetuation of such values may be one mode of adjustment to the frustrations of work. To encourage the development of self-actualization without providing the opportunities would be damaging and dangerous. But the evidence suggests that the potential is there and that workers in fact respond to opportunities for increased skill and control.[1]

The Argyris analysis is strongly psychologically oriented.[2] He draws heavily on ideas about the psychological needs of individuals. An alternative perspective which has been widely used in exploring the relations between individuals and organizations is the concept of *role*. This concept has already been used in discussing occupations in Chapter 4. Examples were given there of the lack of congruence between the needs and expectations of individuals and the demands of organizations. Some scientists, for example, attach importance to autonomy and freedom to publish and experience considerable dissatisfaction with industrial conditions. Foremen occupy an ambiguous status and experience conflicting demands, while teachers experience role strain resulting from conflicting pressures from their

[1] *Ibid.*, pp. 78–86.
[2] He explicitly states the need for integrating the sociological and psychological levels of analysis. *Ibid.*, pp. 281–93.

role-set, the diffuse nature of their role, and conflicting commitments to role and career.[1] Most of these strains and conflicts derive from the fact that occupational roles are performed in an organizational context. These two approaches are in fact very close together. But role analysis would seem to add something to the more psychologically oriented approach adopted by Argyris. For example, strains can arise through role ambiguities, and through conflicting role demands. But Argyris does avoid the weakness usually attributed to the psychological approach which seeks to explain such phenomena as motivation and involvement in work, or apathy, as personality characteristics, rather than as functions of an interaction process between individuals and situations. The sociological perspective sees work attitudes as a function of socially structured roles, and takes account of the characteristics which the individual brings to his role (as a result of previous socialization) his perception of his role, and the organization's role expectations. From this perspective, 'alienation' is not so much a characteristic of an individual, but rather a function of an interaction process.

Role analysis also helps to conceptualize the fact that the role incumbent (worker, teacher, inmate) has a number of social-selves. He is located that is to say, in a number of social roles—as husband, friend, scientist. When acting out any particular role, he does not leave behind completely his other roles, but he carries them with him as a *latent identity*.[2] Thus the committed scientist is also a husband, and however involved he may be in an experiment, is conscious of his other role expectations. Age and sex roles are further examples of latent identities which may affect organizational behaviour. Socially derived values about deference to age and female subordination may contribute to organizational tension if a young woman is put in charge of a section over older men.

SUMMARY AND CONCLUSIONS

Organizations are devices by which the activities of a number of individuals are controlled and co-ordinated for the more effective pursuit of organizational goals. They are faced with two main problems. Firstly, how best to devise an administrative machinery which will co-ordinate the activities of members. Secondly, how best to ensure that individuals act out the roles to which they are allocated.

[1] For references to the literature, see Chapter 4.
[2] A. W. Gouldner, 'Cosmopolitans and Locals: Toward an Analysis of Latent Social Roles', *Admin. Sc. Qu.* 2 (1957), pp. 281–306, 444–80.

In practice, these problems are intertwined, but it can be argued that the problem of compliance presents more difficulties than that of co-ordination.

The analysis of organizations has, in many ways, been a continuous debate with Weber. Weber's model has the merit of being a reasonably logical statement of the structural features of bureaucratic organizations. But later writers have pointed to Weber's failure to take account of the informal or unofficial elements in bureaucracies, and his neglect of their dysfunctional aspects and the unintended consequences of formal organizations. Such studies have shown that the division of labour and hierarchial structuring of roles which is intended to increase efficiency have, in fact, resulted in the development of unofficial sub-systems, pursuing goals which are not those of the formal organization (displacement of goals).

There have been two major lines of development from Weber. The first has stemmed from the recognition that Weber's ideal type construct is only one of a number of possibilities and has lead to the construction of more sophisticated typologies, such as Burns and Stalker's 'organic' and 'mechanistic' types, and Gouldner's 'punishment-centred' and 'representative' bureaucracies. A second major development has been the attempt to isolate a number of distinct dimensions of organizations which are capable of empirical investigation and measurement. From these, it is hoped to be able to construct a series of profiles of organizations. This may make possible the description of some major forms of organization in terms of clusters of structural variables as a basis for the analysis of organizational functioning and effectiveness.

A further development in recent years has been a growing interest in the relations between individuals and organizations, which has focused on the lack of congruence between the needs of individuals and the demands made on them in the pursuit of organizational goals. Such studies have suggested the need for changes in the demands made on individuals by organizations, rather than relying solely on achieving their compliance by incentives or by improved communication, stressed by the 'human relations' school. Such studies have drawn heavily on role analysis, using concepts of role strain and conflict, and have directed attention to the importance of taking account of the characteristics which individuals bring with them into their organizational roles, as well as to any resocialization that may take place within the organization.

QUESTIONS AND EXERCISES

1. Outline briefly Weber's 'ideal type' bureaucracy.
2. 'Weber's analysis of bureaucracy confuses a conceptual model with propositions about its functioning.' Explain and discuss.
3. Examine some of the ways in which Weber's model of an administrative structure has been modified by subsequent research.
4. 'Who says organization says oligarchy.' Discuss with reference to any one organization.
5. What light can sociological researches throw on the problems which face industry in achieving the compliance of semi-skilled machine operatives?
6. 'According to Weber, an official is an expert.' 'Organizations experience special difficulties in the employment of professionals.' Explain and discuss.
7. How far do you think the distinction between 'staff' and 'line' solves the problem of integrating the specialist into the organization?
8. What do you understand by role strain? Illustrate by reference to studies of any one occupation.
9. Under what conditions would you expect informal organizations to form? What functions do they serve?
10. Examine critically attempts to arrive at a typology of organizations.
11. 'Selection and socialization is a major mechanism for achieving conformity with organizational roles.' Discuss.
12. 'Efforts to achieve integration between individuals and organizations must shift from attempts to manipulate individuals to modifications in organizations.' Explain and discuss.

READING

*C. Argyris.—*Integrating the Individual and the Organization* (Wiley, 1964). There is an excellent summary of the impact of organizations on individuals in pp. 110–13.

*P. M. Blau and W. R. Scott.—*Formal Organisations* (Routledge & Kegan Paul, 1963), especially Chapters 2 and 9.

L. Broom and P. Selznick.—*Op. cit.*, Chapters 2, 7, 14.7.

A. Etzioni.—*Modern Organisations* (Prentice-Hall, 1964). An excellent simple outline which summarizes a large amount of the literature on organizations and bureaucracy.

*A. Etzioni.—*Complex Organisation: A Sociological Reader* (Holt, Rinehart and Winston, 1962). A useful collection of extracts from Weber, Merton, Parsons, Blau, Goffman, and many others.

E. Goffman.—*Asylums* (Anchor Books, 1961), especially pp. 1–124, 'On the Characteristics of Total Institutions'.

J. A. Litterer.—*Organisations: Structure and Behaviour* (Wiley, 1964). A useful book of readings, including extracts from 'classical' writers and recent theoretical and empirical work. See especially W. G. Scott, 'Organization Theory: An Overview and an Appraisal'.

J. G. March and H. A. Simon.—*Organizations* (Wiley, 1958).

R. K. Merton, *et al.*—*A Reader in Bureaucracy* (Free Press, Glencoe, 1960).

*R. K. Merton, *et al.*—*Sociology Today: Problems and Prospects* (Harper Torchbooks, 1965), Chapter 18, A. Gouldner, 'Organizational Analysis'.

*D. S. Pugh, D. J. Hickson and C. R. Hinings.—*Writers on Organizations* (London, 1964). A brief summary of the work of twenty leading writers.

*J. Woodward.—*Management and Technology* (HMSO, 1958). A concise but important analysis, comparing management in batch, mass and process production plants.

Chapter 9

DEVIANCE, DISORGANIZATION AND CHANGE

Perhaps at no previous time in human history has man been so aware of the ubiquity of change and of its increasing tempo. And at no other time has it been more important to understand the mechanisms of change. Changes in the technological field are the most rapid and dramatic and have repercussions which it is difficult to foresee. They are providing us with powerful techniques which some fear we may be unable to control. But changes in belief systems and in political systems are equally far reaching. The emergence of new nations in Africa, and the population explosion, for example, may well play as decisive a part in shaping the second half of the century as the steam engine played in the nineteenth century.

PERSPECTIVES

The subject of change is not, of course, being introduced here for the first time. Previous chapters have examined the ways in which changes in the family, the economic and political systems result not only from their internal dynamics, but also from their articulation with other elements in the social system. The perspectives of this chapter, however, will be concerned rather with *social* change, that is, with the nature, direction, and extent of change in the social system as a whole. Moreover, in order to reduce the problem to manageable proportions, we shall concentrate on one major theme— the industrialization and modernization of contemporary societies, and attempt to throw some light on the causes of industrialization as an ongoing process. In doing so, we shall need to take more fully into account the role of strains and tensions in generating innovation and deviance, and the relation of conflicts to disorganization and change.

This chapter will, therefore, look at problems of deviance, conflict, and change from such perspectives. It must be stressed that the framework used for relating these aspects is of necessity tentative. Moreover, it is only one of a number of possible approaches, but it is the one which emerges logically from the framework outlined in Chapter 1 in which three main components of social systems were isolated, the cultural, structural and personality systems.

The study of social change is by far the most complex of any topic in sociology. More than any other, it is necessary to go beyond description to explanation, and to attempt to arrive at generalizations. It is in this field that the claim of sociology to be a science is frequently challenged. The object of science, it is argued, is to be able to predict. And it is the inability of sociology to predict which indicates its immaturity. Such charges can be countered by distinguishing between prediction and prophecy.[1] The sociologist does not claim to be able to foretell the future. Prediction involves being able to say what is likely to happen to other variables in a system when one changes. Nevertheless, the difficulties of dealing with social change underlines the undeveloped state of theory and the paucity of theory-oriented research.

Meaning of change

One major difficulty presents itself at the outset. What precisely do we mean by social change? There is considerable conceptual confusion here, in which a wide variety of terms has been used to refer to various aspects of change, including evolution, development, adaptation, and social process. We must identify both the units for analysis, and the kind of changes which we wish to define as social change. We might, for example, look at the changes in the recruitment of the British cabinet. But this may not involve changes in the structure of the cabinet or its functions and may not, therefore, be considered a significant social change. Again, we may demonstrate the emergence of more equalitarian relations within the family, or the institutionalization of industrial conflict through the establishment of arbitration machinery. These are changes *within* sub-systems and do not constitute major change *of* systems. An example of the latter would be the change from a feudal to a capitalist society. But here again, there are major problems of conceptualization. There is controversy, for example, as to whether the distinguishing features of feudalism are to be found in its economic system or its political system or whether it is a configuration of economic and political variables. We are faced, that is to say, with the problem of devising a classification of types of society.

An alternative approach which avoids such taxonomic problems is to conceive of social change as a process of structural differentia-

[1] K. Popper, *The Poverty of Historicism* (1957).

tion. This is the approach adopted by functionalists such as Parsons.[1] Smelser's[2] study of the industrial revolution, for example, shows how the decline of the domestic economy involved the structural differentiation of the family and the economic system and their functional specialization.

It may also be useful to differentiate between social change and cultural change, and the interrelations between them. In fact, a major controversy in sociology has revolved around such a distinction. Marx, for example, argued that the ideological superstructure of society was built up on the material basis of society, and reflected the techniques of production, and the mode of production to which these techniques gave rise. Ideology could only hasten or retard the process of change but could not in the long run stand against it. Weber, on the other hand, maintained that ideological changes were a necessary pre-condition for the evolution of capitalism, and attributed the emergence of the 'spirit of capitalism' to the influence of protestant sects. Ogburn[3] formulated a theory of 'cultural lag' in which he argued that there was a tendency for the 'non-material' culture to lag behind the 'material' culture.

TRENDS—MODERNIZATION AND INDUSTRIALIZATION

The study of social change has been primarily pre-occupied with change at the macro level—that is with broad trends in the evolution and development of social systems. In the nineteenth century, for example, the theories of biological evolution greatly influenced speculation about the course of human history. Studies of the origin of species in the biological sphere were matched by attempts to reconstruct the natural history of social institutions, such as the origins of religion, the family, and the state. Even more ambitious schemes attempted to discover the laws governing the evolution and development of human societies. Comte, for example, maintained that all societies went through three stages of development from a primitive phase in which theological modes of thought predominate through a metaphysical to a positive (scientific) stage in which the knowledge is based on observation.[4] Many such nineteenth-century theories sought to establish not only the trends of change, but also that this was in an ethically desirable direction. That is to say, laws

[1] See T. Parson, 'A Functional Theory of Change', in A. and E. Etzioni, *Social Change: Sources, Patterns and Consequences* (1964).

[2] N. J. Smelser, *Social Change and the Industrial Revolution* (1959).

[3] W. F. Ogburn, *Social Change* (1922).

[4] For examples of such theories, see A. and E. Etzioni, *op. cit.* (1964), Part 1.

of progress could be discerned.

In more recent years, there has been a shift of attention away from the ambitious task of plotting the course of social evolution to the more limited problem of analysing the transition from pre-industrial to industrial society, discovering the factors which stimulate or retard the process, and exploring the social concomitants of industrialization. Such questions have gained an added significance from their relevance to the rapid emergence of African states and their efforts at modernization.

'Modernization' and 'industrialization' are not synonymous concepts. Modernization refers to attempts to acquire the features which characterize the industrially advanced societies, such as high levels of education, medical services, and a modern civil service. It is clear that such changes are only possible where there is a high level of per capita income, and this, in turn, depends on a high level of application of power to the production processes—i.e. industrialization. But although we can expect some measure of congruence between industrialization and modernization in the long run, in the short run an emerging state may acquire some of the characteristics of a modern society, such as a declining death rate, without having progressed far with industrialization.

There is a fairly extensive literature which compares the characteristics of pre-industrial *traditional* societies with those of industrial *modern* societies. By contrast with traditional societies, modern societies have experienced a demographic revolution with a sharp decline in both birth-rate and death rate, a decrease in the size, scope and pervasiveness of the family, an opening up of the stratification system with the shift from ascribed to achieved status, a levelling of culture with the development of mass communications and mass education, a high level of education, and the secularization and bureaucratization of society.

An alternative conceptualization of the comparison between pre-industrial and industrial society has been developed by R. Redfield, who distinguishes the *folk* society as the polar opposite of the *urban* society.. The folk-type is '. . . small, isolated, non-literate, and homogeneous, with a strong sense of group solidarity . . . Behaviour is traditional, spontaneous, uncritical and personal . . . Kinship, its relationships and institutions, are the type categories of experience and the familiar group is the unit of action. The sacred prevails over the secular; the economy is one of status rather than of the market.'[1]

[1] For a criticism of Redfield's scheme, see H. Miner, 'The Folk-Urban Continuum', in A. and E. Etzioni, *op. cit.* (1964), Chapter 18.

The urban type is the polar opposite, and is characterized by heterogeneity and disorganization, the decay of kinship, the dominance of the secular and of the market. Parsons has described folk society in terms of his four pattern-variables as particularistic, diffuse, collective, affective and ascriptive, while urban society is governed by universalism, specificity, affective neutrality and achievement orientation. As Miner points out, the two concepts are ideal type constructs and must be viewed as the poles of a continuum. Societies combine both folk and urban elements. We have already seen in previous chapters that some aspects of the extended family network persist in urban societies (Chapter 2) while there is evidence of the existence of strong religious communities in large cities (Chapter 6).[1]

These comparisons of the main features of pre-industrial and industrial societies raise a number of further questions. What, for example, are the sources of change? What factors stimulate the process of interrelated changes which characterize the process of industrialization? In other words, what are the conditions and consequences of industrialization? It is, in fact, by no means easy to distinguish between the pre-conditions of industrialization and its consequences. This difficulty can be avoided by adopting the more limited goal of examining empirically the concomitants of industrialization, and the range of variation in the various sub-systems and their functioning.[2] For example, the increasing division of labour which characterizes mechanization, and the organization of the labour force in factory production is normally accompanied by work relations which are functionally specific (confined to specified duties), impersonal, and affectively neutral (based on contractual relations rather than personal loyalties). Yet in many of the smaller factories, kinship relations again play an important part in the recruitment of the labour force, wages often reflect seniority, and employment relations are highly particularistic.[3]

This more limited approach can also help to illuminate the distinction between the pre-conditions and the consequences of industrialization. There is no doubt that major changes in the educational system accompany industrialization. What is less certain is to what extent such changes are pre-conditions or consequences. They may indeed be both. There is little doubt that industrialization

[1] For a discussion of the 'rural-urban' continuum, based on English community studies, see R. Frankenburg, *Communities in Britain* (1966), Chapter 11. This book was published too late for the inclusion of a more detailed discussion.

[2] See, for example, B. F. Hoselitz and W. E. Moore, *Industrialisation and Society* (1960), Chapter 15.

[3] *Ibid.*, and also J. C. Abegglen, *Japanese Factory* (1958).

motivates individuals to seek education as a means of achieving occupational advancement. It is also probable that education contributes to the development of the achievement motivation required by an industrial society. It is also possible to avoid the extreme functionalist position that a change in technology has repercussions throughout the social system. The sub-systems have varying degrees of autonomy. And as we have seen, in the field of education, institutions may resist the demands of the economic system, at least for a considerable time, and may in this way have a feedback affect on the economic system and reduce its rate of change.

There seems little support for the more extreme view that the functional requirements of industrialization will necessarily bring about a substantial homogeneity in the social systems of industrial societies.[1] Nor is there any necessity that the process of industrialization need involve the same steps for all societies. Much will depend on the characteristics of society before industrialization. We have already seen, for example (Chapter 7), that industrialization is consistent with quite considerable differences in systems of stratification, and there is little support for a theory of convergence between stratification systems in industrial societies.[2] The differences are most marked in the political sphere, where highly industrialized societies include a wide variety of political regimes. This does not mean that there are no limits to the range of variations in the social systems of industrial society. The notion of a modern society indicates that there are sufficient common features to make such a concept meaningful. On the other hand, the constraints on variability may well be less than we have hitherto considered as a result of the restriction of industrialization until recently to a relatively small segment of the western world.[3]

SOURCES OF CHANGE AND DISORGANIZATION

There is no absence of literature on the subject of the causes of social change.[4] Indeed, it was a major pre-occupation of the 'founding

[1] Clark Kerr, *et al.*, *Industrialism and Industrial Man* (1964), sees such changes as a part of the logic of industrialization.

[2] J. H. Goldthorpe, 'Stratification in Industrial Society', *Sociological Review Monograph*, No. 8.

[3] For a summary of the concomitants and consequences of industrialization, see W. E. Moore, *Social Change* (1963), pp. 97–105, and B. F. Hoselitz and W. E. Moore, *Industrialization and Society* (1960), Chapter 15, 'Industrialization and Social Change'.

[4] For a summary, see A. and E. Etzioni, *op. cit.* (1964), Parts I and 11, and

fathers'. The close connexion between the origins of sociology and the philosophy of history has left us with a legacy which includes a wide variety of theories of social development, evolution and progress, including Comte's 'law' of the three stages of evolution, Marx's theory of the role of 'modes of production' as the prime-mover, and Weber's emphasis on culture as a key variable. Most early theories were 'monistic' (single factor) theories, attributing change to a single variable, such as technological innovation. Many were not distinctively sociological, but located the prime-mover in factors external to society, such as genetic or climatic factors.[1]

Economic and cultural factors

Among the most influential theories of social change is that which focuses on technology as the independent variable and claims that all other changes are functions of changes in the technological sphere. Of the various forms of this theory, Marx's version is the best known and will be briefly examined here.[2] In Marx's view, it is the stage of technological development which determines the mode of production and the institutions and relationships that constitute the economic system: 'the sum total of these relations of production constitutes the economic structure of society—the real foundation, on which rise legal and political superstructures and to which correspond definite forms of social consciousness.'[3]

There are major difficulties in this theory. The exact degree of determinism is by no means clear from Marx. Moreover, although it is easy to demonstrate a correlation between social and economic changes, Marx certainly failed to demonstrate that the one was the single cause of the other. But by far the most fatal objection is the fact that Marx failed to account for technological innovations (which are essentially changes in culture), and for the appearance of a class of innovating entrepreneurs. Marx oversimplifies the problem of accounting for such innovations and assumes that there are no hindrances to the application of new ideas to the production processes. Moreover, recent examples of emerging states point to the role which the political system may play in stimulating technological developments in the pursuit of modernization as an expression of

W. E. Moore, 'A reconsideration of theories of social change', *A.S.R.*, Vol. 25, Dec. 1960.

[1] A major objection to such theories is that climate and genetic changes occur more slowly than changes in social systems. See M. Ginsberg, *Sociology* (1934).

[2] For a more detailed examination of such theories, including that of T. Veblen, see R. MacIver and C. H. Page, *Society* (1960), Chapter 25.

[3] *Critique of Political Economy*, p. 11.

nationalism. Furthermore, such developments have themselves been profoundly influenced in many cases by the policies of colonial governments which have promoted the development of rational bureaucratic administrative systems in economically underdeveloped countries.[1] In other words, the course of industrialization does not necessarily follow one single line of development.

Marx's neglect of the role of cultural variables in social change stimulated Weber to undertake an elaborate inquiry into the role of culture in which Weber concluded that certain religious forms, notably Protestantism in the West have provided the necessary values and motivations for economic development. He pointed to both the congruence between the values of Protestantism, with its emphasis on hard work, thrift, and abstinence, and those of the entrepreneurs, and to the motivation which Protestantism provided by legitimizing worldly success.[2] Whatever the criticisms and limitations[3] of Weber's explanation, he drew attention to the complexity of the process of economic change, and the role of culture in providing values and legitimation for conduct.

Functionalist theories
By contrast with the mainly monistic theories of the past, contemporary theories stress the systemic nature of society, and accept the possibility that the initiation of change may derive from any one segment, or even several. This approach involves exploring the interactions between elements in the social system in the process of change. We may, for example, accept the view that technological developments within the economic system have been the most influential factors during the process of industrialization. But to explain such changes, we have to account for the appearance of innovations and their application to the production process. This directs our attention to changes in the cultural sphere and also raises questions about the conditions favouring the emergence of innovating personalities.[4] Such considerations raise further questions about the kind of family structures, political and educational systems which facilitate economic growth and lead to an analysis of the interaction between the various elements in a social system undergoing industrialization. Such an approach suggests that the search for a

[1] For a discussion see S. N. Eisenstadt, 'Political Development', in A. and E. Etzioni, *op. cit.* (1964), Chapter 34.
[2] *The Protestant Ethic and the Spirit of Capitalism* (1930).
[3] See R. H. Tawney, *Religion and the Rise of Capitalism* (1926).
[4] This will be examined at the end of the chapter.

single cause may not be very profitable. It indicates concentration rather on the process of change, the factors which facilitate or retard change, and the consequences for other elements in the social system of changes in any one segment.

This essentially functionalist approach has, in turn, attracted criticism. In its most extreme form, functionalism implies that a change in any one element in the social system will lead to adjustive changes in other elements, and in this way, the integration of the system will be maintained. In particular, it is argued, the functionalist approach ignores the existence of conflict, and the role of coercion in maintaining integration. Durkheim, for example, saw society as a system of ways of acting, thinking, and feeling, external to the individual, which exert pressures on the individual to conform. And although he emphasized the coercive elements in society, he placed most emphasis on what he called the collective conscience or consciousness; that is to say, on shared values and norms. Only when these break down, as, for example, during periods of rapid social change, does conflict and coercion appear. Talcott Parsons similarly stresses the role of values as integrative elements in society.

More recently however, sociologists such as Dahrendorf[1] and Rex[2] have criticized such one-sided emphasis on consensus. Wrong[3] has gone farther and argued that the consensus school has placed too much stress on the extent to which the individual has internalized the values and norms of society through socialization. Integrated and co-ordinated social action, he argues, does not necessarily depend on such a high degree of socialization and consensus. Men can work together for what appear to be common goals from quite different motives. Studies of industrial work also suggest that the involvement of workers is slight. Many comply with the rules not because they think they are right, nor because they share the goals of the organization, but simply because work is a source of income.[4]

Such criticisms have prompted replies from the functionalists who have rejected the view that functionalism cannot provide a satisfactory approach for the study of social change. Both Parsons and Smelser have argued that the structural-functional model of social systems can handle the analysis of change. One important

[1] R. Dahrendorf, *Class and Class Conflict in Industrial Societies* (1959).

[2] J. Rex, *Key Problems of Sociological Theory* (1961).

[3] D. Wrong, 'The Over-socialized View of Man', in N. J. Smelser and W. J. Smelser, *Personality and Social Systems* (1963).

[4] Political theorists such as Hobbes and Marx have also emphasized conflicts of interest and the role of coercion.

kind of change is increasing division of labour or differentiation of functions. During industrialization, the functions of socialization and production shift from the family to other agencies. This process requires that the new units which emerge to perform the specialized functions be related to each other. In other words, functional differentiation involves the re-formation of social structures.[1]

An alternative answer to the critics has been put forward by Cancian[2] who points out that the concept of functional requisites for the maintenance of the system can also be used to state the conditions for disintegration, and indicate the corrective changes adopted by the system to restore equilibrium.

Structural strains, and conflict

It is clearly difficult to account for change using a model of society which is preoccupied with demonstrating the integrative functions of norms. Hence, writers such as Rex and Dahrendorf both 'assert that social change is a result of the shifting balance of power between conflict groups'.[3] But as Lockwood has pointed out, however much importance we attach to the role of conflict and coercion we still cannot ignore the importance of value systems and ideologies which play a key role in structuring the individual's definition of the situation and hence his response to it.

It is not, of course, being argued that strains and conflicts necessarily lead to social change. Only some of the possible range of societal responses will have this result. We are simply identifying a possible source of change in the strains and conflicts within subsystems or between structural elements in the social system. Moreover, structural strains are not the same as individual strains. Dissatisfaction with low wages, for example, does not necessarily lead to trade unions and organized industrial conflict. The conditions under which individual dissatisfactions lead to collective action will be examined later. Meanwhile, we will first turn to an analysis of the extent of conflict and its relations to disorganization and change.

[1] T. Parsons, 'A Functional Theory of Change', and N. J. Smelser, 'Towards a Theory of Modernization', in A. and E. Etzioni, *op. cit.* (1964), Chapters 12 and 30.

[2] F. Cancian, 'Functional Analysis of Change', *ibid.*, Chapter 14.

[3] D. Lockwood, 'Social Integration and System Integration', in G. K. Zollschan and W. Hirsch, *Explorations in Social Change* (1964). See also R. Dahrendorf, 'Toward a Theory of Social Conflict', A. and E. Etzioni, *op. cit.* (1964), Chapter 13.

Industrial conflict[1]

One particularly important location for conflict in industrial societies is industry. Employment is the sole source of income for most. Moreover, it is in his daily work that a man may become most conscious of the coercive nature of society and of his relative powerlessness.

Strike statistics provide an index of industrial conflict, although it must be remembered that there are other ways of expressing discontent, such as absenteeism and labour turnover. The broad trend has been a marked decline in the number of working days lost through strikes this century. Peak years were 1912 with 41 million days lost, 1920 with 27 million, and 1921 with 86 million.[2] By contrast, the post Second World War years have had from 2 million to 3 million days lost.

The high figures for the early decades of the century were due to a relatively small number of strikes involving large numbers of workers for a long period. These were the days when industrial conflict came close to a class struggle. Indeed, the general strike was an attempt to achieve political ends by industrial action. These were the years when miners were struggling for adequate basic wages, hours, and conditions of work. The bitterness of the struggle reflected the relative poverty and insecurity of workers in basic industries such as mining and textiles, and the unwillingness of the employers to reach negotiated agreements. Strikes were a show of force in a conflict for power to control market and work conditions.

In recent decades, there have been many more strikes, but of much shorter duration and involving fewer workers. Part of the explanation is the growth of complex negotiating and consultative machinery,[3] so that more disputes are now settled through conciliation and few become overt strikes. There has also been a substantial measure of accommodation by the employers to the demands of the workers. Fewer strikes are over basic issues, and more are frictional disputes over working arrangements. In the strike-prone industries such as mining and textiles, which contributed a disproportionate share to the disputes of the early decades, workers faced special difficulties. These industries were located in areas where there were

[1] See A. Kornhauser (ed.), *et al.*, *Industrial Conflict* (1954), for an extensive discussion of this subject, especially Chapter 40.

[2] K. G. J. C. Knowles, *Strikes: A Study of Industrial Conflict* (1952). The figure for 1926 (the year of the general strike) is, of course, much higher but not typical.

[3] Strikes are more frequent in large pits where the immediate settlement of a dispute is more difficult. S. Wellisz, 'Strikes in Coal Mining', *B.J.S.*, Dec. 1953.

few alternative chances for employment. There was, therefore no escape from frustrating circumstances and unemployment.[1] The post-war policy of industrial diversification has provided an escape for those who would otherwise be pent-up with little alternative.

The significance of industrial conflict for social change and integration depends largely on the extent to which conflict is confined and accommodated within the boundaries of the economic system, and the extent to which it is carried over and articulated as political demands for some radical change in the power structure. And this in turn will reflect the legitimacy of existing arrangements.

Class conflict
The existence of class conflict in society is to some extent a matter of definitions. For Marx, conflicts derive essentially from the ownership and non-ownership of the means of production. Marx believed that the increasing concentration of ownership and the resulting increasing impoverishment of the masses would lead to the growing polarization of society in warring classes, and the eventual overthrow of capitalist owners by the proletarian revolution. Indeed, it was in the class struggle that Marx located the dynamics of social change; 'The history of all hitherto existing society is the history of the class struggle'. But this does not mean that every strike over wages is part of the class struggle. Only if workers define themselves as members of a common class with a common fate and are seeking to change the position of their class by achieving power can such a conflict be defined as a class conflict in Marx's sense.

In fact, industrialization and the growth of per capita income is directly related to weak support for such revolutionary class movements. But it is not poverty alone which generates radicalism. On the contrary, stable poverty tends to be associated with conservatism. It is the awareness of the possibilities of betterment which accompanies industrialization, which is explosive. It is relative deprivation,[2] not absolute poverty which generates discontent. Where industrialization has been accompanied by the extension of the franchise and a party system, it has provided legitimate channels for the expression of discontent.[3]

[1] See also C. Kerr and A. Siegel, 'The Inter-industry propensity to strike', A. Kornhauser, *et al.*, *op. cit.* (1954), Chapter 14.
[2] For a recent discussion of this concept, see W. G. Runciman, *Relative Deprivation and Social Justice* (1966).
[3] S. M. Lipset, *op. cit.* (1959), pp. 61–7, 'Economic Development and the Class Struggle'.

Dahrendorf however, argues that class is essentially a question of power. All associations are co-ordinated by means of an authority structure, and it is the resulting differential distribution of authority which dichotomizes society into those who have and have not power. The class struggle is the struggle for power—including power to dispose of material resources, and to regulate conditions of work. Thus, even in a fully socialized society, the struggle for material resources and to control aspects of the work situation would remain. The 'new class' would be the managers and party officials who exercised control. According to this view, the class struggle is a permanent feature of all organized societies. Its severity can be mitigated and controlled by the reduction of objective differences and by the 'institutionalization' of conflict, but it cannot be entirely abolished.

Social conflict, disorganization and change

The maintenance of social integration depends not only on the existence and extent of conflict, but also on the effectiveness of the mechanisms which exist for its management. Conflicts occur between the structural elements in society. Those occupying dominant roles in one segment of the social system may seek to dominate other segments. The military elite, for example, may attempt to capture the political machinery or the church may seek to dominate the state. This is a struggle between rival elites for dominance over other elites. A second type of conflict occurs within a sub-system of the social structure. There may be conflict for dominance between rival religious groupings, or contending political parties, or between workers and owners in the economic system over the distribution of incomes.

One of the most important factors influencing the intensity of conflict is the existence and perception of objective differences in the distribution of power, income, property, status. But equally important is the meaning attached to such differences. If, for example, the contrast between 'The rich man in his castle, The poor man at his gate' is perceived, it is less likely to become a basis for social conflict if the distinction is judged to be legitimate, as the next two lines of the hymn suggest—'God made them high or lowly, And order'd their estate.'[1] Two further conditions are necessary for the emergence of conflict; firstly, the perception of common interests by those who feel they have grounds for grievance, and finally an awareness of

[1] Hymns Ancient and Modern, 1889 edition. As a previous chapter showed, an important function of belief systems in the culture is to provide individuals with meanings and definitions for the situation in which they find themselves

the possibility of common action. A conflict may remain latent until the situation is defined as favourable for overt action. The severity of overt conflict will depend on the existence of societal machinery for channelling, accommodating and managing conflict—what Dahrendorf[1] calls the institutionalization of conflict. The development of arbitration machinery and industrial law, for example, has channelled and controlled industrial conflict.

Finally, a most important factor influencing the strength of conflict and the possibility of accommodation is the extent to which there is a super-imposition of differences so that they become cumulative and lead to unbridgeable dichotomies. If workers, for example, are members of the same religious groups, then religious similarities will reinforce economic interests and intensify the conflict with opposing groups. Both Lipset and Coser stress the fact that the existence of multiple group affiliations in democracies is a major integrating factor reducing conflict.

Coser stresses the fact that overt conflict is not necessarily dis-integrative. On the contrary, it acts as a safety valve by providing an outlet for accumulated frustrations. Moreover, both Dahrendorf and Coser argue that it leads to the search for associations, coalitions, and machinery for the management of conflict and thus performs an integrative function.[2]

In order to examine the implications of conflict for social disorganization, it is necessary to establish first the criteria for determining its existence. The simplest approach is to start from the notion of organization and consider what we mean by a breakdown of organization. It was shown in Chapter 8 that the essence of organization is the allocation of tasks and their co-ordination for the pursuit of goals in accordance with a set of constituted roles. Disorganization may occur therefore (a) when individuals are not adequately motivated to act out roles, (b) when there is no system of rules which adequately defines the behaviour of actors in the system (anomie). Such breakdowns of organization can, of course, occur in any of the sub-systems of society. But it is when such a breakdown threatens the stability of the total social system that we are faced with the possibility of a major social disorganization.

Thus, as we have seen, conflict does not necessarily threaten disorganization. Much will depend on the responses of the system and the means it adopts to accommodate conflicts of interests. Those

[1] R. Dahrendorf, *Class and Class Conflict in Industrial Society* (1959).
[2] L. Coser, *The Functions of Social Conflict* (1956). See also the discussion of 'cleavage' in Chapter 5.

social systems which have elaborate mechanisms for the articulation and aggregation of interests are less likely to be threatened by a breakdown of organization, and are more likely to have achieved a consensus on ends and means. Conflict may stimulate the development of machinery for its resolution. Arbitration is a means whereby a compromise is reached which is accepted as legitimate by both sides. By such means, conflict may be 'institutionalized', that is to say, regulated by an agreed set of rules. Once the parties act outside the rules, there is a degree of disorganization.

Apart from attempts to modify rules or devise fresh rules to contain actions within an organized framework, efforts may be made to increase the motivations of the individual to abide by the rules. Appeals to higher obligations, efforts to increase the perceived legitimacy of the rules, or the threat of sanctions and coercion, may all contain actions within the framework of rules, while in no way lessening the basic dissatisfactions or conflicts of interest. Adaptations of the social system in these ways may be sufficiently basic to constitute a change within the system. The emergence of machinery for the handling of industrial disputes constitutes a change within the economic system, but not social change in the sense of change in the structure of the social system.[1]

The existence of deviance, such as crime, and social problems, such as divorce, do not therefore, by themselves, indicate social disorganization. While marriages are contracted and terminated within an agreed set of rules, sexual life remains organized. A high rate of family instability, may of course, present a society with problems and hinder the tension-management and latency functions of the family. It may, therefore, indirectly contribute to disorganization, by reducing the motivation of individuals to carry out their roles in the economic system.

INDIVIDUALS AND THE SOCIAL SYSTEM

Strains and conflicts between sub-systems clearly do not exhaust the possible sources of disorganization and change. In the last analysis, strains are experienced by individuals and conflicts are between groups of individuals. We turn now, therefore, to a study of the sources of tensions and strains, and those responses of individuals which take the form of non-conformity or deviant behaviour. But first, we must establish the nature and variety of non-conformity.

[1] See R. Dahrendorf, *Class and Class Conflict in Industrial Society* (1959), for an elaboration of this distinction.

It must be remembered that deviant behaviour is only one kind of non-conformity. Inventors, reformers, delinquents—are all non-conformists. The term 'deviant' is however, reserved for those actions which violate the moral norms of a society. It tells us therefore, something about the society rather than about the individual, since an action which is considered immoral in one society may be acceptable in another (e.g. homosexuality or polygamy).

Conformity requires the pursuit of socially valued ends by socially approved means. Merton identifies four types of non-conformity derived from the differential acceptance of means and ends. In industrial societies such as America and Britain, great emphasis is placed on the achievement of success judged in terms of wealth and status. Such cultural emphasis on success goals plays an important part in encouraging the high levels of motivation which industrial societies require. But it also presents problems for those who are handicapped in the race for success, especially ethnic minorities and the children of manual workers. There is a variety of responses to such stress situations. *Innovation* involves the search for new means in addition to those already recognized and prescribed by the culture. Some such means may be condemned by society, such as fraud and robbery, while others are simply viewed unfavourably, such as institutionalized gambling.

FIGURE 9.1

TYPES OF NON-CONFORMITY*

	Values (Ends)	Norms. (Approved means)
1. Conformity	+	+
2. Innovation	+	—
3. Ritualism	—	+
4. Retreatism	±	±
5. Rebellion	—	—

* R. K. Merton, *op. cit.*

This situation in which there is a lack of agreement on socially recognized means was recognized by Durkheim as an important factor contributing to social disintegration. He described it as a condition of *anomie* (or normlessness) and believed it to be one of the consequences of rapid social change. But Durkheim also stressed that where the social pressure to conform was excessively strong, that such a situation would inhibit change and innovation. This led him to the view that crime is not only normal in society, but also functional, in the sense that it occurs in social systems in which the normative system is not so repressive that it inhibits all deviance. In other words, crime, innovation, and reform, are all functions of social systems which permit deviance.

Ritualism involves giving up the pursuit of ends and the search for security in a ritualistic involvement in means. By an undue emphasis on rules, the timid bureaucrat may allay the anxieties which the exercise of discretion might generate. The *retreatist* abandons both the goals and the sanctioned patterns of behaviour. He retreats from involvement in life to drink, drug addiction, or simply melancholic withdrawal to the role of a fatalistic and passive onlooker. *Rebellion* is the total rejection of both culturally approved ends and means. It may take a political form which involves a rejection of the dominant values of society (for example, the rejection of the aristocracy in the French Revolution) together with an attempt to change the social structure. Or it may take the form of a social movement. Beatniks, for example, reject the traditional values of society, such as material gain and success, and adopt socially disapproved means (drug-taking, deviant styles of dress) to achieve valued ends such as 'creative experiences'.

But Merton's paradigm is not a theory which accounts for conformity or deviance. It simply provides us with a list of the possible forms of nonconformity. We may take the analysis further by examining both the motivation to non-conformity and the constraints on non-conformity. In some cases, the constraints which ensure our conformity are external—legal sanctions with the threat of coercion and punishment, or incentives, such as production bonuses or chances of promotion, or the fear of ridicule which leads us to comply with conventions. In others, the constraints are internal. The child learns through the socialization process that stealing and lying are wrong and accepts these as moral imperatives. The scientist values knowledge and feels impelled to publish his findings without distortion.

The relative importance of internal and external constraints will vary both between individuals and in different circumstances. In our work for example, we may be calculatively involved, we may refrain from exceeding the speed limit simply because we fear a conviction, while we remain faithful to our wife because we think it is right to do so. Riesman[1] has suggested that there are three modes of conformity

---

[1] D. Riesman, *The Lonely Crowd*. Riesman's views have been criticized on theoretical and empirical grounds, but they are valuable for the insights they provide.

and that their relative importance varies in different periods. *Inner-directed* persons, for example, are dominated by conscience and inner drives. They have an internal gyroscope which keeps them on a fixed course. This type was dominant in nineteenth-century America. It corresponds to the rugged individualism of the protestant ethic and the entrepreneur. *Other-directed* persons have a radar-like sensivity to others, particularly to the *significant others* whose opinions they value. They are sensitive to their expectations and adjust readily to social demands. The *other-directed* type is dominant in the modern era in which the emphasis is on consumption and performance in bureaucratic organizations. Conformity has become more important than self-assertion for getting on, and parents and schools have come to emphasize such values and to encourage their development in children. The third *tradition-directed* type is dominant only in relatively static societies.

Conformity then, may be the result of internalized constraints, external pressures such as incentives which satisfy needs, the opinions and expectations of others, or the threat of coercion. But in addition to such pressure, individuals are also caught up in a network of reciprocal obligations and expectations. Malinowski[1] has shown that reciprocity can be a powerful force securing conformity. Present giving at Christmas is perhaps the clearest example. We may at times feel ourselves to be trapped in a ritualistic exchange of gifts in which values are nicely balanced and from which escape is extremely difficult. These 'norms of reciprocity', Gouldner[2] suggests, exists in all societies. But such considerations throw light only on the expression of non-conformity. They do not examine the motivational sources of non-conformity, or to factors which shape particular responses. It is to this problem to which we now turn.

Significant discrepancies between what is expected and what is experienced generate problems for the individual. The response to such *exigencies* may be individual or collective. Individual responses include alcoholism, drug addiction, suicide and many crimes. Eisenstadt refers to responses such as these as the 'retreat from role performance'.[3] An important sociological problem here is to investigate the social factors which determine the rates of various types of deviant behaviour, that is, the *epidemiology* of deviance.[4]

[1] B. Malinowski, *Crime and Custom in Savage Society* (1960).

[2] A. W. Gouldner, 'The Norm of Reciprocity', *A.S.R.*, April 1960.

[3] *Comparative Social Problems* (1964).

[4] This perspective stems from the work of Durkheim, who first demonstrated that suicide was a function of specific social structures. *Suicide* (1952).

Sociological studies have also shown that such problems are widespread in human societies, though their incidence and society's response to them may vary.

Suicide, drug addiction, alcoholism

The most extreme form of retreat from the performance of roles is suicide. It is not only generally regarded in all societies as deviant behaviour (in the normative sense), but constitutes a major form of death, accounting for about one per cent of all deaths in the United Kingdom. Over 5,000 suicides in England and Wales in 1959 far exceeds the 320 deaths by homicide and war.[1] The trends in most countries over the last fifty years have been fairly stable, but there have been more marked fluctuations in recent years.[2]

One of the pioneer works in scientific sociology, Durkheim's *Le Suicide* challenged the view that the explanation of suicide was to be found simply in the psychology of the individual.[3] Durkheim adopted the epidemiological approach to the study of suicide and sought to establish the reasons for varying suicide rates. In a detailed statistical study, he claimed to demonstrate that suicide rates were a function of the integration of the individual in social groups. This, he argues, explains why the single, widowed and divorced, are more prone to suicide than the married. Furthermore, Durkheim maintained, the inverse relation between religious subscription and suicide cannot be explained by the normative condemnation of suicide by religion. Such reasoning cannot explain the high incidence of suicide among Protestants and Jews, and the lower incidence among Catholics since all religions proscribe suicide.[4] The explanation, argues Durkheim is again to be found in the fact that both Catholics and Jews form more close-knit communities, and it is this integration of the individual in a religious community which preserves him from suicide. This view has received some recent support from

[1] United Nations' *Demographic Yearbook* (1961). England and Wales has a lower rate than some other European countries (10·8 per 100,000 population) compared with Austria 22·8, Sweden 17·8, France 15·9, but is higher than Norway 7·4, Italy 6·1.

[2] United Nations, *Epidemiological and Vital Statistics Report*, Vol. 9, No. 4 (1956).

[3] The female rate for mental illness, for example, is higher than the male, yet more males commit suicide.

[4] It is, of course, possible to argue that the consequences of suicide for the Catholic deriving from the doctrine of mortal sin without repentance leads to attempts to avoid accepting deaths in the Catholic community as suicide, if it can be avoided, and hence to unreliable statistics. In fact, the uncertain reliability of statistics is a major weakness hindering adequate analysis.

a study of suicide which showed a positive correlation between the number of single-member households and the suicide rate of London boroughs.[1]

Suicide which results from the lack of integration between the individual and the group Durkheim called *egoistic* suicide. He distinguished this from *altruistic* suicide which results from actual group pressure to commit suicide under some circumstances, such as the Hindu custom of widows committing suicide (suttee). A third type he identified as *anomic* suicide. This occurs when some social crisis, such as economic disaster challenges the established norms and values which regulate society and restrain the actions of the individual. There is a collapse of what he calls the *collective conscience*, and the individual finds himself in a normless vacuum.

Such a disturbance of the norms and values of society, Durkheim maintains, may occur not only during periods of economic depression, but also during times of growing prosperity. This, he argues, may explain the higher incidence of suicide among the upper income groups, and the evidence which Durkheim claimed showed an increase near the peak of the economic cycle as well as the trough. This aspect of Durkheim's theory has, however, been challenged by more recent researches which find suicide to be associated with periods of business contraction.

An alternative explanation argues that both suicide and homicide are aggressive responses to frustration.[2] But whereas suicide increases with depression, homicide increases with prosperity among Negroes, and declines for whites. Moreover, suicide is concentrated in the high status categories, while homicide characterizes low status categories. A tentative explanation is sought in the explanation that suicide and homicide are both responses to 'extreme frustration arising from loss of position in the status hierarchy relative to the status position of others in the same status reference group'.[3] It is further argued that relative status deprivation is highest among high status categories during business depression, since they have much to lose, hence the increase in suicide, while frustration is lowest among lower-class Negroes during business contraction, hence the decrease in their homicide rate.

The argument is too complex and the data too scanty for a full treatment here, but enough has been said to outline the possibility of alternative hypotheses which remain basically sociological, since they

[1] P. Sainsbury, *Suicide in London* (1955).
[2] A. F. Henry and J. F. Short, Jnr, *Suicide and Homicide*, 1954.
[3] *Ibid.*

identify the *aetiology* of suicide in the individual's role in the social system.

More recent studies have shown that other aspects of Durkheim's theory are challenged by more complete statistics.[1] There are many cases, for example, in which Jews have higher rates than Protestants (Netherlands), or Catholics higher than Protestants (Toronto).[2] Moreover, although women generally have lower rates than men, the ratio varies extremely widely. But the search for alternative theories has so far failed to yield a satisfactory explanation of the variations between societies and statuses. The attempt to relate suicide to social disorganization, for example, is often essentially tautological since both are conceptualized as lack of conformity to social norms.[3] Nor does secularization account for high rates, since some highly secularized societies such as the United States, Australia and England have only moderate rates. All that we can say with any confidence is that psychological explanations which attribute suicide to some form of mental disorder fail to account for the frequent wide difference between the sexes, religions, occupations, and societies.

Drug addiction is a form of deviant behaviour which also appears to be primarily an escape from the strains of living. In America, it is particularly prevalent among negroes and adolescents, and is heavily concentrated in communities characterized by low socio-economic status, low proportions living in family groups and high rates of variety of social problems including crime and delinquency.[4] Within these areas, drug addiction is highest 'where income and education were at their lowest and where there was the greatest breakdown of normal family living arrangements'.[5] But this is not the only factor. Such facts do not by themselves explain why individuals turn to this particular form of retreatism. An additional consideration appears to be the sub-cultural stress on the search for 'kicks', together with support for behaviour which is contrary to the prevailing norms. The use of narcotics, together with criminality and violence in various forms, are sub-culturally approved means of enjoying the sub-culturally prescribed goal of excitement, which appeals to those

[1] There are also a number of methodological objections. For example, Durkheim's judgment of social integration is purely impressionistic, nor does he provide a definition of integration.

[2] J. P. Gibbs, 'Suicide', in R. K. Merton and R. A. Nisbet, *Contemporary Social Problems* (1961), Chapter 5.

[3] *Ibid.*, p. 252.

[4] J. A. Clausen, 'Drug Addiction', in R. K. Merton and R. A. Nisbet, *Contemporary Social Problems* (1961), Chapter 4.

[5] *Ibid.*, p. 192–3.

who find difficulty in enjoying the more approved forms of satisfaction, or who experience the insecurity, sexual disturbance, and other behavioural disorders associated with a disturbed background.[1]

Drug addiction is not such a serious problem in England as in the USA.[2] This may be due in part to the stronger cultural prohibitions in England. A contributory factor may be the much smaller size of an ethnic minority frustrated in their attempts to achieve socially approved success goals and seeking retreat into fantasy as a tension-management mechanism. The British system of drug control which permits the limited prescription of a maintenance dose on medical grounds has also helped to minimize the growth of an illicit traffic by drug-pushers and the associated criminality.

The control of drug addiction presents particular difficulties which reflect its aetiology in the social role of the addict. Synthetic drugs have been developed which minimized the abstinence syndrome (acute physical and psychological distress) which otherwise locks the sufferer in a vicious circle of addiction. But such treatment alone does nothing to alleviate the pressures to retreatism, and the return to a dependence on the in-group for support is almost inevitable, since addiction generally leads to alienation from the conventional culture. Consequently, recidivism is high.

Closely related to narcotic addiction is alcoholism, which presents similar problems of a withdrawal syndrome. Again, widespread group differences in its incidence indicate the existence of social factors. It is predominantly a male phenomenon, and strongly associated with ethnic groups in the USA, where the Irish and Scandinavians have high rates, and Southern Italians and Jews low rates. Snyder[3] has suggested three main factors which may account for such differences. Firstly, there are *dynamic factors*, which refer to the level of acute psychic tensions within the group.[4] Secondly, there are *normative orientations*, including the norms, ideas and sentiments related to drinking in different groups. Thirdly, there are *alternative factors*; those culturally patterned behaviours which may act as functional alternatives. These factors together constitute the 'pressure' towards alcoholism. There are, for example, marked differences between Americans, Irish and Jews in the normative

[1] See B. M. Spinley, *The Deprived and the Privileged: Personality Development in English Society* (1953).

[2] 350 compared with about 50,000 addicts: Merton and Nisbet, *op. cit.*, p. 218.

[3] 'A Sociological View of the Etiology of Alcoholism', in S. N. Eisenstadt, *op. cit.* (1964), pp. 16–19.

[4] Cross cultural studies provide tentative support for this view. See D. Horton, 'The Functions of Alcohol in Primitive Societies', *ibid.*, pp. 20–5.

orientations toward drinking. Among Jews, 'cultural tradition locates the act of drinking squarely in the network of sacred ideas, sentiments, and activities'.[1] Drinking is primarily expressive and religiously symbolic. Socialization to this pattern begins early in life, and the orthodox Jew 'learns how to drink in a highly controlled, ritualized manner'.[2]

By contrast, in Irish culture, drinking is not associated with a network of religious ideas and sentiments. Moreover, cultural traditions define the meaning of drinking so that the individual is likely to drink in situations of stress, simply to meet his needs to adjust as an individual.

This is a very tentative and hypothetical approach, but it does suggest that the current tendency to treat alcoholism simply as a disease resulting from chemical changes due to excessive drinking is likely to have only partial success. However, the attempts to establish support for alcoholics by the formation of 'alcoholics anonymous' groups may go some way to provide functional alternatives.

Crime and delinquency

We need to remind ourselves that crime is a social category. It refers to that class of actions that a particular society defines as illegal and as attracting legal sanctions. Many acts considered to be immoral are not crimes. And there would not be consensus about the immorality of all crimes. It is also important to remember that the majority of individuals are never indicted for criminal offences. The interesting problem therefore from the sociological point of view is why so many conform rather than why the few are deviant.[3] Nevertheless, the actions of a few have a high nuisance value, and are defined as a serious social problem.

We have a substantial volume of statistical data on the epidemiology of crime. It is outstandingly a male characteristic. The rate for men in all societies is very much higher than that for women. In some societies, such as Algeria and Ceylon, the ratio is several thousands to one, but in societies in which there is substantial

[1] *Ibid.*, p. 17.
[2] *Ibid.*, p. 18.
[3] One study, however, has shown that 91 per cent of a sample of (mainly) New Yorkers admitted having committed at least one of a list of forty-nine offences for which they could have been imprisoned. Moreover, Sutherland has argued that a large number of 'white collar' crimes do not appear in the official statistics but are dealt with by administrative tribunals and civil courts. For a discussion of criminal statistics, see Merton & Nisbet, *op. cit.*, pp. 26–30 and 8 –5.

equality and freedom for women, the ratio is nearer ten to one.[1] Crime rates are also higher among young people in the lower social classes, and in some areas of large cities.

Any theory of crime must therefore account for such major variations. The view which attributes crime to poverty, for example, fails to account for the fact that women have very low crime rates. One major class of explanation seeks to account for crime in terms of the characteristics of the criminal. Biological theories stem from the work of Lombroso, who believed that criminals actually exhibited physical stigmata of degeneracy. More recently, there have been attempts to demonstrate that criminals were characterized by low intelligence or mental defect. More recent studies, however, have failed to substantiate that the criminal population differs in any significant way from the non-criminal. Psychoanalytic theories have sought to explain criminal acts as meeting unconscious needs for punishment, or as expressions of repressed aggressive or sexual drives. Again, such theories fail to account for the sex, class, ethnic and ecological variations in crime rates and for temporal changes.

The major criticism of sociologists, however, is that such theories, by focusing on the characteristics of the actor, fail to take account of the other variable in the equation: the situation in which he finds himself.[2] Moreover, they do not explain why the individual adopts a specifically criminal or delinquent solution to his problems. The sociological approach therefore, has looked for an explanation of criminal and delinquent acts to the same social mechanisms by which it seeks to explain non-criminal acts, and to investigate the roles which individuals play in the social system, their socialization for such roles, and the strains to which they are exposed, and to seek an explanation of the aetiology and epidemiology of crime and delinquency in terms of such variables.

One such approach starts from the position that a functional necessity in all societies is the existence of processes which ensure that individuals are socialized to adopt socially defined roles and must be adequately motivated to play such roles. This perspective therefore focuses on learning and motivation and seeks to explain how some individuals come to embrace deviant roles. As we have seen in the analysis of occupations, a major problem facing the individual is to achieve congruence between his self-image (identity) and role demands. Many aspects of male delinquency can be explained in these terms. Being tough, adventurous, daring—are all

[1] *Ibid.*, pp. 33–5.
[2] $b=f(a+s)$: i.e. behaviour is a function of the actor in a situation.

consistent with the way in which modern industrial societies define masculinity. Hence the boy who steals for 'kicks', (and much delinquency falls into this pattern) is seeking to express and establish his masculinity. Girls, by contrast, steal in a more rational way—typically clothing, cosmetics, jewellery. Such behaviour is *role-supportive* rather than *role-expressive*.[1] This theory may go some way to account for the peak years for delinquency in Britain occuring during the final year of compulsory education.[2] As Carter[3] has shown, these are years of boredom for many, and delinquency may under some circumstances, provide the compensatory kicks, and act as an expression of masculinity for those who resent the authority relations and subordination of many schools.[3]

As we have seen in Chapter 2, an important element in the socialization process is the influence of others on our self-images. We are particularly influenced by *significant others*, those whose opinions we value and whom we accept as reference groups. Cohen and Short[4] distinguish between *normative reference groups* by which we measure the rightness of our behaviour. Such groups may provide justification for ambiguous actions, such as industrial stealing which is sanctioned by the norms of the work group. *Status reference groups* function in a similar way to confer acceptance and respect, in return for conformity to their standards. Committing an offence, and being on probation, for example, have been observed as achieving status and respect in some delinquent groups. Such theories stress the fact that criminal roles are learned by the same mechanisms as non-criminal roles. A well-known version of this view is Sutherland's theory of 'differential association' which argues that persons become criminals because they have frequent contacts with criminal behaviour patterns and because of isolation from anti-criminal patterns.[5] It is the ratio of associations with definitions of situations favourable to law violation which is the significant variable.

Such theories contribute to an understanding of the aetiology of crime. A second major sociological perspective emphasizes the

[1] For a more detailed account of this and related researches, see A. K. Cohen and J. F. Short, 'Juvenile Delinquency', in Merton and Nisbet, *op. cit.*, Chapter 2.

[2] In the age group 14–17, 1,548 per 100,000 were found guilty of indictable offences, compared with 975 and 250 for the groups 17–21 and over 30. *Criminal Statistics for 1954.*

[3] *Home, School and Work.*

[4] *Ibid.*, pp. 101–3.

[5] E. H. Sutherland and D. R. Cressey, *Principles of Criminology* (1955). For a summary and critique of Sutherland's theory, see Merton, Broom and Cottrell, *op. cit.*, pp. 510–13.

broader cultural pressures to criminality rather than socialization and learning helps to explain the epidemiology (distribution) of criminal behaviour. We have already seen that Merton's theory stresses the discrepancy between socially approved goals and the distribution of opportunities available for the achievement of success.[1] This theory helps to explain the higher incidence of crime among the working-class in industrial societies. Moreover, it takes account of alternative reactions to the frustration of success goals in the form of various retreatist activities including drug addiction and its supportive criminality (e.g. theft) with which this is frequently associated.

A somewhat similar theory has been put forward by Taft[2] to explain the high crime rates of some nations such as America. He stresses the existence of 'criminogenic' influences in American culture, including its emphasis on material success, the destruction of primary group controls, rapid social change generating confusing definitions of morality, and a gulf between precept and practice which permit large-scale 'social swindles' to go unpunished. Such a culture will generate criminality, though its impact will vary between different segments of society and account for their specific form of criminal response. This explains the excess of male crime, since females are relatively protected from the stress of competition. Moreover, families which give security and affection provide more protection for their members from the criminogenic culture.

It is clear that no one theory can explain all the known facts. Theories which stem from the perspective of socialization for social roles are more successful in accounting for the aetiology of crime and why some individuals become criminals. Theories stressing cultural pressure, culture conflict, disorganization and anomie are more successful in explaining the epidemiology of crime and its differential distribution between nations, classes, and city areas. Moreover, the theories so far examined have tried to explain crime as a general category of behaviour, without distinguishing between various types of crime. It is hardly likely, for example, that a theory which explains larceny will be equally good at accounting for crimes against the person.

A study of criminal areas in Croydon (Surrey) is particularly interesting as an attempt to combine more than one approach. It establishes that a hard core of 'psychiatric delinquency' is 'related to

[1] 'Social Structure and Anomic', discussed above.
[2] D. R. Taft, *Criminology* (1956). For a summary, see D. R. Cressey, 'Crime', in Merton and Nisbet, *op. cit.*, Chapter 1, pp. 61–3.

serious emotional disturbance in the family or mental ill health'.[1] About one quarter of all the cases in each class are associated with such factors as parental disharmony, rejection, or separation, and inconsistent, severe, or lax discipline. But the residue is attributed to the cultural milieu and regarded as 'social delinquency'. Morris argues that the sub-culture of those 'at the bottom of the pile' is essentially criminal. Children exposed to a culture in which 'knocking-off' is a legitimate activity learn to comply with such normative expectations.[2] Moreover, housing policy and economic factors which combine to segregate 'unsatisfactory' tenants into homogenous enclaves virtually ensures the perpetuation of the delinquent sub-culture. A child reared in these enclaves 'grows up in an atmosphere in which restraint is often conspicuous by its absence. . . . Punishment and indulgence follow in swift succession . . . play will be largely in the street in which he will form an autonomous social group with boys of his own age. . . . Whereas the middle-class way of life tends to inhibit spontaneity, working-class culture tends to encourage it. In particular, aggression is seldom the subject of social disapproval'.[3] Furthermore, the working-class child is more likely to encounter the stressful situations with which he is ill-equipped to cope. Tensions and disagreements over money and sex occur publicly in the overcrowded conditions of sub-standard housing, while the single family living room is a further source of discord and conflict. It is such factors which account for the higher incidence of crime among lower working-class families, who are also to be found concentrated in delinquent enclaves in towns and cities.

Downes[4] similarly finds that the norms, values and beliefs of delinquents in East London do not differ markedly from those of the adult lower working-class, though their emphasis on leisure justifies reference to the existence of sub-cultural variations. But he also identifies specific motivations to delinquent behaviour. Failure at school and at work for the lower working-class boy leads to the displacement of his search for achievement to non-work areas. The working-class 'corner boy' depends on leisure as a source of satisfying exploits. In other words, dissociation is the working-class male adolescent's normative response to semi and unskilled work. It is to

[1] T. Morris, *The Criminal Area* (1957), Chapters 10 and 11.
[2] See also J. B. Mays, *Growing Up in the City* (1954). Such areas are not 'disorganized' in the sense that they lack normative integration. On the contrary, there may be a high degree of consensus.
[3] *Ibid.*, pp. 171–3.
[4] D. M. Downes, *The Delinquent Solution* (1966).

leisure that he turns for achievement. He starts out in a delinquency-prone situation. And the cultural values of the lower working-class areas help to shape the search for meaningful leisure.

Innovation, achievement motivation, and social change
The individual responses to strain which have been examined may threaten the stability of society and certainly may lead to pockets of disorganization. But not all responses to discrepancies between the actual and the ideal take the form of retreat from role performance or deviance. An alternative is increased effort to achieve satisfaction by legitimate means. The struggle against the challenge of the environment, for example, may lead to innovation and invention, to overcome pain, suffering and hunger, or simply to increase the level of satisfaction.

Recent studies have focused on attempts to discover the social situations which lead to innovation and invention and stimulate the motive to achieve. Although Merton's paradigm does not explain innovation and non-conformity, it contains the germ of an explanatory theory.[1] A number of writers have suggested that the source of innovation is to be found in socially structured strains experienced by the individual. Individuals experience needs which are not adequately satisfied by existing arrangements. We have already seen in Chapter 6 that the evidence on scientists suggests that they were drawn predominantly from individuals whose social position led them to see the desirability of change. A somewhat similar theory has been put forward by Everett Hagen,[2] who argues that the innovators in a number of societies were individuals who experienced threats of status deprivation. They were the sons of fathers whose position in society was being undermined and who could not therefore provide their sons with an adequate role model.

Somewhat similar studies by McClelland, and Rosen and D'Andrade[3] have sought to explore the sources of high levels of achievement motivation and their connexion with economic growth. McClelland considers that the entrepreneurs discussed by Weber were probably characterized by the need for high levels of achievement and were examples of a more general phenomenon in which levels of achievement motivation are correlated with economic

[1] A. K Cohen, 'The Study of Social Disorganization and Deviant Behaviour', in Merton, Broom and Cottrell, *op. cit.* (1959).
[2] *On the Theory of Social Change* (1961).
[3] David C. McClelland, 'The Achievement Motive in Economic Growth', in B. F. Hoselitz and W. E. Moore, *op. cit.*, Chapter 4, and *The Achieving Society* (1961).

growth. For historical periods, the existence of a high level achievement motivation was measured by the content analysis of imaginative literary documents or folk tales and found to correlate strongly with economic growth and the existence of entrepreneurs. Comparable studies of contemporary nations confirmed this association between achievement motivation and economic growth. McClelland also demonstrates that those with high scores on achievement motivation, in fact, possess the characteristics of entrepreneurs—willingness to innovate and to take risks. Fluctuations in achievement motivation scores are too rapid to be attributed to heredity. McClelland considers that the sources of high motivation must be attributed to parental influences.[1] A study by Inkeles of Russian emigrants also found that parents responded to extreme social changes resulting from the revolution by a marked decline in emphasis on traditional values in the upbringing of their children.[2] Moreover, he found that in the area of occupational choice, there was a marked decline in the importance attached to family traditions and an increased emphasis on self-expression and free choice.[3] His study however, failed to find evidence of increased emphasis on achievement, but this he attributes to the possible greater importance attached to political considerations by his sample of refugees. The study does, however, serve to demonstrate the way in which parents respond to changing circumstances by mediating the values appropriate to the new situation which their children will face, rather than those to which they were themselves exposed during childhood.

It is interesting to speculate on the possible connexions between innovation and deviance. Much innovation in the economic sphere is a form of deviance in the sense that it involves behaviour opposed to prevailing norms; that is, non-traditional. There are many historical examples of such deviance, for example the financial entrepreneurship which was opposed by the official medieval doctrines on usury. The expected rewards of deviancy must be attractive and are likely to appeal therefore, to those who have strong motives to succeed or who find their position in the social order unrewarding. Such positions would include social marginality. Again, there is some evidence to support this view of marginality as a source of deviance. For example, early moneylenders were often foreigners, while ethnic

[1] See Chapter 7 for a discussion of the literature. See also D. F. Swift, 'Social Class and Achievement Motivation', *Educational Research*, Feb. 1966.

[2] A. Inkeles, 'Social Change and Social Character: The Role of Parental Mediation', A. and E. Etzioni, *op. cit.* (1964), Chapter 37.

[3] *Ibid.*, p. 350.

minorities play a dominant role as businessmen in the economics of Africa and Latin America.[1]

It is not sufficient, however, to locate the sources of innovating personalities in a social system. We still need to explain under what conditions innovations are taken up and become *institutionalized* and in this way result in changes in the social system. Zollschan and Hirsch have elaborated a theoretical framework which identifies the major steps in the transformation of what they call *exigencies* into system changes. An *exigency* is defined as 'a discrepancy . . . between a consciously or unconsciously desired or expected state of affairs and an actual situation. To eventuate in social system changes, . . . such exigencies must trigger a series of phase processes, namely, articulation—action—institutionalization'.[2] The discrepancies may be *cognitive* (between what is expected to happen and what happens), *evaluative* (between a legitimate arrangement and an extual situation), or *affective* (between what it desired and what it achieved). *Articulation* involves the expression of what would otherwise remain as a free-floating discomfort. Articulation depends on the measure of discomfort generated by the exigency (saliency), the extent to which the sources of discomfort can be identified and specified (*specification*). Moreover, there must be some measure of normative support for the articulation of a need (*justification*). Somewhat similar conditions are necessary before articulated needs evoke actions (valence, application, legitimation).

Collective action results when an action involves one or more others. Institutionalization is likely to occur when others bring to the situation similar needs and where the resulting interaction is mutually satisfying. A second variety of collective action occurs when the goal requires more than one person and where co-operation aids individuals in the achievement of similar or congruent goals. The collective activity which results does not necessarily achieve a state of equilibrium. There may, for example, be unintended (latent) consequences and in this way, the creation of fresh exigencies. The existence of a stable state is, in fact, a special case since actions will create new exigencies. The theory does not, therefore, posit any fixed categories of needs.[3] Moreover, it takes account of the fact that

---

[1] See B. F. Hoselitz, 'Main Concepts in the Analysis of the Social Implications of Technical Change', in B. F. Hoselitz and W. E. Moore, *op. cit.* (1966), Chapter 1, pp. 25–7.

[2] G. K. Zollschan and W. Hirsch, *Explorations in Social Change* (1964), p. 89.

[3] Cf. Parson's notion of functional imperatives. The authors argue that 'social systems continue to satisfy functional requirements only as long as potential

exigencies emerge within the framework of established social systems with existing institutionalized patterns. The socialization process will have ensured that such institutionalized 'definitions of situations' and normative expectations are 'built in' to the personalities of members of society, and will function to determine the kind of responses adopted to an exigency.[1] The emergence of collective action does not necessarily lead to social change. Much will depend as we have seen, on the societal response to such action. A full discussion of this requires us to move from an emphasis on the personality sub-system to the structural level of analysis,[2] and takes us back to the earlier discussion on structural strains.

SUMMARY AND CONCLUSIONS

With the present state of sociological knowledge on social change, it is difficult to do more, in an introductory text, than to indicate what appear to be some promising perspectives and lines of inquiry. There are signs that the distinction between the study of stability and change first put forward by Comte (who divided sociology into social statics and social dynamics) is breaking down and that the same perspectives being developed for the study of stability, conformity and organization can be applied to the study of change, deviance and disorganization. There has been a decided shift away from the earlier monistic theories which sought to discover the causes of change in one main variable such as technology or culture, to attempts to use the 'systems' model of society. This model leads to the view that the stimulus to change may be derived from a variety of sources, and to a study of the system responses to change, and to the investigation of the concomitants and consequences for the total system of changes in any one segment of the system.

The criticisms levelled against this essentially functionalist approach to the study of change by those who argue that it neglects the role of

failures to meet them become exigencies. . . . States of equilibrium are special cases of dynamics . . .' (p. 122).

[1] 'It is in the socialization process that horizons of expectations and horizons of justification are formed in individuals. We are . . . suggesting that there exists a feedback process in which institutionalization leads to socialization of persons. . . . The horizons of expectations and horizons of justifications of socialized individuals thereupon enter into the determination of new articulations of exigencies and new patterns of institutionalization.' (ibid., p. 114).

[2] Much will depend too on the kind of control which a society exercises over innovations. For a discussion of this, see A. Boskoff, 'Functional Analysis as a Source of a Theoretical Repertory and Research Tasks in the Study of Social Change', in Zollschan and Hirsch, op. cit. (1964), pp. 231-4.

conflict and coercion in the maintenance of integration, have led to renewed attention to the problem of change by the functionalists, and to an extension of functionalist theory to embrace a more dynamic view of society. The study of social conflict has therefore acquired a fresh significance as a possible source of change. Moreover, recent world trends have resulted in a growing interest in the problems of industrialization and modernization, with a consequent focus of attention on this narrower problem of change. Consequently, we now have a growing literature on the differences between traditional and modern societies, and on the distinctions between folk and urban communities. Resulting foci of contemporary controversy arise over the extent to which industrialization takes similar paths in societies which begin from different bases and the extent to which there is substantial convergence in the social systems of industrial societies.

There is a growing interest in the relation between individuals and social systems, and to the role of innovating personalities and the conditions from which they emerge. One result has been an interesting convergence between psychology and sociology through studies which seek to discover the social sources of the high levels of motivation to achieve and take risks which characterize key figures such as entrepreneurs and innovators, and to a renewed interest in social marginality as a source of innovation and deviance.

But despite such probable connexions between the conditions which underly both deviance and change, not all deviant responses necessarily contribute to change. As Merton has shown, one form of non-conformity is the retreat from role performance. Studies of suicide, drug addiction and crime have documented some of the factors which lead to these particular responses to individual strain, which constitute threats to the organization of society. Some preliminary explorations have also been made into the conditions which facilitate the transition from individual to collective responses to strains, and which underly the development of structural strains and conflicts as a possible source of change.

QUESTIONS AND EXERCISES

1. 'By his distinction between social statics and social dynamics, Comte set sociology on a false trail from which it is only now recovering.' Explain and discuss.
2. Examine the distinction between changes *in* social systems and changes *of* social systems.

3. Examine the problems involved in arriving at a satisfactory definition of social change.
4. Explain and discuss the distinctions between (a) traditional and modern societies, (b) folk and urban societies.
5. 'Industrialization and modernization are not synonymous concepts.' Discuss.
6. Examine critically technological theories of social change.
7. Give a critical account of the view that culture is a major source of social change.
8. 'We cannot expect the course of industrialization in new nations to parallel that of the older European societies.' Discuss.
9. Examine the view that functionalism cannot provide a satisfactory approach to the study of social change.
10. What part is played by social conflict in social change?
11. 'Strike trends are a useful index for the study of social conflict and integration.' Discuss.
12. Account for the main trends in strike statistics over the last fifty years.
13. What evidence would you consider in examining the extent of class conflict in contemporary industrial societies.
14. 'Social conflict may contribute to social integration.' Discuss.
15. 'Deviance is only one of a number of possible varieties of non-conformity.' Explain.
16. Examine the social factors which underly any one form of deviant behaviour.
17. Give an account of the social determinants of either alcoholism, or drug addiction, or suicide.
18. How far can the notion of delinquent sub-cultures explain the aetiology and epidemiology of delinquency?
19. Examine the social factors which generate high levels of achievement motivation.
20. Examine the connexion between achievement motivation and economic growth.
21. What evidence is there that social marginality contributes to deviance and innovation?

READING

A. C. Crombie.—*Scientific Change* (Heinemann, 1963). An advanced text; a collection of papers presented at a symposium. See especially Part 7.

R. Dahrendorf.—*Class and Class Conflict in Industrial Society* (Routledge, 1959).

D. M. Downes.—*The Delinquent Solution* (Routledge, 1966), Chapters 1, 5, 7, 8.

S. N. Eisenstadt.—*Comparative Social Problems* (Collier Macmillan, 1964).

*A. and E. Etzioni (ed.).—*Social Change: Sources, Patterns and Consé-quences* (Basic Books, 1964). A collection of readings. See especially the introduction to sections and Chapters 12, 13, 14, 18, 20, 30, 31, 34, 37, 41, 48, 51.

E. E. Hagen.—*On the Theory of Social Change* (Tavistock, 1964).

P. Halmos (ed.).—*Sociological Review Monograph No. 8: Industrialization and Society* (Keele, 1964).

*B. F. Hoselitz and W. E. Moore.—*Industrialization and Society* (Unesco, 1963). A collection of conference papers. See especially Chapter 15.

Clark Kerr, *et al.*—*Industrialism and Industrial Man* (OUP, 1964).

A. Kornhauser, *et al.* (eds.).—*Industrial Conflict* (McGraw-Hill, 1954). See especially Chapter 40 for an 'overview'.

*R. M. MacIver and C. H. Page.—*Society* (Macmillan, 1950), Book III: 'Social Change', especially Chapter 25.

*R. K. Merton, L. Broom and L. S. Cottrell.—*Sociology Today: Problems and Prospects* (Harper, 1965).

*R. K. Merton and R. A. Nisbet.—*Contemporary Social Problems* (Hart-Davis, 1965).

*W. E. Moore.—*Social Change* (Prentice Hall, 1963). An introduction and review of the literature. See especially Chapters 1, 4 and 5.

T. Morris.—*The Criminal Area* (Routledge, 1957).

G. K. Zollschan and W. Hirsch.—*Explorations in Social Change* (Rout-ledge, 1964). A more advanced text. See especially Introduction and Chapters 8, 9, 14, 21, 26, 31.

INDEX

TABLES AND FIGURES

INDEX

SUBJECT AND AUTHOR

GEORGE ALLEN & UNWIN LTD

Head Office:
40 Museum Street, London, W.C.1
Telephone: 01–405 8577

Sales, Distribution and Accounts Departments
Park Lane, Hemel Hempstead, Herts.
Telephone: 0442 3244

Athens: 7 Stadiou Street
Auckland: P.O. Box 36013, Northcote Central, N.4
Barbados: P.O. Box 222, Bridgetown
Beirut: Deeb Building, Jeanne d'Arc Street
Bombay: 103/5 Fort Street, Bombay 1
Calcutta: 285J Bepin Behari Ganguli Street, Calcutta 12
Cape Town: 68 Shortmarket Street
Delhi: 1/18D Asaf Ali Road, New Delhi 1
Hong Kong: 105 Wing on Mansion, 26 Hankow Road, Kowloon
Ibadan: P.O. Box 62
Karachi: Karachi Chambers, McLeod Road
Madras: 2/18 Mount Road, Madras 2
Mexico: Villalongin 32, Mexico 5, D.F.
Nairobi: P.O. Box 30583
Pakistan: Alico Building, 18 Motijheel, Dacca 2
Philippines: P.O. Box 157, Quezon City, D–502
Rio de Janeiro: Caixa Postal 2537–Zc–oo
Singapore: 36c Prinsep Street, Singapore 7
Sydney: N.S.W.: Bradbury House, 55 York Street
Tokyo: C.P.O. Box 1728, Tokyo 100–91
Toronto: 81 Curlew Drive, Don Mills

INTRODUCTION TO THE SOCIAL SCIENCES

MAURICE DUVERGER

Professor Duverger at last provides the student with an overall view of the methodology of the social sciences. He briefly traces the origin of the notion of a social science, showing how it emerged from social philosophy. Its essential elements and pre-conditions are described; the splintering of social science into specialist disciplines is explained, and the need for a general sociology affirmed.

The techniques of observation used by social scientists are dealt with in some detail and the unity of the social sciences is illustrated by examples of the universal application of these techniques. Documentary evidence in its various forms (archives, the Press, official publications, etc.) are described along with the basic analytical techniques, including quantitative methods and content analysis. Other methods of gathering information through polls (there are sections on sampling, the design, administration and processing the results of questionnaires), interviews, attitude scales and participant observation are all described.

Under the heading 'systematic analysis' Professor Duverger brings together the different kinds of analysis used to assess the information thus gathered. Arguing that observing and theorising are not two different stages or levels of research, he examines the practical value and difficulties of general sociological theories, partial theories and models and working hypotheses. He both describes and assesses the limitations of experiment and the scope of comparative methods in the social sciences. He then gives elementary instructions for using and assessing the value of mathematical techniques. The possibilities of presenting social phenomena through graphs and charts are also explored. There are useful book lists and diagrams.

When the French original was reviewed in *Political Studies*, a strong plea was made for an English translation, a plea which was echoed by all those teaching in the field of the social sciences whom the publishers consulted. Hitherto, English students have lacked an authoritative, systematic introduction of this kind.

Dr Anderson, of the Department of Government, University of Manchester, has slightly shortened the work in his terse English vision. The author is Professor à la Faculté de Droit et des Sciences Economiques de Paris. He is famous as one of the most eminent and courageously outspoken French political scientists of today.

GEORGE ALLEN & UNWIN LTD